【英汉对照】

当代国际商务文化阅读丛书

Readings for Modern International Business Culture

公开的赌注
——『商务演讲』篇

Public Stakes
Business Speeches

吴斐 编著

武汉大学出版社

图书在版编目(CIP)数据

公开的赌注:"商务演讲"篇:英汉对照/吴斐编著. —武汉:武汉大学出版社,2016.5
当代国际商务文化阅读丛书
书名原文:Public Stakes:Business Speeches
ISBN 978-7-307-13992-3

Ⅰ.公…　Ⅱ.吴…　Ⅲ.商务—演讲—英、汉　Ⅳ.H019

中国版本图书馆 CIP 数据核字(2014)第 181989 号

封面图片为上海富昱特授权使用(ⓒ IMAGEMORE Co.，Ltd.)

责任编辑:郭园园　金 军　　责任校对:鄢春梅　　版式设计:韩闻锦

出版发行:**武汉大学出版社**　(430072　武昌　珞珈山)
(电子邮件:cbs22@ whu.edu.cn 网址:www.wdp.com.cn)
印刷:武汉中远印务有限公司
开本:880×1230　1/32　印张:11.125　字数:244 千字
版次:2016 年 5 月第 1 版　　2016 年 5 月第 1 次印刷
ISBN 978-7-307-13992-3　　定价:28.00 元

前　言

　　人类社会进入 21 世纪后，国家间的商务往来更加频繁，商务交际手段随着互联网的诞生和电子信息的进步日新月异，国际化企业的文化和理念千差万别，商务话题的表达和沟通能力无疑是人们所遇到的最大障碍。　在我们熟知的生活英语、学术英语之外，商务英语不仅是我国目前从事或即将从事涉外商务人员英语实际应用能力不可多得的辅助工具，更是商务工作人员在这个国际化的高科技时代商务竞争能力、外贸业务素质和英语水平的重要体现。《当代国际商务文化阅读》（英汉对照）丛书以从事国际商务活动所必需的语言技能为经，以各种商务活动的具体情景作纬，将商务精神和商务元素巧妙融合，展示时尚而又经典的商务文化世界流行风，为广大读者提供一套语言规范、内容新颖、涉及面广、趣味性强、具有实用价值、富于时代精神的读物，既注意解决人们在国际商务环境中因遇到不熟悉的专业词汇而无法与外国合作者就工作问题交流沟通的难题，又着力解决人们学外语单纯地学语言而缺乏商务专业知识的弊端。

　　《当代国际商务文化阅读》（英汉对照）丛书由 10 个单行本组成：《拥抱新欢亚马逊（**Embracing Amazon Service**）——电子商务篇

前　言

（E-Commerce）》、《华尔街梦魇（Nightmare on Wall Street）——商界风云篇（The Business Circles）》、《路易斯·波森的朋克摇滚（The Punk Rock of Louis Posen）——商界精英篇（Business Elites）》、《希波克拉底誓言（Hippocratic Oath）——商务交际篇（Business Communication）》、《强烈的第一印象（A Powerful First Impression）——商务礼仪篇（Business Etiquette）》、《企业帝国继承权之争（Corporate Empires' Grappling with Succession）——商务文化篇（Business Culture）》、《紫色血液（The Purple Blood）——商务心理篇（Business Psychology）》、《多米诺骨牌效应（The Domino Effects）——商务知识篇（Business Knowledge）》、《公开的赌注（Public Stakes）——商务演讲篇（Business Speeches）》、《伊斯特林悖论（The Easterlin Paradox）——感悟财富篇（Comprehension of Wealth）》。　这套丛书的编写旨在帮助读者在国际商务环境下，能够读懂英文的商务信息和商务新闻，并能对某一商务话题的知识有全面透彻的了解，领悟当代时尚商务文化成长的环境和思维方式，提高在全球化高科技时代的商务竞争能力、外贸业务素质和英语交际水平。　丛书中的阅读材料力求做到题材广泛、内容精辟、语言规范，遵循趣味性、知识性和时效性原则，培养读者在商务环境下的英语竞争能力和综合应用能力。　丛书融时代性与经典性为一体，内容经得起时间考验，文字经得起反复咀嚼，保证其可读性。　读者在阅读过程中接收大量的语言输入，为合理组织和娴熟运用英语语言表达自己的思想打下牢固的基础。　丛书的单行本包括以一个主题为中心的 30 篇文章，每篇文章包括题记、英语原文、汉语译文、生词脚注和知识链接。"题记"用丰富生动的语言点评文章的精髓，对文

章的内容起到提炼和画龙点睛的作用。"英语原文"主要摘自当代国际主流报纸杂志,具有语言规范、内容新颖、涉及面广、趣味性和时代感等特点。"汉语译文"力求准确流畅,既关注译文的文化语境及其内涵,也重视译文的外延和现当代标志性语言符号。"生词脚注"的难度把握在大学英语六级和研究生英语词汇程度,以帮助读者及时扫清阅读障碍。"知识链接"根据文章内容,或精解一个专业术语、或阐释一种新的商务理念、或介绍叱咤商界的企业或公司,以帮助读者培养游弋商海、运筹帷幄的能力,具备洞悉中西文化的国际视野。

《公开的赌注》(Public Stakes)——商务演讲篇(Business Speeches)给读者展示了商界领袖和政界领袖的公众演讲能力。 惠普、埃克森美孚、康柏电脑、联想、可口可乐、嘉吉、IBM、德国默克集团等全球著名企业和公司的董事会主席兼首席执行官的演讲,向人们诠释了全球经济版图变迁之时,公司对未来技术发展的美好憧憬和发明创造的激情,掀开了商界对世界金融、货币和贸易实体经济结构变化的深度解读,对世界贸易合作伙伴关系的重新定位,对企业价值目标相关度的垂直考察和重建。 比尔·盖茨的演讲论证了创造性资本主义具有的双重使命:赚钱赢利和让那些无法充分享受市场好处的人群生活也得到改善,让全人类都能享受到资本主义发展带来的福利。 迈克尔·戴尔在演讲中透露了自己成功的秘密:对消费者顶礼膜拜。 这些成功创建全球著名企业的商界名人站在巨人的肩膀上,追求卓越,在不经意间叩开了成功的大门。 美国前总统布什、联合国秘书长潘基文、英国财政大臣、美国财政部长、英国金融服务管理局主席、英国前首相戈登·布朗等掌管全球和国家

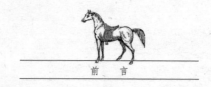

金融命脉的政治家，在全球金融危机面前彰显了运筹帷幄的大家风范。 美国政府宣布接管陷入困境的美国住房抵押贷款融资机构房利美和房地美，尽全力缓解因金融危机而引起的投资者担心，以便稳定金融体系，从而促进金融市场恢复运转，推动经济的复苏；英国政府为稳定银行系统采取了三个步骤，即解决银行之间的资金流动，支持银行筹集追加资本和允许银行在市场上自筹资金，旨在恢复大众对金融系统的信心和信任，使英国的银行体系建立在更加健全的基础之上，为未来的发展蓄积力量。 威尔士王子查尔斯殿下、香港贸易发展局局长林郑月娥、英国石油公司替代能源部执行副总裁和首席执行官维维恩妮·考克斯等以经济学家的眼光对未来环境和未来能源的和谐发展阐述了自己的观点。 查尔斯王子已经成为保护海洋环境事业的领军人物，海滩监管代表了查尔斯王子的所有环保哲学。 当埃克森美孚远离拥抱替代能源的时尚潮流之际，英国石油公司仍然沉浸在崇尚环保的浓浓绿意之中，为"超越石油"、加速转向可替代能源奔走相告，呼吁国际社会共同努力和合作，创建可靠的、能够消费得起的清洁能源。

五彩纷呈的商务演讲展现了企业家的个人魅力，是传递团队管理理念、赢得员工追随、获得商业认可、树立形象名片的途径。 让我们跟随时代潮流，掌握商务演讲的语言技巧，提高商务沟通效果，赢得商业成功和个人发展机遇，享受世界流行文化创造的快乐、荣誉、价值和成就感！

作　者

2016 年 1 月

目 录

目 录

目　录

目　录

目　录

目　录

题　记

　　英国为了顺利渡过金融危机，将赌注押在重新规划金融体系的结构上，这无疑是雪上加霜。如果这个建立更加一体化的监管框架的尝试失败了，市场可能会对苏格兰皇家银行和哈利法克斯-劳埃德银行的前景失去信心，也会鼓励资本重整计划、抵押担保、英格兰银行的流动资金等逃离机构治理和金融监管实体，产生持续支离破碎的压力。在这场瞬息万变的金融游戏中，政府随时要有深思熟虑的创新：将膨胀的资产价格回落至可持续的水平；私营行业去杠杆化；认可金融业由此出现的损失以及向金融体系注资。英国的公开赌注能否使其经济重返持续性的增长轨道，不幸的是这一问题的答案仍然不能确定。

Public Stakes
—A Speech by Lord Turner,
Chairman of the FSA

Good morning!

In April of this year everybody knew that something pretty big had happened to the world's financial system. What we had no idea, bluntly, was how extreme it was going to be. I think what really happened from the Lehman weekend, which was the weekend before I joined, until Friday last week, was an extreme intensification of the crisis, which turned into — for the first time that anybody can remember — what was getting close to a complete seizure of the money markets. Therefore you get a whole system which is heading towards huge amounts of overnight lending, which is then on a complete trigger① because you are having banks that start the day with enormous funding needs to get to by 4: 30 in the afternoon. And it really did start with Lehman, and it was intensified with Washington Mutual. And I think the Americans know, in retrospect, that Lehman was a mistake. There was a desire to draw a line somewhere on the moral hazard issue, but actually it was that

---

① trigger [ˈtrigə] n. 触发器

公开的赌注

——英国金融服务管理局主席特纳勋爵的演讲

早上好！

今年四月，人人见证了世界金融系统发生了一些重量级的大事。坦白地说，我们手足无措，不知道这些事情会发展到何种极端的程度。我认为，危机的极度加剧取决于雷曼周末发生的真实情况，这些事情发生在我参加会议前的周末，直到上周五才结束。危机接近完美地袭击着货币市场，第一次让所有人刻骨铭心。你掌控的整个金融体系正在接洽巨额的隔夜贷款，随之却彻底溃不成军，因为你掌控的银行早上一开门即面临大量的资金需求，并一直延续到下午四点半。这种状况的的确确始于雷曼，在华盛顿互惠银行愈演愈烈。回想起来，我认为美国人明白雷曼是个错误。人们希望能在某处给道德风险问题画一条界限，但实际上这种做法又将事情拖入真实的信任危机，人们开始说不，甚至交易关系或大型金融机构的存款也处于危机四伏之中，只剩下急剧消退的信心。

如果你在这个时间点匆忙地试图开始重新规划金融体系的结

that put the thing into a real crisis of confidence, and people beginning to say no, even in counterparty relationships or deposits of very major financial institutions are at risk, and there was just an extraordinary drying up of confidence.

There is a danger here if you start at a point in time and try to start to redraw the architecture of the financial system in a hurry. There are two things that you can get wrong, but the first one you mustn't actually worry too much about, in the sense of which there are a set of crisis actions taken: the recapitalization scheme, the guarantees, the Bank of England liquidity, where I think it is inevitable that somebody at the end of it will be able to say: if you had done it precisely this other way it might have been better. Maybe somebody will be able to prove that in some detail X would have been better than Y, but actually what matters is to get something which is 90 percent right, done. And I am confident that even if the economic historians suggest that there could have been something slightly different, what was done and the three key elements of it: recapitalization, guarantees and central bank liquidity, were what had to be done, and what had to be done to prevent what was a tailspin① of confidence in the whole financial system.

It was done in the UK, it was followed up at the weekend by the US and Europe. And I do think that, although there are still going to be macroeconomic consequences of what has occurred, I think we are past the point of the danger of where we were last week, where we could have had a fundamental systemic meltdown of the core plumbing of the world

---

① tailspin *n.* 混乱

构，无疑是雪上加霜。 你会在两件事上出错。 首先，你没有必要过度担心一系列的危机行动举措，包括资本重整计划、抵押担保、英格兰银行的流动资金等。 我认为最终有人可能会说：如果你完全按照另一种方法来做，结果可能会更好。 这是不可避免的。 也许有人能够证明在某些细节上 X 比 Y 好，但是实际上，重要的是保持90%的做事正确率。 即使经济历史学家们说明了可能存在的细微差别，我也很自信。 已经采取的措施和它的三个关键元素是：资本重整计划、抵押担保、英格兰银行的流动资金。 这些是必须要做的事，实施这些举措是为了防范整个金融体系中的信用恐慌。

英国采取了行动，美国和欧洲在周末时随之采取行动。 我确实认为，即使仍然会存在已经发生的宏观经济后果，我相信我们已经渡过了上周所处的危险期，当时世界金融体系的核心流通渠道可能已经从根本上系统地分崩离析。 匆忙而非完美的行事有危险吗？是的，当然会有危险，但是达到90%的正确率远比不停地辩论完美和逃避完美更重要。

现在，如何使金融体系长期正确地运行是一个完全独立的问题。 我认为没有必要在一个星期、两个星期、三个星期和四个星期里公布什么政策。 这样做需要时间。 首先，因为该发生的事已经在国际上发生了，那么即将发生的事最好也按国际规则来处理。 坦率地说，争取国际协议和讨论协议的过程非常复杂，包括相当复杂的制度参与者：有金融稳定论坛、巴塞尔银行监督委员会，欧洲扮

financial system. Is there a danger that in doing things in a hurry you don't do things perfectly? Yes, of course there is, but it is far more important to get something 90 per cent right than to go on debating perfection and avoid it.

Now, there is a completely separate issue about what has to happen to the system to get it right for the long term. And there, I don't think, there is a need to promulgate① something in a week, two weeks, three weeks, four weeks; it will take time. First of all because some of what has to happen must happen internationally; most of what has to happen is best done internationally. And the process of getting international agreement and of debating it is very complicated with, frankly, quite a complicated set of institutional players: there is the Financial Stability Forum, there is the Basel Committee on Banking Supervision, Europe has a role, and the US independently has a role.

It is a complicated institutional infrastructure for making progress, and I think it is capable of making progress, but I think it is a challenge of the next three to six months and not the next week, because frankly the structure of the world financial system and what happens for the immediate future will be heavily driven by the emergency measures that have been taken. So, in the UK the structure of our financial system is going to be heavily influenced by the fact that we have very large public stakes in two of the banks, Royal Bank of Scotland and HBOS-Lloyds that we will end up with at the end of this process.

In a sense it doesn't actually matter very much what happens in the

---

① promulgate ['prɔməlgeit] *vt.* 发表

演着角色，美国也起着独立的作用。

这是一个为了取得进展的复杂的制度建设，我认为它能够取得进展，但我认为这是接下来三到六个月、而不是下个星期的一场挑战，坦率地说，因为已经实施的紧急措施在很大程度上驱动着世界金融体系的结构和不久的将来出现的情况。 所以，在英国，金融体系的结构将受到一个事实的重大影响，即我们在两家银行——苏格兰皇家银行和哈利法克斯-劳埃德银行——拥有非常庞大的公共股权，我们将在这个过程消失时结束这种状况。

在某种意义上，接下来的几个月发生什么、世界是否赞同已有的长期资本充足率的管理体制，这些实际上并不太重要。 危机的解决方式存在着稳定性。 作为多少有点独立的手段，我们可以辩论必须要辩论的事情，包括会计制度、整体公允价值、按市值计价、银行条款辩论、资本充足率、前周期性和反周期性的辩论。 我们如何有效地调控流动资金？ 流动资金应该类似于为资本而存在的资金，是实际数量测定形式，或者是一组原则和富有成效的监督讨论、整体报酬结构、着眼于整体的放款加转销证券化模式。 有些人对此持不同的看法，例如，麦克理维专员认为，在这场他称之为肤浅的游戏中，必须要有深思熟虑的创新，有些人只愿意分享他们可以保留一部分的资源。 还有些人认为，实际上，证券化模式出现的根本问题准确地说明了风险不会真正地危及投资者，大量的风险处于进退两难的困境。

举例来说，如果你实实在在地查看国际货币基金组织发布的最

next few months what the long-term capital adequacy regime which the world agrees is or is not, as it were; there is stability in the solution of crisis. And we can, as a somewhat separate exercise, debate the things that have to be debated, which are accounting, the whole fair value, mark-to-market, banking provision debate, capital adequacy, the pro-cyclicality versus counter-cyclicality debate. Liquidity, how do we effectively regulate liquidity, should that take the form of actual quantitative measures similar to those which exist for capital or is a set of principles and a rich supervisory discussion, the whole remuneration structure, and a whole look at the whole originate-and-distribute securitization model where some people are arguing, for instance Commissioner McCreevy, that there has to be deliberate creation of what he calls skin in the game, people only distributing stuff where they keep a slice of it. Other people are arguing that actually the fundamental problem of what has gone wrong with the securitization model is that precisely the risk wasn't really passed through to investors, that a hell a lot of it stuck in the middle.

And indeed if you look, for instance, at the latest IMF global financial stability report, and you look at what percentage of their predicted losses on securitized instruments are going to be suffered by banks, you realize how little real pass-through had actually occurred. That is an interesting debate. I think one has got to be open-minded about it, but one mustn't rush to judgment on those sorts of things.

(1,023 words)

新全球金融稳定报告，了解银行对他们预期的证券化工具造成多大比例的损失，你就会意识到，实际发生危机转嫁的几率是多么渺茫。这是一场有趣的辩论。我认为大家应该对此思路开阔，但一定不能草率地对这些事情做出判断。

知识链接

Lord Turner 特纳勋爵是英国金融服务管理局（FSA）主席、全球金融稳定理事会（FSB）成员、二十国集团（G20）国际监管改革机构的负责人。他工作踏实肯干，做事非常坚持原则，在他的领导下，金融服务管理局始终坚持它的目标——为国家和人民服务。

FSA 英国金融服务管理局（Financial Services Authority）。英国金融服务管理局于1997年由证券投资委员会（Securities and Investments Board, SIB, 1985年成立）改制而成，是一个独立的非政府组织，直接向财政部负责。金融服务管理局的宗旨是对金融服务行业进行监管，致力于保持高效、有序、廉洁的金融市场，同时帮助中小消费者取得公平交易机会。它的目标是维护英国金融市场及业界信心，促进公众对金融制度的理解，了解不同类型投资和金融交易的利益和风险，确保从业者有适当的经营能力及健全的财务结构。

题 记

　　美国政府宣布接管陷入困境的美国住房抵押贷款融资机构房利美和房地美的消息，似乎给处于动荡和压力漩涡的金融市场和金融机构注入了一剂强心针。政府以霹雳手段遏制信贷危机继续扩大，这可能成为有史以来美国政府干预房地产市场的最大规模行动。接管方案根据四个步骤有条不紊地展开：两房的投资组合以每年10%的速度缩减，并最终稳定在一个较低的、风险不大的水平上；将优先股股东置于普通股股东之后承担损失的位置；建立新的信用信贷担保，资助两房在资本市场的日常经营活动；制定购买两房按揭债券的临时计划。无论政府是在创造"最糟糕的公费资本主义"，还是真心实意伸出金融援助之臂，此举都将可能成为目前信贷危机的一个"转折点"。

Protecting Financial Markets and Taxpayers

— A Speech by U.S. Secretary of the
Treasury Henry Paulson

Good morning. I'm joined here by Jim Lockhart, director of the new independent regulator, the Federal Housing Finance Agency (FHFA).

In July, Congress granted the Treasury, the Federal Reserve, and FHFA new authorities with respect to the GSEs, Fannie Mae and Freddie Mac. Since that time, we have closely monitored financial market and business conditions and have analyzed in great detail the current financial condition of the GSEs, including the ability of the GSEs to weather a variety of market conditions going forward. As a result of this work, we have determined that it is necessary to take action.

Announcing Four Steps based on what we have learned about these institutions over the last four weeks-including what we learned about their capital requirements-and given the condition of financial markets today, I concluded that it would not have been in the best interest of the taxpayers for Treasury to simply make an equity investment in these enterprises in

保护金融市场和纳税人
——美国财政部长亨利·鲍尔森的演讲

早上好。 我与新的独立监管机构——联邦住房金融机构（FHFA）的执行长吉姆·洛克哈特一道，在此向大家说明情况。

今年 7 月，国会批准了财政部、联邦储备委员会及联邦住房金融机构对两房（房利美和房地美）的新权力。 自那时起，我们就已经密切监控金融市场和商业情况，并非常详细地分析了两房目前的财务状况，包括两房平安通过多变的市场环境并向前发展的能力。鉴于以上工作，我们下决心采取必要的行动。

基于过去四周对这些机构的情况调查，包括了解它们对资本的需求，以及当前金融市场的环境，我们现在宣布四项行动计划。 我认为，以这些公司目前的状况对其进行股权投资，对财政部来说，并没有让纳税人的利益最大化。

我支持董事长必要而恰当的决定，并向他进言，托管是唯一的形式，我同意按这种方式将纳税人的钱提交给两房。

我一直认为，房地产市场造成了我们经济的最大风险。 它拖累了经济增长，使我们的金融市场和金融机构处于动荡和压力的漩涡。

their current form.

I support the director's decision as necessary and appropriate and had advised him that conservatorship① was the only form in which I would commit taxpayer money to the GSEs.

I have long said that the housing correction poses the biggest risk to our economy. It is a drag on our economic growth, and at the heart of the turmoil and stress for our financial markets and financial institutions.

Portfolio Reduction

To promote stability in the secondary mortgage market and lower the cost of funding, the GSEs will modestly increase their MBS portfolios② . Then, to address systemic risk, their portfolios will begin to be gradually reduced at the rate of 10% per year, largely through natural run off, eventually stabilizing at a lower, less risky size. With this agreement, Treasury receives senior preferred equity shares and warrants③ that protect taxpayers. Additionally, under the terms of the agreement, common and preferred shareholders bear losses ahead of the new government senior preferred shares.

These preferred stock purchase agreements were made necessary by the ambiguities in the GSE Congressional charters, which have been perceived to indicate government support for agency debt and guaranteed MBS.

---

① conservatorship [kən'səvətəʃip] n. 英国管理委员的职位
② portfolio [pɔːt'fəuljəu] n. 投资组合
③ warrant ['wɔrənt] n. 授权证

投资缩减

为了促进二级抵押贷款市场的稳定和降低资金成本，两房将小幅增加抵押贷款支持证券投资组合。 届时，为了解决系统性风险，他们的投资组合将开始以每年 10% 的速度逐步减少，主要呈自然流失的方式，并最终稳定在一个较低的、风险不大的水平上。 在这个协议下，财政部获得高级优先股和认股权证，以保护纳税人。 此外，根据协议的条款，普通股和优先股股东承担政府购买高级优先股之前的损失。

有必要根据模棱两可的两房国会特许条例制定这些优先股购买协议，这已被视为表明政府支持机构债务和担保的抵押贷款证券。

普通股股东最危险

当股东既能承担投资风险又能获得投资回报时，市场规律即达到最佳状况。 虽然托管并没有消除普通股股票，但就企业资产债权而言，它确实置后了普通股股东的权益。

同样，托管并没有消除外部的优先股，但它确实将优先股股东置于普通股股东之后，即承担损失的位置。 联邦金融机构正在评估银行和房利美和房地美的风险敞口。

走向稳定

优先股投资者应该认识到，两房不同于其他的金融机构，因此，两房的优先股也不能在更广泛的意义上代表金融机构的优先股。 稳定两房才能使他们能够更好地履行自己的使命，现在的行动应该加快稳定房地产市场，并最终使金融机构受益。

财政部现在采取的第二个步骤是建立新的信用信贷担保，从而可以向房地美、房利美和联邦住房贷款银行提供帮助。 考虑到我们

Common Shareholders Most at Risk

Market discipline is best served when shareholders bear both the risk and the reward of their investment. While conservatorship does not eliminate the common stock, it does place common shareholders last in terms of claims on the assets of the enterprise.

Similarly, conservatorship does not eliminate the outstanding preferred stock, but does place preferred shareholders second, after the common shareholders, in absorbing losses. The federal banking agencies are assessing the exposures of banks and thrifts to Fannie Mae and Freddie Mac.

Moving Toward Stabilization

Preferred stock investors should recognize that the GSEs are unlike any other financial institutions and consequently GSE preferred stocks are not a good proxy[①] for financial institution preferred stock more broadly. By stabilizing the GSEs so they can better perform their mission, today's action should accelerate stabilization in the housing market, ultimately benefiting financial institutions.

The second step Treasury is taking today is the establishment of a new secured lending credit facility which will be available to Fannie Mae, Freddie Mac, and the Federal Home Loan Banks. Given the combination of actions we are taking, including the preferred share purchase agreements, we expect the GSEs to be in a stronger position to fund their regular business activities in the capital markets.

Finally, to further support the availability of mortgage financing for

---

① proxy ['prɔksi] n. 代表权; 代理权(尤指投票)

正在采取的联合行动，包括优先股购买计划，我们期待两房处于更强大的地位，资助他们在资本市场的日常经营活动。

最后，为了给成千上万的美国人抵押贷款融资的可用性提供进一步的支持，财政部正在发起一项购买两房按揭债券的临时计划。在房市持续调整的过程中，两房的投资组合已经受到自身资本状况和应对系统性风险监管的限制。

防范系统性风险

通过我们目前已经采取的四项行动，美国联邦住房金融局和财政部履行了我们的职责，我们必须保护包括抵押信贷市场在内的金融市场的稳定，并最大限度地保护纳税人的利益。

让我阐明当前的行动对美国人和他们的家庭意味着什么。房地美和房利美在我们的金融系统中是如此庞大和如此盘根错节，以致它们中的任何一家倒闭都会引起国内金融市场、乃至全球金融市场的剧烈动荡。

工作仍在继续

尽管我们期望这四个步骤的行动能为市场参与者提供更大的稳定性和确定性，为两房债务和按揭证券的投资者提供长期的透明度，但我们的集体工作尚未完成。财政部临时权力在明年年底到期，两房投资组合将开始逐渐流失，他们将开始向政府支付一笔费用，对纳税人提供补偿以获得通过优先股购买协议提供的持续支持。

在今后的几个星期，我将对长期改革陈述我的观点。我期待参与及时和必要的辩论。

millions of Americans, Treasury is initiating a temporary program to purchase GSE MBS. During this ongoing housing correction, the GSE portfolios have been constrained, both by their own capital situation and by regulatory efforts to address systemic risk.

Protecting Against Systemic Risk

Through the four actions we have taken today, FHFA and Treasury have acted on the responsibilities we have to protect the stability of the financial markets, including the mortgage market, and to protect the taxpayer to the maximum extent possible.

And let me make clear what today's actions mean for Americans and their families. Fannie Mae and Freddie Mac are so large and so interwoven in our financial system that a failure of either of them would cause great turmoil in our financial markets here at home and around the globe.

Work Not Complete

While we expect these four steps to provide greater stability and certainty to market participants and provide long-term clarity to investors in GSE debt and MBS securities, our collective work is not complete. At the end of next year, the Treasury temporary authorities will expire, the GSE portfolios will begin to gradually run off, and the GSEs will begin to pay the government a fee to compensate taxpayers for the ongoing support provided by the preferred stock purchase agreements.

In the weeks to come, I will describe my views on long-term reform. I look forward to engaging in that timely and necessary debate.

(818 words)

保护金融市场和纳税人

知识链接

Henry Paulson 亨利·保尔森，美国前财政部长。亨利·保尔森 1946 年 3 月 28 日生于美国佛罗里达州充满阳光的美丽棕榈海滩，1970 年从哈佛大学商学院毕业，后在尼克松总统任职期间，出任总统幕僚助理和白宫内务委员会成员。1974 年他加入高盛芝加哥分部，在芝加哥分部担任银行业务助理，合伙人，由于工作表现突出，1999 年正式出任高盛集团董事长兼首席执行官。在保尔森的领导下，高盛集团成为华尔街最赚钱的投行。保尔森 2006 年就任美国第 74 任财政部长。他造访中国不下 70 次，被视为在华美国企业的中国问题专家和银行领域的"中国通"。

题 记

　　金融的自由化和促进交易更快捷的技术发展使金融与人类社会结合得更为紧密，并带来了更为深刻的变革。然而，"此涨彼伏"的金融危机却日益渗透到社会的各个层面，每一次大规模的金融危机都会带来既有金融格局的大洗牌。英国首相戈登·布朗在对小企业的演讲中呼吁重建全球金融体系，包括结构重组，帮助人们从劳动力过剩的岗位调整到新的工作中去；解决资源压力，满足人们对石油、粮食和商品的需求；信贷紧缩，将流动资金交给急需用钱的小企业和一般企业。全球性的问题需要全球性的解决方案，重建全球金融体系，意味着重新调整银行的资本，意味着给找工作的任何人提供帮助，意味着帮助小企业重塑对未来金融体系的信任和信心。

Rebuilding the Financial System Globally

— A Speech by British Prime Minister Gordon Brown on small businesses

Can I say first of all, it is a great pleasure to be here today and to be back in the region and to be talking about some of the challenges that we face, some of the challenges that are global, some that are national, some that are local.

It is very funny for me also to be in what seems to be like an old university lecture theatre.

I wanted to talk today however about what is happening to the global economy and how it impacts on what is happening here. I am very grateful that so many distinguished business leaders are here with us today to talk about the issues.

When people look at the last year or so, I think they will say this is the first financial crisis of the new global economy, and I think they will look back also at what happened with oil prices when they went up to $ 150 and they will say that is the first resources crisis of the new global

重建全球金融体系
——英国首相戈登·布朗对小企业的演讲

　　首先，我想说我很高兴今天能够站在这里，回到这个地方来探讨一些我们所面临的挑战。 有些是全球性的挑战，有些是国家性的挑战，还有些是地区性的挑战。

　　这对我来说也是非常有趣的，就像是在一个古老的大学演讲厅做报告。

　　我今天想谈谈全球经济究竟发生了什么事，以及它对这里产生着什么样的影响。 我非常感谢今天有这么多杰出的商界领袖与我们一起在此讨论这个问题。

　　人们回顾过去一年时，我想他们会说这是新型的全球经济的第一次金融危机，我想当石油价格上升到 150 美元的时候，他们还会回头看到石油价格发生了什么样的变化，而且他们会说这是新型的全球经济的第一次资源危机。

　　现在我们看到的是我们还必须处理所谓的全球化的初期困难，最重要的是，这些都是全球正在进行的大规模工作和产业重组。

23

economy.

Now we are seeing we have to deal with what you might call the teething troubles of globalization as well, and these are first of all a massive restructuring of jobs and businesses that is taking place around the world. So China, as you know, has become a great manufacturing centre producing half the electronics of the world; equally at the same time we are seeing a restructuring of jobs, manufacturing jobs that were once in America and Europe are now the jobs that are being taken in lower cost production in China.

We have three big problems. One is the restructuring I am talking about, so we have to help people move from jobs that are redundant into new jobs. The second is the pressures on resources, and that is really what happened in the last year, but the demand for oil, the demand for food, the demand for commodities that grew and the supply was inadequate to meet it, so we had a higher oil price, we had higher food prices, it affected people's standards of living in this country and in all countries, and that is the second feature that is a problem of the global economy and we have got to deal with that by having a better relationship between oil producers and oil consumers.

But the third problem is the one that we are now dealing with, and is often called the credit crunch① , and that is that we have got a global financial system now where there are global flows of capital all over the

---

① crunch [krʌntʃ] *n.* 紧缩状态

重建全球金融体系

众所周知，中国已经成为一个巨大的制造业中心，生产全球一半的电子产品。 同样，我们在同一时间看到了工作岗位的调整，曾经在美洲和欧洲的制造业工作现在转移到了中国，因为那里的生产成本更低。

我们有三大问题。 其一是我所说的结构重组，我们必须帮助人们从劳动力过剩的岗位调整到新的工作中去。 其二是来自资源方面的压力，这确实是去年发生的事情，但是对石油的需求、粮食的需求和商品的需求正在增长，而供给的不足根本无法满足这些需求，因此，我们只得接受较高的石油价格，我们只得接受较高的粮食价格，它影响了这个国家和所有国家的人们的生活水平，这是全球经济的第二个方面的问题，要想处理好这个问题，我们必须在石油生产国和消费国之间建立更好的关系。

但是，第三个问题是我们目前正在处理的问题，它常被人称为信贷紧缩，就是我们现在有一个全球金融体系，世界各地的资本在这个体系中流动，但是我们实际上仅有国家手段来监管这些全球流动资金。 银行目前还不能（在某些情况下不愿意、也不能）将流动资金交给急需用钱的小企业和一般企业，家庭和家族企业，特别是交给抵押贷款持有人，让他们获得贷款。

我们面临的问题是发生在世界上每个国家的问题。 银行正在调整资本，我们代表英国政府在银行购买股份，美国现在发生着同样

25

world, but we don't actually have anything other than a national way of supervising these global flows. The banks are now unable, and in some cases unwilling and unable, to give the flow of money that is necessary for small businesses and businesses generally, and for households and families, particularly mortgage holders, to get their money.

We have been faced with this problem in every country of the world. The banks are being recapitalized, we are buying shares as a British government in banks, it is happening in America now, it is happening in Europe, it is happening in Korea, Australia, all the major countries are realizing that they must have far stronger banks to enable them to withstand the problems that they face.

But most of all I think we have seen a loss of trust in the financial system that has got to be rebuilt, and rebuilt quickly, because if banks are not prepared to lend to each other and then not prepared to be trusted by members of the public, then the essential element of the financial system, which does depend on trust and confidence, is eroded and things come to a halt.

This is therefore a global problem that needs global solutions, and that is why I have been so keen that we have international leadership, and there will be a meeting of international leaders over the next few weeks. To build confidence in the system for the future we will have to show people that we have rooted out all the abuses that have caused problems in the past, that is off-balance sheet activities, a lack of transparency and disclosure,

重建全球金融体系

的事，欧洲发生着同样的事，韩国和澳大利亚发生着同样的事，所有的国家都意识到，他们必须拥有更强大的银行，使他们能够承受面临的问题。

但是最重要的是，我认为我们已经见证了金融体系的信誉损失，必须重建金融体系，而且要迅速重建金融体系，因为银行如果不打算互相借贷，也就是不打算获得大众的信任，那么完全依赖信任和信心的金融体系的基本要素就会受到侵蚀，事情就会停滞不前。

这就是为什么全球性的问题需要全球性的解决方案，这就是为什么我一直如此热衷于我们要有国际性的领导权，在未来几周还有一个国际领导人之间的会议。 为了重塑对未来体系的信心，我们必须向大家展示，我们已经根除了造成以往问题的全部流弊，包括资产负债表外活动，缺乏透明度和信息披露，某些情况下缺乏适当的监管，没有根据勤奋工作、努力、进取心和承担风险等条件制定高管薪酬方案等。

这对我们在未来的几个月里应该做的事情意味着什么？ 我们可以做稳定系统的工作，我们也可以做重新调整银行资本的工作，而且我们可以做启动借贷的工作。 但是我们应该做的远不止这些，我很高兴今天皮特也来到了这里，因为他已经宣布了一些措施，我们可以通过这些举措帮助小企业渡过这段困难时期。

27

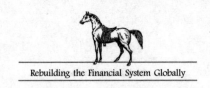

Rebuilding the Financial System Globally

a lack of proper supervision in some cases, executive remuneration①
packages that are not based on hard work, and effort and enterprise and
responsible risk-taking.

What does that mean for what we can do over the next few months?
We can work to stabilize the system, we can work also to recapitalize the
banks and we can work to start lending. But we have to do more than
that, and I am glad that Peter is here today because he has announced
some of the measures that we can take to help small businesses through
this difficult period.

And we also want to help home owners and we also want to help to
make sure that anybody who is at risk of losing their job, or anybody who
is looking for a job, gets the best possible opportunity to do so.

As far as small businesses are concerned, we are trying to access
what is actually a 24 billion euro fund in Europe so that we can have more
capital flowing to businesses in this country. We have increased the money
available in the Small Firms Loan Guarantee Scheme so that people can get
access to that more easily. Peter has made a decision that government
departments will pay within 10 days, and that means that instead of late
payment we will have the earliest possible payment to businesses. We are
asking local authorities to do likewise, we are asking the Health
Authorities to do similarly, and I know the Regional Development
Agencies are asking people in their areas that are public authorities to do

---

① remuneration [rimjuːnəˈreiʃən] *n.* 报酬

我们也希望帮助业主，我们也希望为面临失去工作危机的任何人、或者正在找工作的任何人提供帮助，使他们都可以得到最好的机会去这么做。

就小企业而言，我们正在试图与欧洲一个 240 亿欧元的基金接触，以使我们能够有更多的资金流入这个国家的企业。我们已经增加了小企业贷款担保计划的可流动资金，以使人们能够更容易获得贷款。皮特已经做出了决定，政府部门 10 天之内付款，这意味着我们会尽快给企业付款，不再拖延。我们要求地方当局这么做，我们要求卫生当局这么做，而且我知道，地区投资发展机构正在要求本地政府当局的人也同样这么做。

在未来的几个星期里，我们会主动实施更进一步的措施，此外，还要大幅削减正在进行全球协调的基本利率。

但是我们必须解决我们目前遇到的问题，而且要做得完全彻底，这就是为什么我们将尽一切力量来推动事情的进展。在很多情况下，这意味着必须要与其他国家合作，因为除非我们稳定、改善和加强全球金融体系，否则人们在未来的日子里会对这个体系失去信任。

但是，无论是就业，还是帮助小企业，或解决住房和抵押贷款等问题，我们都要殚精竭虑。

但是我认为，尽管我们经历了各种各样的困难，尽管世界上各

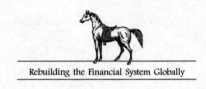

exactly the same.

And we will come forward over the next few weeks with further measures, in addition obviously to the cut in the basic rate of interest that has happened on a coordinated basis worldwide.

But we have to get through the problems we have got today, and we have got to get through that fairly and that is why we will do whatever it takes to move things forward. In many cases that means working with other countries to make the chances that are necessary, because unless we stabilize and improve and strengthen the financial system globally, then people will not have the confidence in it that they should for the years to come.

But whether it be on jobs, or whether it be on helping small businesses, or on housing and mortgages, we will do whatever we can.

But I think despite all the difficulties that we are going through, and despite the harder times that every continent in the world is facing, we should be confident about our future because our basic skills, our basic strengths, our scientific genius, and also our stability are a very good guide to how we can do well in the future. So we must come through these difficult times and we must come through them fairly, and I look forward to your questions and giving answers today.

Thank you very much.

(1,204 words)

个大陆正面临着更为艰难的时刻，我们应该对我们的未来充满信心，因为我们的基本技能、我们的基本优势、我们的科学天才、还有我们的稳定性能够指导我们在将来如何表现卓越。因此，我们必须走过这段艰难的时刻，我们必须安然度过这段时光，现在，我期待你们的问题，并期待你们给出答案。

非常感谢。

知识链接

Gordon Brown 戈登·布朗，前英国财政大臣以及英国首相。戈登·布朗1951年2月20日出生于苏格兰，1982年获得爱丁堡大学经济学博士学位。戈登·布朗1997年出任英国财政大臣，并创下连任财政大臣的纪录。当托尼·布莱尔于2007年正式向英国女王递交辞呈、辞去英国首相职务时，布朗接任英国首相，入住唐宁街10号。北京时间2010年5月12日，布朗向英国女王提出辞职，保守党和自由民主党组建联合政府，卡梅伦出任新首相，工党13年的统治在这一天画上了句号。布朗在任期间提出了"公仆政府"和"政府服务于人民"的执政方针，为英国的子民做出了杰出的贡献。

题　记

　　全球经济版图的变迁引起了信息技术领域的震动。六十多年来，倡导"以员工为导向"以及"企业价值观"、"企业目标"和"策略与执行"三位一体精神的惠普公司，从未停止过创新和变革的步伐。当年的惠普公司怀着对未来技术发展的美好憧憬和发明创造的激情开始了硅谷的创新之路，当世界经济增长的重心从发达国家转向新兴经济体之时，惠普在变化中的世界大刀阔斧，成为最早在中国成立办事处的外资企业之一。在人们还未料到中国有可能引领世界的卓越程度之时，惠普已经预见到中国即将向世界展示的能力和精神。新千年大张旗鼓地掀开了惠普对世界金融、货币和贸易实体经济结构变化的深度解读，对世界贸易合作伙伴关系的重新定位，对企业价值目标相关度的垂直考察和重建。

A World of Change

— A Speech by Carly Fiorina, CEO of HP,

at Asia-Pacific Economic Cooperation Shanghai

Thank you. Good afternoon, everyone.

One of the things they teach in business school is that positioning is crucial. How you position yourself in relation to your competitors can mean the difference between success and failure. Applying this principle to today's program, I keep wondering how it is that I got positioned to speak in the slot before the President of the Russian Federation — on the subject of change, no less.

Hewlett-Packard has been at the center of a lot of change in our 62-year history. But President Putin was elected president in the first democratic transition in Russia in 1,000 years. Talk about giving new meaning to the word "invent."

All the same, I am honored to be here in Shanghai, not only to attend this conference, but to celebrate an anniversary.

FROM THE START

It was 20 years ago next month-on November 9, 1981 — that Hewlett-

变化中的世界

——惠普公司首席执行官卡莉·费奥瑞纳
在亚太经合组织上海峰会上的演讲

谢谢,大家下午好!

定位是至关重要的,这是商学院教给我们的事情之一。 如何确定自己与竞争对手的位置可以带来成功和失败两种不同的结局。 我老是在琢磨,为什么我有勇气在俄罗斯总统面前谈论变革的话题,将定位原则运用于今天的这种场合,我就不再紧张了。

在 62 年的历史进程中,惠普一直处于无数变革的漩涡。 但是,普京总统却是俄罗斯 1 000 年来第一次民主转型后当选的总统。 这一重大历史事件为"创新"一词赋予了新的含义。

同样,我很荣幸地来到上海,不仅是为了参加这次会议,而且是庆祝一个周年纪念日。

开端

那是 20 年前的下一个月,即 1981 年 11 月 9 日,惠普在中国开办了第一家办事处,地点设在北京的一个旧厂房中。 开业的前一天,地板上还残留着木屑,我们的两个工程师非常努力地做准备工作,通宵在折叠床上睡觉。 正式运营时,我们成为中华人民共和国

Packard opened our first office in China, in an old municipal① factory building in Beijing. A day before the opening, there was still sawdust on the floor, and two of our engineers worked so hard to get our systems ready that they slept overnight on folding cots. When we opened, it was the first partnership of its kind to be sponsored by the government of the People's Republic of China in conjunction② with a foreign company.

One newspaper recalled that the day was marked by "much handshaking and drinking of tea." At the ceremonial dedication, our representative at the time, Bill Doolittle, said that it was our hope that by exchanging experiences, not only would we contribute to the friendship between our countries, but to the progress of our industries and the growth of our economies. In short, that we would both do better by working together than either could do by working apart.

Twenty years later, I am proud to say that we have fulfilled that hope. And I think that statement perfectly describes the spirit in which we all meet here this week. I don't think anybody back in 1981 could have imagined that less than a generation later-thanks in part to the work of the people in this room-Asia-Pacific Economic Cooperation (APEC) nations would account for a combined $18 trillion in Gross Domestic Product (GDP) and conduct 44 percent of the world's trade.

And I'm certain that nobody that day-even though they knew firsthand the talent and spirit that still defines China today-could have imagined the remarkable degree to which China would be helping to lead

---

① municipal [mjuˈnisipəl] *adj.* 市的
② conjunction [kənˈdʒʌŋkʃən] *n.* 联合

政府赞助的首家此类外资合伙企业。

一家报纸回顾了当天的盛况，称人们"不断地握手和喝茶"。当时的我方代表比尔·杜利特尔在庆典仪式上宣称，我们希望，交换经验不仅有助于国家间的友谊，而且有助于行业的进步和经济的发展。简而言之，对我们双方来说，共同工作比任何一方单打独干都会做得更好。

20 年后，我可以自豪地说，我们已实现了这个愿望。我认为，这个声明完美地阐释了本周我们所有人在此开会的精神。我认为，重回 1981 年，没有人会想象，不到一代人的时间，亚太经合组织（APEC）国家的国内生产总值（GDP）已达 18 万亿美元，占世界贸易额的 44%。这部分要感谢与会的所有人员。

我确信，即使有人预见了今天中国展现出的能力和精神，当时没有人会想到中国有可能引领世界的卓越程度。这座城市就是一个杰出的范例，它展示了世界上最古老的文明之一正在充分利用世界上某些最新的观念。

新的起点

时值我们庆祝惠普在中国的办事处成立 20 周年之际，中国将成为世界贸易组织（WTO）中的一员，惠普为此感到特别自豪。中国经济改革和加入世界贸易组织的决策将会使其经济和人民受益。

我同样赞赏中国加入"信息技术协定"（ITA）的决策，这样可以在接下来的几年里消除 IT 产品的所有进口关税。在未来 4 年内，预计单是中国的所有互联网用户就将占亚太地区的 42%。将"信息技术协定"加入亚太经合组织，会给环太平洋地区的每个国家的公

the way. This city is a shining example of how one of the world's oldest civilizations is helping to make the most of some of the world's newest ideas.

NEW BEGINNINGS

It is a special point of pride for HP that during the year that we celebrate the 20th anniversary of our first office in China, China will become a member of the World Trade Organization (WTO). The decision China has made to transform its economy and become part of the world's trading system will benefit its economy and its people.

I also want to applaud China's decision to join the Information Technology Agreement (ITA), to eliminate all import duties on IT products over the next few years. Over the next four years, China alone is expected to account for 42 percent of all Internet use in the Asian Pacific region. By joining other APEC economies in the ITA, it will bring more positive change for citizens in every country of the Pacific Rim.

I am pleased to announce that we are celebrating our 20th anniversary in China by launching a major software development center here in Shanghai next month. The center will work together with our partners here in China to develop software for the worldwide market and find application solutions for the domestic enterprise market. We're especially pleased that the project will create another 1, 500 jobs for software professionals in Shanghai.

A few months ago, when I was invited to speak here, I planned to come and make the case that the next global economic upturn will be enabled by a whole new generation of information technology. I was going to talk about how that new wave of technology will empower customers — transforming the ways we do business, creating value and revolutionizing

变化中的世界

民带来更多积极的变化。

我高兴地宣布，在庆祝惠普中国办事处成立 20 周年之际，我们下个月将在上海这儿建立一个主要的软件开发中心。 中心将与我们这里的中方伙伴合作，为全球市场开发软件，为国内企业市场找到应用解决方案。 我们尤其高兴的是，该项目将会给上海的软件专业人员创造 1 500 个职位。

几个月前，当我接受邀请在这儿演讲时，我原计划来解释完整的新一代信息技术有可能导致未来全球经济复苏的理由。 我打算谈一谈新一波的技术将如何给用户授权：新的信息技术将会转变我们做生意的方式，创造价值，彻底改变整个行业。 我当然打算向大家说明，在打造所有人都可得到的技术及其效益的领域，领导者的责任。 我认为，这些仍然是值得探讨的话题。

当然，我们并不是生活在 5 周前的那一个世界中。 人们一直认为，如果千年标志着一个瞬间，那么 9·11 事件标志着历史的一个转折点。

走到一起

我从一个举国哀痛的国家来到你们面前。 今天我们在这里开会，纽约和华盛顿特区的救援人员仍然在挖掘废墟，寻找那些失踪的遇难人员。 和你们一样，我的心仍然在悲伤，为所有的父母、兄弟姐妹、儿女和朋友，他们还在等待答案，他们的生活变得从此不一样。 我的祖国正在经历一种不安全感，中东和北爱尔兰的公民们数十年来就活在这种恐怖之中。

当然，这不仅仅是对美国的攻击，这是在攻击整个文明世界。大家都心知肚明，80 多个国家，包括今天在场的许多国家，在这场

39

A World of Change

entire industries. And I certainly intended to talk about the responsibility of leaders in shaping a world in which technology and its benefits are accessible to all. I think these are still worthy topics of discussion.

But of course we don't live in the same world as we did five weeks ago. It's been said that if the millennium① marked a moment in time, the events of September 11 marked a turning point in history.

COMING TOGETHER

I come to you from a nation in mourning. As we meet here today, rescue workers in New York and Washington, D.C., are still digging through the rubble to find the remains of those who are missing. Like yours, my heart still aches for all the mothers and fathers, brothers and sisters, sons and daughters and friends who are still waiting for answers, whose lives will never be the same. My country is now experiencing a sense of insecurity that citizens in the Middle East and Northern Ireland have known for decades.

Of course, this wasn't just an attack against America. This was an attack against the entire civilized world. As we all know too well, more than 80 nations-including many of the nations represented here today-lost somebody in those brutal attacks. All of us are feeling more uncertain than we did five weeks ago. While we may be more anxious than we have ever been, we are also more united than we have ever been.

(970 words)

---

① millennium [mi'leniəm] n. 一千年

野蛮的攻击中失去了亲人。 与 5 周前相比，我们所有人都更加忧心忡忡。 虽然我们前所未有地更加忧虑，但是我们也前所未有地更加团结。

知识链接 🔍

Carly S. Fiorina 卡莱顿(卡莉)·菲奥莉娜，惠普公司前董事会主席兼首席执行官。卡莱顿·菲奥莉娜 1954 年 9 月出生于一个经济条件优越的家庭，先后从马里兰大学、麻省理工大学、斯坦福大学取得了学位，毕业后从事过秘书、教师等工作，后来投身美国电话电报公司的销售电话服务。1995 年，卡莱顿参与美国电话电报公司分拆朗迅科技的工作，由于工作表现出色于 1998 年升为朗迅科技的全球服务供应业务部行政总监，管理一个占公司总收入达 6 成的部门。1999 年，卡莱顿出任惠普公司首席执行官，成为道琼斯工业指数成分股企业中唯一的女性总裁，2001 年，惠普与康柏公司达成一项总值高达 250 亿美元的并购交易，卡莱顿出任新惠普公司首席执行官。2005 年，卡莱顿结束了在惠普的 6 年职业生涯，卸下惠普主席兼首席执行官的职务。在这个男权至上的商业时代，卡莱顿·菲奥莉娜以她的聪明才智在商业上取得了丰硕的成就，为当代女性树立了崇高的典范。

题　记

　　香港地处中国内地与邻近亚洲国家的要冲，既在珠江三角洲入口，又位于经济增长骄人的亚洲太平洋周边的中心，可谓占尽地利。香港是从太平洋驶来的巨型远洋船和从珠江驶来的较小型沿岸内河船、更是新加坡与上海之间唯一充分开拓的现代化深水港，因而成为华南所有海上贸易活动的集中地。港湾和谐发展是香港港口跻身世界大港之列的必备条件，它包括6条城市设计原则，即多样性和活力、港湾和谐开发的强度、尊重自然环境和现有的城市结构、易于通行和行人往返、尊重文化遗产以及促进保护生态环境的设计和绿化。当人们真正有机会享受海滨提供的乐趣之时，也是香港成为最具效率的港口之日。

Development in Harmony with the Harbourfront

— A Speech by the Secretary for Development, Mrs. Carrie Lam, at the Harbour Business Forum

Vincent（Cheng）, Jon （Addis）, Distinguished guests, ladies and gentlemen,

Thank you for the invitation to join you for lunch today. Or more accurately, I thank the Harbour Business Forum （HBF） for granting me my request to come to speak to you on a subject very close to our hearts, following the launching of the Stage 2 public engagement on the Urban Design Study for the New Central Harbourfront. It is always a pleasure, and an enlightened experience for me to meet people who care deeply about Hong Kong and share a passion for our most precious natural resource, the Victoria Harbour.

Since its establishment several years ago, the Harbour Business Forum has played an important role in promoting new ideas on how best to manage the harbour from a holistic① perspective. I am particularly

---

① holistic [həuˈlistik] *adj.* 整体的

港湾和谐发展

——香港贸易发展局局长

林郑月娥在港商论坛上的演讲

文森特（程），乔恩（亚的斯亚贝巴），尊敬的各位来宾，女士们，先生们：

非常感谢你们邀请我参加今天的午餐。 或者更准确地说，我感谢港商论坛（HBF）应我的要求让我来给你们讲解一个非常贴近我们内心的话题，之前我们发起了第二阶段公众参与的"新中央港湾城市设计研究"。 对我来说，能够看到公众十分关心香港、并且热情参与我们最宝贵的自然资源——维多利亚港湾的建设是非常荣幸和开心的经历。

港商论坛自几年前建立以来，在如何运用新思维促进海港管理的最佳化和全盘化方面发挥了重要的作用。 我特别感谢海港工商论坛，自从去年7月发展局成立以来，它作为主要的研究型智囊团，在优化港湾的建设方面为香港特区政府做出了富有成效的工作和重大贡献。 在几个月内，海港工商论坛发布了三份易读和有价值的报

grateful to the Forum, as primarily a research driven think tank, for its productive output and significant contribution to the HKSARG's work in enhancing the harbourfront since the setting up of the Development Bureau last July. Within a few months, HBF has published three very readable and relevant reports, namely the Land Use Study for Hong Kong's Harbour-front entitled "What is on Hong Kong's Harbour"; Sustainable Transport Opportunities for the Harbourfront entitled "Balancing the Need to Travel with the Need to Improve Our Quality of Life"; and Organisational Structures & Harbourfront Management entitled "Managing the Vision". The tasks ahead of us to deliver the vision in these reports are daunting. But I can assure you that these reports will not be left to dust in the "too difficult tray". They will be valued as guiding documents for our harbour conservation work.

For some who have been closely following our work on the Central Harbourfront's Urban Design Study, you may be aware that the launching of the Stage 2 consultation① has been put back by a few months. This is justified such that we can take into account our latest initiatives in reducing development density as announced by the Chief Executive in his Annual Policy Address, in enhancing air ventilation, in better controlling total GFA, etc. It is well intended such that we could find inspiration from the community-driven design competition undertaken by Designing Hong Kong, and supported by HBF, which has attracted very high quality local

---

① consultation [ˌkɔnsəlˈteiʃən] n. 磋商

告，即题为"香港的港湾有什么"的香港海港土地利用研究报告、题为"平衡旅游需要与改善生活质量需要"的港湾可持续交通机遇报告以及题为"管理视野"的组织结构与港湾管理报告。这些报告拓宽了我们的视野，摆在我们面前的将是艰巨的任务。但我可以向你们保证，这些报告不会放在"太难的托盘"里被灰尘掩盖。它们是海港保护工作有价值的指导文件。

对于一些一直密切关注我们中央海滨城市设计研究工作的公众，你们可能知道，第二阶段的磋商启动工作已经推迟了几个月。这是合理的，正如特首在年度施政报告中宣布的那样，我们可以考虑我们的最新举措，降低开发密度，加强空气流通，更好地控制建筑面积等。我们有意从海港工商论坛支持、"创建香港"协会举办、社区公众参与的设计大赛中寻找灵感，这个竞赛吸引了高质量的本地和国际项目。新中环海滨优雅城市设计框架和具体地点的规划参数列入了第二阶段的文件，他们是公众在第一阶段参与收集的，也反映了公众的意见，与公众的诉求相一致。

精确的框架包括6条城市设计原则。他们是——

1. 多样性和活力

2. 港湾和谐开发的强度

3. 尊重自然环境和现有的城市结构

Development in Harmony with the Harbourfront

and international entries. The refined urban design framework and the planning parameters for specific sites in the New Central Harbourfront included in the Stage 2 document have also reflected public views collected in the Stage 1 public engagement and has responded to public aspirations.

The refined framework has embraced six urban design principles. They are —

1. Diversity and vibrancy

2. Development intensity in harmony with the Harbourfront

3. Respecting the natural context and existing urban fabric

4. Ease of access and pedestrian connectivity

5. Respecting cultural heritage

6. Promoting environmentally friendly design and greening.

One of the implementation issues that we have asked the Harbourfront Enhancement Committee to address and advise is management model for the harbourfront. Here, we have been presented with a range of options based on overseas experience. There is no doubt in my mind that a single entity able to pull together, not necessarily command, different levels and functions of government and to harness the support of the community is highly valuable. Indeed, a couple of weeks ago, with the formal approval of the Legislative Council, we have set up in Development Bureau an Office of the Commissioner for Heritage which is exactly performing that "pulling together" and "community focus" functions. We will review this experience down the road to see its applicability to managing the harbourfront.

48

4. 易于通行和行人往返

5. 尊重文化遗产

6. 促进保护生态环境的设计和绿化。

我们已经要求共建维港委员会解决和提议的实施问题之一是港湾区的管理模型。 在这里，我们根据国外的经验已经提出了一系列的选项。 毫无疑问，在我看来，单个实体能够使各级政府和职能部门齐心协力，无需强制命令，利用社区的支持是非常宝贵的。 实际上，几个星期前，在立法局正式批准后，我们已经在开发局成立了一个保护遗产专员办事处，就是履行"齐心协力"和"社区集中"的职能。 我们将在一段时间之后检验这些经验，考察它对管理港湾模式的适用性。

虽然公众参与、规划和体制讨论正在进行，但我们仍然在寻找某种"速赢"方案。 这些将让人们真正有机会享受海港，不再等待和观望。"速赢"方案的一个好例子就是湾仔海滨长廊，它在开发前是湾仔公共工程货运区。 我们有时称之为"宠物园"，因为它的设计符合宠物主人的思想，此地大受遛狗人的青睐。

我很高兴在担任民政事务局常任秘书长时亲自参与了湾仔区议会建立"宠物园"的工程。 虽然这项工程的规模相对较小，存在一些内在的无障碍环境限制，但它给人们已经带来了很多乐趣，而感

Development in Harmony with the Harbourfront

While the public engagement, planning and institutional discussions are going on, we are looking for some "quick wins". These will give people a real chance to get to enjoy the harbour without further waiting and watching. A good example of a "quick win" is the Wan Chai Promenade, developed on the former Wan Chai Public Works Cargo Area. We sometimes call this the "Pet Garden" because it is designed with pet owners in mind and has rightly become very popular with people out walking their dogs.

I am pleased to have been personally involved in establishing the "Pet Garden" initiated by the Wan Chai District Council in my former capacity as the Permanent Secretary for Home Affairs. Although this is on a relatively small scale and has some inherent accessibility limitations, it has brought a lot of enjoyment to people, not only just pet owners and lovers. It is a rare chance for people to get close to the waterfront. I have invited several District Councils to work with us in identifying similar "quick win" projects. I am confident we can come up with more of these so that more people can enjoy the harbourfront.

To give my colleagues and me further inspiration in this area of work, I took them on a visit to the North Tsing Yi Promenade on a Saturday morning last month. This particular promenade is commended in HBF's Study as a good example of vibrant and accessible harbourfront area-it is very popular and is a joy to walk down by residents as well as visitors. It is the creation of public private partnerships, and the envy of people living along the waterfront on the Tsuen Wan hinterland. With

50

受到这些乐趣的不只是宠物主人和情侣。 它为人们亲近海滨提供了难得的机会。 我已经邀请了几个区议会与我们携手合作，制定类似的"速赢"项目。 我相信，我们可以拿出更多的这种项目，使更多的人可以享受海滨。

为了让我的同事和我对这方面的工作产生进一步的灵感，上个月周六的一个早晨，我带他们走访了北青衣海滨。 海港工商论坛的研究推荐过这种特殊的海滨长廊，它是充满活力和开放的海滨地区的一个好例子，它非常受欢迎，它给来此散步的游客和居民带来了欢乐。 它是建立公私伙伴关系的好去处，荃湾腹地的人们过着令人羡慕的水边生活。 良好的推进计划、与私人开发商合适的共同努力是该项目成功的关键，我认为这个成就可以在其他地方推广。

现在，我猜想没有人会羡慕一名高级官员的工作。 我们承载着不断增长的需求和压力、规模庞大和复杂的政府工作，我们需要平衡各种各样的利益，我们需要对付闻风而动的媒体。 这些有时会使我质疑，为什么人们仍然愿意谋求这个职位。 我想我已经在一篇文章中找到答案。 这是一篇题为"你究竟为什么在 21 世纪加入公务员的行列"的文章，由前英国常任秘书长菲利普·海登爵士撰写。 这篇文章发表在一部散文集中，以庆祝 150 年的英国公务

good advance planning and suitable joint efforts with private developers, I think this success can be replicated elsewhere.

These days, I suppose nobody envy the job of a senior official. The growing demands and pressure placed on us, the sheer scale and complexity of government work, the diverse interests we need to balance and a very vigilant media we need to handle sometimes prompt me to ask why one would still like to take this position. I think I have got the answer from an article entitled "Why on Earth would you join the Civil Service in the 21st Century" written by a former UK Permanent Secretary, Sir Philip Hayden. In concluding his article which was published in a collection of essays to celebrate the 150 years of the UK Civil Service Commissioners system, Sir Philip said that people would still join the civil service now as he did several decades ago because they are still able, as individuals, to make a difference to the real world. For harbour protection and conservation work in Hong Kong, I would want to be that individual making a real difference.

Thank you.

(1,074 words)

港湾和谐发展

员事务专员制度，菲利普爵士认为，现在人们仍然像在几十年前一样加入公务员队伍，因为他们仍然可以作为个人在现实世界中有所作为。 为了香港的港湾保护和维护工作，我想成为这种个体，做出真正的改变。

谢谢大家。

知识链接 🔍

Hong Kong Trade Development Council 香港贸易发展局于 1966 年成立，是专责拓展香港特别行政区对外贸易的法定机构，活动范围覆盖世界各地市场。香港贸易发展局在全球 30 个国家及地区设有办事处，每年举办超过 350 项贸易推广活动，在香港会议展览中心举办 15 项大型国际贸易展览会，接待约 550 个访港贸易团体，年贸易咨询个案已突破 100 万。

题 记

个人的力量是渺小的。当人们面对突如其来发生的严重和破坏性的飓风、全球金融危机、气候变化、全球健康问题和恐怖主义等重大问题时，个人的力量尤其显得苍白无力。但是，正如霍勒斯曼对人类的呼吁一样："如果不为人类赢得某种胜利，至死也会羞愧"。作为联合国秘书长的潘基文，保护全球金融危机时期的共同利益当是责无旁贷，义不容辞。他在约翰·肯尼迪政治学院的演讲中，主要强调了全球具有挑战性的五个重大问题，包括全球金融危机、气候变化、全球健康问题以及恐怖主义和裁军。在这个全球化的时代，人们成为了全球金融稳定和繁荣的受益者，保护全球金融危机时期的共同利益，理所当然地考验着人类的勇敢和智慧。

Securing the Common Good
in a Time of Global Crises
— A Speech by Secretary-General Ban
Ki-moon at the John F. Kennedy School

Thank you for your very kind introduction Dean Ellwood.

Distinguished Faculty Members, Students and dear friends,

It's a great honour and pleasure for me to be back to the John F. Kennedy School. This is a really great opportunity for me, in my new capacity as Secretary-General of the United Nations, to return to visit my old school.

I must start by expressing my great regret at having had to postpone my visit here this past May. There was the very serious and devastating① Cyclone Nargis in Myanmar, so I had to rush to talk with the Myanmar authorities. With my direct intervention, fortunately, people have been able to receive all humanitarian assistance, and even until today this humanitarian assistance is flowing. Thank you very much for your

---

① devastating ['devəsteitiŋ] *adj.* 破坏的

保护全球金融危机时期的
共同利益
——联合国秘书长潘基文在
约翰·肯尼迪政治学院的演讲

埃尔伍德院长，谢谢你热情洋溢的介绍。

尊敬的老师们，同学们和亲爱的朋友们：

对我来说，回到约翰·肯尼迪政治学院是一份伟大的荣幸和快乐。对我来说，这真是一个千载难逢的机会，让我以联合国秘书长的新身份重返母校。

我必须首先对今年5月不得不推迟的来访表达深深的歉意。当时缅甸遭受了非常严重、颇具破坏性的强热带风暴纳尔吉斯的袭击，所以我不得不急于拜访缅甸当局。幸运的是，由于我的直接干预，人们已经能够接收所有的人道主义援助，甚至直到现在，这种人道主义的援助仍然源源不断。非常感谢你们对我迟到的理解。

现在，我很高兴地说，重返校园、会见我的教授——艾丽森院长，让我感到多么荣幸。我甚至在这里见到了我的教授，他曾经是我的老师。注视着年轻的学子们的脸庞让我回想起我在学校的时

understanding for that postponement.

Now I am pleased to say how much I am honoured to be back again, meeting with my professor, Dean Allison. I even have here my professor, who used to be my teacher. Looking at the faces of the young students reminds me of my school days which I still regard as the golden times of my life. I have never had such a great time in my previous life. I have been always busy, but that does not mean that I did not study much. But it was a real golden time for me. Last time I visited the Kennedy school was in September 2005 when I was Foreign Minister. At that time I brought some "good news" of the very historic announcement of the Six Party Talks Agreement. At that time I brought some very good news as well as some answers. But this time, unfortunately, I have to bring you some questions and a call to action on our common challenges. These are some things that I would like to discuss with you today. Of course I will state what I think in my capacity as Secretary-General, but I am here to learn more from you, to learn some very fresh, creative ideas from young students as well as professors.

I have had a two-hour long- I think almost three-hour long discussions with the very distinguished prominent professors of Harvard University on major issues pertaining① to our common challenges-the global financial crisis, climate change, global health issues, terrorism and disarmament. All these are the common issues, the common global

①　pertaining [pə(:)'teiniŋ] *adj.* 与……有关系的

光，我仍然认为那是我生活中的黄金时代。 在我以前的生活中，我从未有过这样一段伟大的时光。 我一直很忙，但这并不意味着我没有很多时间学习。 对我来说，那是一个真正的黄金时代。 我上次访问肯尼迪政治学院是 2005 年 9 月，那时我是外交部长。 我当时带来了一些"好消息"，即极具历史意义的"六方会谈协议"公告。 我当时既带来了一些非常好的消息，也提供了一些答案。 不幸的是，我这次必须带给你们一些问题，并呼吁大家采取行动，应对我们的共同挑战。 这些都是我今天想和你们一起讨论的一些事情。 我当然会以秘书长的身份来宣讲，但我在这里更多的是向你们学习，向青年学生以及教授们学习一些非常新鲜、有创意的思想。

我与哈佛大学非常杰出的著名教授们讨论了两个小时，我认为差不多近三个多小时，就我们共同面临的、具有挑战性的重大问题交换了意见，包括全球金融危机、气候变化、全球健康问题以及恐怖主义和裁军。 所有这些都是共同的问题，我们必须一起面对的全球性共同问题。 这正是我今天要与你们讨论的问题。

我也想借此机会表达我对梅森学者项目全体师生员工的衷心祝贺，梅森学者项目即将在下个月举行 50 周年庆典。 作为哈佛社区中的肯尼迪政治学院中的一员，我一直为此感到非常骄傲，但更重要的是，我还是梅森学者项目的一名成员。

据我所知，梅森研究员中有几位已经担任部长，目前至少有四到五位出任国家元首或政府首脑，还有一位，在很大程度上是由于出色的教学，已成为联合国的秘书长，我非常感谢学院带给我的荣誉。

problems which we have to address together. That is exactly what I am going to discuss with you today.

And I would like to also take this opportunity to express my sincere congratulations to all Mason Fellows who will soon be celebrating the 50th anniversary next month. I have been very proud as part of the Harvard community as part of the Kennedy School and more importantly as a member of the Mason Fellows.

Among Mason Fellows I understand that several have become Ministers and there are at least four or five Heads of State or Government at this time, and one, in no small part due to excellent teaching, has become Secretary-General of the United Nations, and I am very much grateful for this honour.

As I said we come together today at a time of intense crisis — unrelenting① waves buffeting② the world's people and institutions. Many months ago, when I spoke of a "triple crisis" — soaring food and fuel prices, climate change, and also development emergencies. Now all these triple crises have been compounded by the global financial crisis. Today, with increased evidence of the effects of all three crises around the globe, compounded by the ongoing shock waves of the financial crisis, my call to arms now seems distant and all too modest.

Now more than ever we must be bold. In these times of crisis, when we are tempted to look inward, it is precisely the time when we must

---

① unrelenting [ˌʌnriˈlentiŋ] *adj.* 无情的
② buffeting [ˈbəˈfei] *vt.* 冲击，与……搏斗

保护全球金融危机时期的共同利益

　　正如我所说的，我们今天在此相聚，面临一场严峻的危机——无情的冲击波正肆虐着世界各国的人民和机构。许多个月前，我谈过持续增长的食品和燃料价格、气候变化以及突发事件等"三重危机"。现在，全球金融危机掺杂到所有的这些三重危机之中。今天，全球所有的三重危机效应愈演愈烈，与正在进行的金融危机的冲击波叠加，我呼吁大家武装起来的号令似乎遥不可及，太微不足道了。

　　我们现在必须比以往任何时候都要更加勇敢。在危机时期，当我们倾向于保护自己的时候，正是我们必须把追求共同利益置于最高议程的时候。为了所有人的利益，全球团结是必要的。追求共同利益需要解决一系列的全球性挑战，这是我们共同未来的关键。我愿意强调五个问题：确保全球金融稳定是达到全民生活繁荣的第一步；解决气候变化问题；推进全球健康；反击恐怖主义；防止核扩散和裁军。

　　最近几年的繁荣带来了日益增长的全球化，它似乎来得太容易了，让我们理所当然地成为全球金融稳定和繁荣的受益者。但是，繁荣时期团结我们的全球化进程同样在不景气的时候深深伤害着经济，特别是那些承受能力最差的企业。虽然最近我们听到了很多关于这个国家的问题，包括华尔街风暴如何影响了主街上无辜的人们，但是我们需要更多地考虑世界各地没有街道栖身的人们。华尔街、主街、没有街道——我们设计的解决方案必须对所有人适用。

move pursuit of the common good to the top of the agenda. Global solidarity is necessary and in the interest of all. Pursuing the common good will require addressing a set of global challenges that hold the key to our common future. I would like to highlight five issues: ensuring global financial stability as an intentional first step toward prosperity for all people; addressing climate change; advancing global health; countering terrorism; and ensuring non-proliferation and disarmament.

In the recent boom years brought about by increasing globalization, it became all too easy for us to take for granted global financial stability and the prosperity it facilitated. But the same threads of globalization that united us in the good times, are now biting deep in the bad times, especially for those who can least afford it. While recently we have heard much in this country about how problems on Wall Street are affecting innocent people on Main Street, we need to think more about those people around the world with no streets. Wall Street, Main Street, no street-the solutions devised must be for all.

Dean Ellwood, Faculty members, students and friends,

America's great educator, Horace Mann, summoned humankind to "be ashamed to die until you have won some victory for humanity." Achieving disarmament is one such goal. Achieving financial stability and prosperity for all, addressing climate change, global health and international terrorism are others. Let us ensure we are equal to the task.

Thank you very much.

(887 words)

保护全球金融危机时期的共同利益

埃尔伍德院长，全体教职员工，同学们和朋友们：

美国伟大的教育家贺拉斯·曼曾经呼吁人类："如果不为人类赢得某种胜利，至死也会羞愧"。实现裁军就是这样的一个目标。实现财政稳定和各方繁荣、解决气候变化、促进全球健康和打击国际恐怖主义是其他目标。让我们确保我们都有平等的任务。

谢谢！

知识链接 🔍

Ban Ki-moon 潘基文(韩语：반기문，1944年6月13日–)，大韩民国外交官、政治家。他于2007年1月1日出任联合国秘书长一职，任期直至2011年12月31日。2012年1月1日连任联合国秘书长。他是第八位联合国秘书长，第二位来自亚洲的联合国秘书长。

题 记

    建立之初的"布雷顿森林体系"给战争重创之下的国际货币金融体系带来了曙光，并在"二战"之后三十多年的时间内有效地维持了国际金融秩序，促进了战后各国经济的恢复和发展。作为具有里程碑意义的国际货币体系，"布雷顿森林体系"以其合理的运行机制规范着国际货币金融秩序的有效运行。随着历史的发展，"布雷顿森林体系"的内在缺陷不断地暴露出来，并最终导致其不可避免地走向崩溃。当美国的次贷危机逐步演变为全球的金融危机之时，自由市场经济的风险彰显无遗，人们呼唤新"布雷顿森林体系"的回归，包括调整银行资本、阻止变现流、找到刺激经济的其他方法、通过监管改革重拾信心以及创建一个有效的多边机构。

A New "Bretton Woods Moment"

— A Speech by Economist Joseph Stiglitz on the Financial Crisis

Ladies and gentlemen:

Good evening. The amount of bad news over the past weeks has been bewildering for us in the world. Stock markets have plunged; banks have stopped lending to one another, and central bankers and treasury secretaries appear daily on television looking worried. Many economists have warned that we are facing the worst economic crisis the world has seen since 1929. The only good news is that oil prices have finally started to come down.

While these times are scary and strange for most of us, a number of people in other countries feel a sense of deja vu[①]. Asia went through a similar crisis in the late 1990s, and various other countries (including Argentina, Turkey, Mexico, Norway, Sweden, Indonesia and South Korea) have suffered through banking crises, stock-market collapses and credit crunches.

Capitalism may be the best economic system that man has come up

---

① dejavu *n.* 似曾相识的感觉

新"布雷顿森林时刻"

——经济学家约瑟夫·斯蒂格利茨
应对金融危机的演讲

女士们，先生们：

晚上好。 在过去的几周里，大量的坏消息一个个接踵而至，令我们惊慌失措，无所适从。 股票市场陷入瘫痪，银行停止了相互借贷，每天出现在电视中的央行行长和财政部长看上去忧心忡忡。 许多经济学家不断地警告我们：我们正处在 1929 年以来最严重的经济危机之中。 唯一的好消息就是石油的价格终于开始下跌。

虽然我们中的大多数人对这种状况感到害怕和陌生，但是其他国家的很多人都曾有过这种感觉。 亚洲在 20 世纪 90 年代末期经历过类似的危机，并且其他很多国家（包括阿根廷、土耳其、墨西哥、挪威、瑞典、印度尼西亚和韩国）也正经历着银行危机、股票市场崩溃和信贷紧缩。

资本主义也许是人类建立的最佳经济体制，但是没有人说过它会一直稳定下去。 事实上，在过去的 30 年间，市场经济已经经历了 100 多次危机。 这就是为什么我和许多其他经济学家都认为政府

with, but no one ever said it would create stability. In fact, over the past 30 years, market economies have faced more than 100 crises. That is why I and many other economists believe that government regulation and oversight are an essential part of a functioning market economy. Without them, there will continue to be frequent severe economic crises in different parts of the world. The market on its own is not enough. Government must play a role.

It's good news that Treasury Secretary Henry Paulson seems to finally be coming around to the idea that the U.S. government needs to help recapitalize our banks and should receive stakes in the banks that it bails out. But more must be done to prevent the crisis from spreading around the world.

All of us are concerning about how to fix the crisis. As we know, we are now facing a liquidity problem, a solvency problem and a macroeconomic problem. We are in the first phase of a downward spiral. It is, of course, part of the inevitable process of adjustment: returning housing prices to equilibrium levels and getting rid of the excessive leverage (debt) that had kept our phantom economy going.

Even with the new capital provided by the government, banks won't want to, or be able to, lend as much as they did in their reckless past. Homeowners won't want to borrow so much. Savings, which have been near zero, will go up-good for the economy in the long run but bad for an economy going into recession. While some large firms may be sitting on a bundle of cash, small firms depend on loans not just for investment but even for the working capital to keep going. That's going to be harder to come by. And the investment in real estate, which played such an important role in our modest growth of the past six years, has reached

管制和督察是市场经济有效运行必不可少的一部分。没有这些管制和督察,世界不同的地方仍然会频繁地出现严重的经济危机。市场本身不足以解决所有的问题。政府必须发挥作用。

财政部长亨利·鲍尔森似乎终于表示美国政府需要帮助银行调整资本,应该给银行注入国有股,帮助他们摆脱困境。这是一个好消息。但是,政府还必须做更多的工作,阻止危机在世界范围内蔓延。

我们所有人都很关心怎样渡过这场危机。众所周知,我们现在面临流动资金问题、偿付能力问题和宏观经济问题。我们处在螺旋式下降的第一阶段。当然,这是调整时期不可避免的一部分:恢复住房价格的均衡水平,摆脱维持我们有名无实的经济增长的过度杠杆(债务)。

虽然政府提供了新的资本,但是银行不愿意、也不可能不计后果地出借过去那样多的债务了。购房者不愿意借太多。我们的储蓄一直接近于零,以后将会上升,长期来看,这种状况对经济有好处,但不利于进入衰退期的经济。虽然有些大型企业可能坐拥大捆的现金,但依赖贷款的小企业不仅需要投资,甚至需要营运资本才能维持生存。这使经济变得更加艰难。在过去6年对推动经济适度增长起着重要作用的房地产投资,已达到20年来的最低点。

政府从一个半生不熟的解决方案转到了另一个方案。华尔街惊慌失措,白宫也坐卧不安。在一片恐慌之中,他们很难弄清楚要做什么。保尔森和布什面对大规模的反对,花了几个星期推行保尔森

69

A New "Bretton Woods Moment"

lows not seen in 20 years.

The Administration has veered from one half-baked solution to another. Wall Street panicked, but so did the White House, and in that panic, they had a hard time figuring out what to do. The weeks that Paulson and Bush spent pushing Paulson's orignal bailout plan-in the face of massive opposition-were weeks that could have been spent actually fixing the problem. At this point, we need a comprehensive approach. Another failed faint attempt could be disastrous. I will give some suggestions.

1. Recapitalize banks. With all the losses, banks have insufficient equity. Banks will have a hard time raising this equity under current circumstances. The government needs to provide equity. In return, it should have voting stakes in the banks it helps. But equity injections also bail out bondholders. Right now the market is discounting these bonds, saying there is a high probability of default. There needs to be a forced conversion of this debt to equity. If this is done, the amount of government assistance that will be required will be much reduced.

2. Stem the tide of foreclosures① . The original Paulson plan is like a massive blood transfusion to a patient with severe internal hemorrhaging②. We won't save the patient if we don't do something about the foreclosures. Even after congressional revisions, too little is being done. We need to help people stay in their homes, by converting the mortgage-interest and property- tax deductions into cashable tax credits; by reforming

---

① foreclosure [fɔːˈkləʊʒə(r)] *n.* 丧失抵押品赎回权
② hemorrhage [ˈheməridʒ] *n.* 出血

的救市计划。 实际上，那几个星期本可以解决些问题的。 在这一点上，我们需要一套综合的解决方案。 那些失败的、没多大影响力的尝试可能会损失惨重。 我将给出一些建议：

1. 调整银行资本。 经历所有这些损失之后，银行的股本已经不足。 银行在现有形势下增加股本困难重重。 政府需要提供资本。作为回报，政府可以在其帮助的银行中拥有投票股权。 但是注资股本也可以帮助债券持有者摆脱困境。 现在市场上的债券价值正在下降，据说存在高昂的违约概率。 这也迫使这部分债权转变为股权。如果这样做的话，要求政府援助的数量将会大大减少。

2. 阻止变现流。 保尔森最初的计划好比将大量的血液注入一个严重内出血的病人体内。 如果我们没有针对止血的政策，就无法挽救病人的生命。 即使国会修订保尔森的计划之后，所做的还是太少了。 我们需要将住房抵押贷款利率和财产税减免转换成可变现的税收抵免；我们需要修改破产法律，加快结构调整，这样当房屋价格低于其抵押价值时，可能会使抵押价值下降；政府甚至可以将其低成本的基金和储备借给贫穷的和中产阶级的购房者。 这些措施可以帮助人们居有定所。

3. 找到刺激经济的其他方法。 帮助华尔街和阻止变现流都只能解决一部分问题。 美国面临严重的经济衰退，需要一个大的刺激。我们需要增加失业保险。 如果各州和地方政府不愿出手相助，人们会随着税收收入的大幅下跌减少支出，而他们减少的支出会导致经济的进一步紧缩。 但是为了刺激经济，华盛顿未来必须进行投资。

bankruptcy laws to allow expedited① restructuring, which would bring down the value of the mortgage when the price of the house is below that of the mortgage; and even government lending, taking advantage of the government's lower cost of funds and passing the savings on to poor and middle-income homeowners.

3. Pass a stimulus that works. Helping Wall Street and stopping the foreclosures are only part of the solution. The U.S. economy is headed for a serious recession and needs a big stimulus. We need increased unemployment insurance; if states and localities are not helped, they will have to reduce expenditures as their tax revenues plummet, and their reduced spending will lead to a contraction of the economy. But to kick-start the economy, Washington must make investments in the future. Hurricane Katrina and the collapse of the bridge in Minneapolis were grim reminders of how decrepit② our infrastructure has become. Investments in infrastructure and technology will stimulate the economy in the short run and enhance growth in the long run.

4. Restore confidence through regulatory reform. Underlying the problems are banks' bad decisions and regulatory failures. These must be addressed if confidence in our financial system is to be restored. Corporate-governance structures that lead to flawed incentive structures designed to generously reward CEOs should be changed and so should many of the incentive systems themselves. It is not just the level of compensation; it is also the form-nontransparent stock options that provide incentives for bad accounting to bloat up reported returns.

---

① expedite ['ekspidait] vt. 加速
② decrepit [di'krepit] adj. 衰老的

卡特里娜飓风和明利阿波利斯大桥的倒塌严峻地提醒我们，我们的基础设施是多么不堪一击。 对基础设施和技术的投资不仅可以在短期内刺激经济，而且可以促进经济的长期增长。

4. 通过监管改革重拾信心。 潜在的问题是银行的错误决策和监管失败。 如果要恢复金融系统的信心必须解决这些问题。 应该改革公司的治理结构，这种结构导致了有缺陷的用来慷慨地奖励首席执行官的激励结构。 很多激励制度本身也是如此。 这不仅仅是补偿的标准，也是一种形式，即不透明的职工优先认股权为坏账粉饰虚增利润提供激励。

5. 创建一个有效的多边机构。 随着全球经济变得越来越相互依赖，我们需要更好的全球监管。 如果我们 50 个州的管理者各自为政，难以想象美国的金融市场能够有效运行。 但我们正在全球层面尽力从根本上做好监管。

最近的危机给我们敲响了警钟：由于一些外国政府为他们的存款提供了全面担保，资金开始流向看似安全的避风港。 其他国家也不得不做出反应。 一些欧洲政府在考虑需要做什么方面远比美国政府深思熟虑。 甚至在危机向全球蔓延之前，法国总统尼古拉斯·萨科奇就在欧盟呼吁召开世界峰会，为更多的国家规定奠定基础，以取代当前的自由放任政策。 也许我们又到了一个新的"布雷顿森林时刻"。 随着世界摆脱大萧条和第二次世界大战的结束，整个世界意识到它需要一个新的全球经济秩序。 这种秩序持续了 60 多年。很长时间以来，人们清楚地意识到这种秩序不再适合全球化的新世

5. Create an effective multilateral agency. As the global economy becomes more interconnected, we need better global oversight. It is unimaginable that America's financial market could function effectively if we had to rely on 50 separate state regulators. But we are trying to do essentially that at the global level.

The recent crisis provides an example of the dangers: as some foreign governments provided blanket guarantees for their deposits, money started to move to what looked like safe havens. Other countries had to respond. A few European governments have been far more thoughtful than the U.S. in figuring out what needs to be done. Even before the crisis turned global, French President Nicolas Sarkozy, in his address to the U.N., called for a world summit to lay the foundations for more state regulation to replace the current laissez-faire approach. We may be at a new "Bretton Woods moment." As the world emerged from the Great Depression and World War II, it realized there was need for a new global economic order. It lasted more than 60 years. That it was not well adapted for the new world of globalization has been clear for a long time. Now, as the world emerges from the Cold War and the Great Financial Crisis, it will need to construct a new global economic order for the 21st century, and that will include a new global regulatory agency.

This crisis may have taught us that unfettered markets are risky. It should also have taught us that unilateralism can't work in a world of economic interdependence.

I hope it's helpful for you. Thank you.

(1,235 words)

界。 现在，随着世界走出冷战和大金融危机，它将需要为 21 世纪建立一个新的全球经济秩序，并且应该包括一个新的全球管理机构。

这次危机也许已经告诉我们，自由放任的市场充满风险。 它也告诉我们，单边主义在这个经济相互依赖的世界里难以奏效。

我希望对大家有所帮助。 谢谢大家！

知识链接

Joseph Stieglitz 约瑟夫·斯蒂格利茨。斯蒂格利茨出生于 1942 年，获麻省理工学院博士学位，此后在剑桥大学从事研究工作。1969 年，年仅 26 岁的斯蒂格利茨被耶鲁大学聘为经济学教授。1979 年，他获得了美国经济学会两年一度的约翰·贝茨·克拉克奖，该奖项用于表彰对经济学作出杰出贡献的 40 岁以下的经济学家。1988 年起他在斯坦福大学任经济学教授，自 1993 年开始成为克林顿总统经济顾问团的主要成员，并且从 1995 年起任该团主席。1997 年起任世界银行副总裁、首席经济学家。现任美国布鲁金斯学会高级研究员。2001 年约瑟夫·斯蒂格利茨和美国经济学家乔治·阿克洛夫、迈克尔·斯彭斯，因为对信息经济学发展的突出贡献，共同获得当年的诺贝尔经济学奖。

题　记

　　"采掘业透明度行动计划"已经成为世界资源业迈向可持续发展的一个里程碑和重要推动力。"采掘业透明度行动计划"的初衷是使开发自然资源过程中的收入分配和资源致富透明化，这样可以更有效和更公平地使用自然资源及其财富，以减少资源浪费，抑制腐败，同时有利于政府的财政计划和宏观经济规划，并使资源国更容易获取经济发展所需要的国际融资。埃克森美孚迎合这个标准的方法始于其简单的商业模式、监管结构和坚定的道德标准，公司坚信"为谨小慎微的交易打下良好基础的信誉是无价的企业资产"。这种对透明度的承诺给予投资者对整体经济环境的信心，践行了"谨慎使用自然资源财富是实现经济可持续增长重要引擎"的原则。

The Future of EITI:
Forward with Focus

— Remarks by Stuart R. McGill,
Senior Vice President, Exxon Mobil Corporation

Ladies and gentlemen:

It is a pleasure to join you for the Extractive Industries Transparency Initiative's third summit conference. ExxonMobil is proud to support EITI, and we look forward to serving on its Governing Board next year. I also look forward to the announcements this afternoon of additional governments' endorsement of EITI. They are taking an important step in ensuring their countries' resources will better the lives of their countries' citizens.

The number of countries committed to EITI has increased to more than half of the IMF's list of 53 resource-rich nations, representing millions of people who stand to benefit from the initiative's successful implementation. This testifies to EITI's value and the lessons learned as its structure was shaped. By developing a process for effective disclosure of payments and revenues that is workable, useful, and respectful of

进一步关注"采掘业透明度行动计划"的未来

——埃克森美孚公司高级副总裁斯图尔特·R.麦吉尔的演讲

女士们,先生们:

很高兴参加"采掘业透明度行动计划"的第三次峰会。 埃克森美孚公司为支持"采掘业透明度行动计划"感到自豪,我们期待明年在管理委员会轮值。 我也很期待今天下午的公告,将有更多的政府宣布加入"采掘业透明度行动计划"。 他们正在制定一项重要的决策,确保他们国家的资源更好地提升国民的生活水平。

加入"采掘业透明度行动计划"的国家已经增加到 53 个,超过了国际货币基金组织列出的资源丰富国家的半数,代表了成千上万受益于成功执行这个计划的民众。 随着其架构的形成,这也证明了"采掘业透明度行动计划"的价值观和获得的经验。 通过开发过程中对支付和收入进行有效的披露,我们已经奠定了坚实的基础。 这种方式表达了对参与国家的主权和支持公司自治的一种尊重,具有

participating countries' sovereignty and supporting companies' autonomy, we have laid a firm foundation.

That is a tribute① to all the stakeholders who worked together in this process, and especially the leadership provided by the U.K.'s Department for International Development. We now have the opportunity to build on this foundation and further advance EITI's founding principles through its effective expansion and improved implementation. These are the recommendations of the International Advisory Group under consideration at this year's summit, recommendations that ExxonMobil supports.

In my remarks this morning, I will discuss the best means of implementing these recommendations and of moving EITI forward with focus. And in doing so, I will comment on what we have learned from EITI implementation to date. If, as we expand our ranks and strengthen our procedures, we stay true to the core mission of EITI and not stray from our current course, this initiative can continue to play an instrumental role in promoting effective transparency that facilitates responsible resource development.

Good corporate citizenship by EITI's supporting companies is very important to the initiative's continued successful implementation. Sound corporate governance and adherence to high ethical standards is imperative. Our industry strives constantly to meet this standard. We try to learn from each other in industry forums by sharing best practices, many

---

① tribute ['tribjuːt] *n.* 称赞

进一步关注"采掘业透明度行动计划"的未来

可行性和实用性。

我们赞美所有在这个过程中一起努力的股东们，特别是英国国际发展部的领导层。 我们现在有机会通过有效扩张和实时改进在这个基础上建立和进一步发展"采掘业透明度行动计划"的基础原则。 这些是国际咨询集团在今年的峰会上正在考虑的建议，埃克森美孚支持这些建议。

在我今天早上的讲话中，我将讨论执行这些建议的最佳手段和有重点地推进"采掘业透明度行动计划"的发展。 我还会据此对"采掘业透明度行动计划"至今为止的发展做出评论。 如果我们扩大队伍和强化规章制度，我们就会忠实于"采掘业透明度行动计划"的核心任务，不会偏离我们当前的目标。 这种首创精神在促进有效透明度以推进可依赖资源开发方面发挥着重要的作用。

"采掘业透明度行动计划"的配套公司具有良好的企业公民意识，这一点对继续成功执行这项计划非常重要。 健全的公司治理和遵守高度的道德标准是必要的。 我们的行业发展一贯与这个标准相吻合。 我们试图在行业论坛中通过分享最佳实践范例互相学习，今天在场的非政府组织、国际组织和政府提出了很多实践方法。

埃克森美孚迎合这个标准的方法始于我们简单的商业模式、我们的监管结构和我们坚定的道德标准。 我们公司的每一位员工，从高级管理层到底层员工都必须遵守我们的商业标准，这个标准有 18

of which were suggested by NGOs, international organizations and governments represented here today.

ExxonMobil's approach to meeting this standard starts with our straightforward business model, our governance structure, and our uncompromising ethics. Each and every employee within our organization, from senior management to entry level, must comply with our Standards of Business Conduct, which encompass 18 foundation policies ranging from equal employment opportunity, to safety and the environment, to conflicts of interest, to gifts and entertainment. We believe that "a well-founded reputation for scrupulous① dealing is a priceless corporate asset." This ethic of accountability is embedded in all our management systems, demonstrated through our training and discipline, and clearly tied to our business objectives and planning. It is also reflected in our safety, health and environmental performance, as well as our approach to community relations. And it is reflected in our dealings with resource-owning governments with whom we partner. ExxonMobil has long supported transparency, on a bilateral basis as well as through multilateral initiatives such as EITI.

ExxonMobil is also partnering with four other petroleum-rich countries participating in transparency initiatives-Azerbaijan, Kazakhstan, Nigeria, and Sao Tome and Principe. We are working with the Governments of Equatorial Guinea and Angola to encourage their

---

① scrupulous ['skruːpjuləs] *adj.* 绝对正直的

条基本原则,包括平等就业机会、安全和环境、利益冲突以及礼物和娱乐。 我们坚信"为谨小慎微的交易打下良好基础的信誉是无价的企业资产"。 这种道德责任感深入我们管理系统的各个方面,通过我们的培训和规范训练得到证明,并明显地与我们的业务目标和规划相关联。 它还体现着我们的安全、健康和环保性能以及我们处理社区关系的方式。 它体现着我们与拥有资源的政府打交道的方式,作为合作伙伴,埃克森美孚根据双边原则和"采掘业透明度行动计划"等多边倡议,一贯支持透明度。

埃克森美孚还与其他四个石油资源丰富、且参与"透明度行动计划"的国家进行合作,他们是阿塞拜疆、哈萨克斯坦、尼日利亚和圣多美普林西比岛。 我们与赤道几内亚和安哥拉等国政府合作,鼓励他们参与其中,我们继续支持世界银行和英国国际发展部举办的世界范围的透明度专题讨论会,我们支持八国集团的透明度行动计划。 我们欢迎美国政府在八国集团的倡议诞生过程中所起的作用,感谢其在"采掘业透明度行动计划" 诞生之初给予的建设性支持。

公司和政府的参与支持使"采掘业透明度行动计划"获得了成功,他们无论是口头上还是行动上均致力于自身透明度的发展。 这个拥有大笔资金支持的项目已经延续了几十年的生命周期,在品质方面极其复杂。 考虑到这些实际情况,无论是现在还是未来,稳定

participation, we are continuing to support the World Bank's and the U.K.'s Department for International Development transparency workshops worldwide, and we are supporting the G-8 transparency initiative. We applaud the U. S. Government for its role in giving birth to the G-8 initiative and for its constructive support for EITI from its beginning.

The EITI is succeeding with the support of participating companies and of governments, committed to transparency themselves in word and deed. The projects which such massive sums support have lifecycles spanning decades and are exceedingly complex in character. Given these realities, stable business frameworks-today and tomorrow-are imperative. A country's commitment to transparency gives investors confidence in its overall business environment. This economic rationale also underscores the importance of keeping EITI focused on its core mission.

It is counterproductive to make a commitment to transparency regarding revenues to help ensure those revenues benefit citizens in the best way possible and then commit to an oil and gas licensing system in the name of transparency that does not maximize the long-term value of those revenues. To do so would contradict EITI's first founding principle- that the "prudent use of natural resource wealth should be an important engine for sustainable economic growth."

Some say that natural resource wealth is a "curse," inevitably leading to economic practices that ultimately impoverish the nations endowed with it. In fact, when managed properly, natural resource wealth is a blessing, not a curse. The Extractive Industries Transparency

的商业构架势在必行。 一个国家对于透明度的承诺给了投资者对整体经济环境的信心。 这个经济基本原理也强调了持续关注"采掘业透明度行动计划"核心使命的重要性。

根据财政收入承诺透明度，以帮助确保这些收益使公民的利益最大化，然后以透明度的名义提交给石油和天然气授权系统，却没有将这些财政收入的长期价值最大化，这种做法是达不到预期目标的。 这样做就违背了"采掘业透明度行动计划"的最初原则，即"谨慎使用自然资源财富应该是实现经济可持续增长的重要引擎"。

有人说自然资源财富是"祸害"，会不可避免地导致资源丰富的国家最终滑向贫穷的经济边缘。 事实上，只要管理得当，自然资源财富是福音，而不是祸害。"采掘业透明度行动计划"是确保资源丰富国家的所有公民分享这份福音的部分解决方案。

虽然有必要实施"采掘业透明度行动计划"，我们还需要法治、公民自由和公众的声音来帮助抵制糟糕的经济政策和贫困。 这些优秀的管理政策将与透明度计划一道，阻止腐败，鼓励更好的资源管理，改善拥有丰富资源的社会。

我知道，今天到场的很多人一直在积极追求良好的治理职责。这些策略非常重要。 作为推进透明度的一个论坛，"采掘业透明度行动计划"已经显示出进步，而这种进步让支持它的埃克森美孚感

Initiative is part of the solution to ensuring all citizens in resource-endowed countries share in this blessing.

EITI is necessary, but it is not sufficient. The rule of law, civil liberties, and a public voice, are also needed to help combat poor economic policies and poverty. Together with transparency, such good governance policies discourage corruption and encourage the better management of resources to the betterment of the societies endowed with them.

I know that many of you here today have been active in pursuing these factors of good governance accountability. They are important. As a forum for promoting transparency, the EITI has shown progress, progress ExxonMobil is proud to support. To continue this progress, we must maintain the initiative's integrity and stay true to our mission. As we move forward, we must do so with focus.

Thank you.

(934 words)

到自豪。 为了这种进步的持续，我们必须维持项目的完整性，忠于我们的使命。 在我们前进的路途中，我们必须专心致志地做好这件事。

谢谢大家。

知识链接 🔍

EITI 采掘业透明度行动计划。2002 年，在约翰内斯堡举行的"可持续发展世界峰会"上，英国前首相布莱尔倡议设立针对资源行业可持续发展问题的"采掘业透明度行动计划"（Extractive Industries Transparency Initiative，简称 EITI）。这一计划成为全球资源行业迈向可持续发展的一个重要里程碑。"采掘业透明度行动计划"被提出之后，英国国际开发署牵头成立了"采掘业透明度行动计划"国际组织，建立了矿业公司公布向政府的付款和政府披露由矿业获取的收入等方面的全球标准。虽然基于自愿原则，但是一个国家一旦加入"采掘业透明度行动计划"，在该国进行采掘活动的所有公司，包括外国公司、本国公司，不论大小，都必须遵守"采掘业透明度行动计划"条款。

题　记

　　"百年一遇"的金融危机引发了美国经济衰退的可能性，持续成为一股"腐蚀性"的力量，直至摇摇欲坠的房地产价格日趋稳定。美国次贷危机爆发一年之际，美国五大投行的一家已经破产，一家面临破产，几乎所有的金融机构家家自危。美国在金融危机中市场流动性锐减，市场信用普遍降低，股市大跌，危机还将诱发全球一系列的经济动荡。为重建投资者信心，美国政府紧急救市，但是市场信心的重建是一个长期的工程。为稳定全球和美国人的恐慌情绪，美国总统布什不失时机地出面表示，政府将会尽全力采取多项有力的措施，缓解因金融危机而引起的投资者担心，以便稳定金融体系，从而促进金融市场恢复运转，推动经济的复苏。

We Are Acting

— A Speech by President Bush for Restoring
Stability to Financial Markets in Washington

Good morning.

Over the past few days, we have witnessed a startling① drop in the stock market — much of it driven by uncertainty and fear. This has been a deeply unsettling period for the American people. Many of our citizens have serious concerns about their retirement accounts, their investments, and their economic well-being.

Here's what the American people need to know: that the United States government is acting; we will continue to act to resolve this crisis and restore stability to our markets. We are a prosperous nation with immense resources and a wide range of tools at our disposal. We're using these tools aggressively.

The fundamental problem is this: As the housing market has declined, banks holding assets related to home mortgages have suffered

① startle ['stɑ:tl] vt. 使惊愕

我们正在行动

——布什总统在华盛顿呼吁恢复金融市场的稳定

早上好。

在过去的几天中，我们目睹股市令人吃惊地下降，大部分是由不确定性和恐慌造成的。 这是一个令美国人民不安的时期。 我们的许多公民严重地关切他们的退休账户、他们的投资和他们的经济福利。

下面是美国人民需要了解的内容：美国政府正在采取行动。 我们将继续行动，化解此次危机，恢复市场的稳定。 我们是一个繁荣的国家，拥有巨大的资源和可供我们使用的广泛的工具。 我们正在积极地使用这些工具。

基本问题是这样的：随着住房市场的衰退，持有住房抵押贷款相关资产的银行蒙受严重亏损。 由于这些损失，许多银行缺乏资本或彼此之间贷款的信任。 我们的信用系统继而遭到冻结，这种状况阻碍了美国商业日常交易的金融活动，造成国家经

serious losses. As a result of these losses, many banks lack the capital or the confidence in each other to make new loans. In turn, our system of credit has frozen, which is keeping American businesses from financing their daily transactions — and creating uncertainty throughout our economy.

This uncertainty has led to anxiety among our people. And that is understandable — that anxiety can feed anxiety, and that can make it hard to see all that is being done to solve the problem. The federal government has a comprehensive strategy and the tools necessary to address the challenges in our economy. Fellow citizens: We can solve this crisis — and we will.

Here are the problems we face and the steps we are taking:

First, key markets are not functioning because there's a lack of liquidity① — the grease necessary to keep the gears of our financial system turning. So the Federal Reserve has injected hundreds of billions of dollars into the system. The Fed has joined with central banks around the world to coordinate a cut in interest rates. This rate cut will allow banks to borrow money more affordably — and it should help free up additional credit necessary to create jobs, and finance college educations, and help American families meet their daily needs. The Fed has also announced a new program to provide support for the commercial paper market, which is freezing up. As the new program kicks in over the next week or so, it

---

① liquidity [li'kwiditi] n. 流动性

我们正在行动

济的不确定性。

这种不确定性导致了国人的焦虑。 这是可以理解的。 焦虑情绪能够滋长，它使人们很难看到政府正在做的就是在解决问题。 联邦政府制定了全面的战略和必要的工具，以应对我们经济中的挑战。 各位公民：我们可以解决这场危机。 我们能够解决这场危机。

以下是我们面临的问题和我们正在采取的步骤：

第一，关键市场由于缺乏流动资金无法运营，而这是保持金融系统不断运转的必不可少的润滑剂。 因此，美联储对这个系统注资数千亿美元。 美联储已经联合世界各大央行，协调降低利率。 利率下调将允许银行借钱时有更多的实惠，它有助于释放额外的信贷，创造就业机会，资助大学教育，并帮助美国家庭满足日常生活需求。 美联储还宣布了一项新的计划，用于支持已经冻结的商业票据市场。 当新的计划大约在下周开始执行时，这将有助于恢复美国企业和金融机构短期融资的关键客源。

第二，有些美国人担心他们的钱是否安全，因此，联邦存款保险公司和全国信用社管理局已明显扩大了保险储蓄账户的金额，并正在核对账目和审核存单。 这意味着，如果你在其中的一个保险账户中存款高达 25 万美元，那么每一分钱都是安全的。 财政部也在

93

will help revive a key source of short-term financing for American businesses and financial institutions.

Second, some Americans are concerned about whether their money is safe. So the Federal Deposit Insurance Corporation and the National Credit Union Administration have significantly expanded the amount of money insured in savings accounts, and checking accounts, and certificates of deposit. That means that if you have up to $ 250,000 in one of these insured accounts, every penny of that money is safe. The Treasury Department has also acted to restore confidence in a key element of America's financial system by offering government insurance for money market mutual funds.

Thirdly, we are concerned that some investors could take advantage of the crisis to illegally manipulate the stock market. So the Securities and Exchange Commission has launched rigorous enforcement actions to detect fraud and manipulation in the market. The SEC is focused on preventing abusive practices, such as putting out false information to drive down particular stocks for personal gain. Anyone caught engaging in illegal financial activities will be prosecuted.

Fourth, the decline in the housing market has left many Americans struggling to meet their mortgages and are concerned about losing their homes. My administration has launched two initiatives to help responsible borrowers keep their homes. One is called HOPE NOW, and it brings together homeowners and lenders and mortgage services and others to find ways to prevent foreclosure. The other initiative is aimed at making it

94

我们正在行动

采取措施，通过提供金融市场共有基金的政府保险，重振美国金融体系关键部门的信心。

第三，我们担心有些投资者会利用这场危机非法操纵股市。 因此，美国证券交易委员会已经启动了严厉的执法行动，检测市场中的欺诈和操纵行为。 证交会的重点是防止滥用的做法，如为谋取个人利益推出虚假信息，推动个别项目的股市下跌。 任何被发现从事非法金融活动的人都将受到起诉。

第四，房地产市场的萎缩已使许多美国人竭力还清抵押贷款，并担心失去自己的房屋。 我的行政部门已经推出了两项举措，以帮助有责的借贷方不会失去房屋。 一项举措被称作"希望联盟"，它汇集了业主、贷款者、抵押服务机构和其他方，共同寻求丧失抵押赎回权的方式。 另外一项举措旨在使有责的房屋业主更容易负担联邦住房管理局担保的抵押贷款再融资。 到目前为止，这些计划已经帮助 200 多万美国人保住了自己的房屋。 关键是：如果你正在努力偿还抵押贷款，总会找到各种获得帮助的方法。

第五，我们已经发现，美国金融体系中的问题不是孤立的，他们也影响到了全球的其他国家。 因此，我们正致力于与全球伙伴密切合作，确保我们行动的协调和有效。 明天，我将会见七国集团的财政部长、国际货币基金组织和世界银行的首脑。 亨利·保尔森财

easier for responsible homeowners to refinance into affordable mortgages insured by the Federal Housing Administration. So far, these programs have helped more than 2 million Americans stay in their home. And the point is this: If you are struggling to meet your mortgage, there are ways that you can get help.

Fifth, we've seen that problems in the financial system are not isolated to the United States. They're also affecting other nations around the globe. So we're working closely with partners around the world to ensure that our actions are coordinated and effective. Tomorrow, I'll meet with the finance ministers from our partners in the G7 and the heads of the International Monetary Fund and World Bank. Secretary Henry Paulson will also meet with finance ministers from the world's 20 leading economies. Through these efforts, the world is sending an unmistakable signal: We're in this together, and we'll come through this together.

And finally, American businesses and consumers are struggling to obtain credit, because banks do not have sufficient capital to make loans. So my administration worked with Congress to quickly pass a $700 billion financial rescue package. This new law authorizes the Treasury Department to use a variety of measures to help bank rebuild capital — including buying or insuring troubled assets and purchasing equity of financial institutions. The Department will implement measures that have maximum impact as quickly as possible. Seven hundred billion dollars is a significant amount of money. And as we act, we will do it in a way that is effective.

我们正在行动

长还将会见世界 20 个主要经济体的财政部长。 通过这些努力,世界正在发出一个明确无误的信号:全球处于危机之中,我们将一起渡过危机。

最后,因为银行没有足够的资金发放贷款,美国企业和消费者都难以获得信贷。 因此,我的政府与国会将尽快通过一项 7 000 亿美元的金融救援计划。 这一新法规授权财政部使用各种各样的措施帮助银行重建资本,包括购买或投保问题资产以及购买金融机构的资产等。 财政部将尽快采取措施,实施最大的影响力。 7 000 亿美元是一笔数额巨大的资金。 我们在采取行动时,将以行之有效的方式执行这些计划。

我们正在执行的计划是雄心勃勃的救市计划。 这是个正确的计划,需要时间验证它的全部影响力。 它有足够的灵活性适应形势的变化。 它大得足够运行。 联邦政府将会继续采取必要的行动,重振金融市场的稳定和经济的增长。 我们有一个由财政部长汉克·保尔森、美联储主席伯南克、美国证券交易委员会主席考克斯以及联邦存款保险公司主席希拉拜尔领导的杰出的经济团队执行这项工作。 在美国历史上这个重要的时刻,我感谢他们和他们的特别行动小组做出的贡献。

这是一个焦虑的时期,但美国人民可以相信我们未来的经济。

We Are Acting

The plan we are executing is aggressive. It is the right plan. It will take time to have its full impact. It is flexible enough to adapt as the situation changes. And it is big enough to work. The federal government will continue to take the actions necessary to restore stability to our financial markets and growth to our economy. We have an outstanding economic team carrying out this effort, led by Secretary of the Treasury Hank Paulson, Federal Reserve Chairman Ben Bernanke, SEC Chairman Chris Cox, and FDIC Chair Sheila Bair. I thank them and their dedicated teams for their service during this important moment in our country's history.

This is an anxious time, but the American people can be confident in our economic future. We know what the problems are, we have the tools we need to fix them, and we're working swiftly to do so. Our economy is innovative, industrious and resilient because the American people who make up our economy are innovative, industrious and resilient. We all share a determination to solve this problem — and that is exactly what we're going to do. May God bless you.

(1,057 words)

我们正在行动

我知道我们的问题是什么，我们拥有我们需要解决这些的工具，我们正在努力地尽快这样做。 我们的经济是创新的经济、勤劳的经济和富有活力的经济，这是因为创造经济的美国人民善于创新、勤奋努力和充满活力。 我们大家决心共同解决这个问题——这也正是我们要做的事情。 愿上帝保佑你们。

知识链接 🔍

George Walker Bush 乔治·沃克·布什为美国第 43 任总统。布什在 2001 年就职，并且在 2004 年的选举中获得连任。在担任总统之前，布什于 1995 年至 2000 年间担任第 46 任的德州州长。布什家族很早就开始投身共和党以及美国政治，布什的父亲是之前曾担任第 41 任总统的乔治·赫伯特·沃克·布什，他的弟弟杰布·布什也曾是佛罗里达州的州长。由于与父亲同样都是美国总统，因此又常被称为"小布什"以示区别。

题 记

　　也许每个慈善家的慈善事业都有一个"高尚的原因"和一个"真实的原因"，但是，他究竟做了什么，远比他为什么做更为重要。微软公司的董事长比尔·盖茨在圣何塞技术创新博物馆接受该博物馆颁发的詹姆斯·摩根全球人道主义奖时，抒发了自己"君子有财，捐之有道"的理念。他希望世界在分配资源时心照不宣，让每个人的生命具有同等的价值，以减少由不平等造成的苦难。他希望借助美国联合慈善总会的活动将雇员们聚集到一起，帮助他们观察微软之外的世界，并将这种放眼世界的胸怀变成企业文化的一部分。市场做不到的事，慈善事业可以弥补。运用技术改善人们的生活，回报社会，满足人类的需求已经成为比尔·盖茨从事慈善事业的最佳境界。

The Way We Give

— A Speech by Bill Gates at James C. Morgan
Global Humanitarian Award Ceremony

Ladies and gentlemen:

I always thought philanthropy① was something I would do when I was much older, after I retired. However, as Microsoft became increasingly successful, I realized that the amount of money I would be able to give back to society as I got older was steadily increasing.

One of the people who helped me start to think about how to give back in the smartest way was Warren Buffett. He told me he didn't think it was a good idea to give so much wealth to children, and I agreed with him. Of course, my children weren't old enough to understand the implications and argue against that idea.

I also thought that doing philanthropy and running a company at the same time might make me a little crazy. After all, during the day I'd make money, and then at night I'd go home and give it away. I was worried I'd

---

① philanthropy [fi'lænθrəpi] n. 慈善

我们回报社会的方式

——比尔·盖茨接受詹姆斯·摩根
全球人道主义奖时的演讲

女士们，先生们：

我以前一直这么想：再过几十年，等我年长一些、退休之后再去做慈善事业。可是，随着微软公司日渐成功，我发现，随着我的年龄增长，我能够回馈社会的金钱也在稳步增多。

在促使我开始考虑如何以最明智的方式回报社会，沃伦·巴菲特是其中之一。他对我说，他不觉得把这么多财富留给子孙是件好事，我赞成他的想法。当然，我的子女当时年龄还小，不能理解这样做的含义，也不会和我就此争辩。

我以前还想过一边做慈善一边经营公司，同时做这两件事也许会显得我多少有点疯狂。毕竟，我白天要赚钱，然后晚上回家，接着又把钱捐出去。我担心我会感到困惑，不清楚自己在做什么，为什么要这样做。

但是，后来发生的事情打动了我，说服我开始认真地做起了慈

get confused about which thing I was doing and why.

But some things happened that persuaded me to start serious philanthropy. One was working with the United Way. I learned about the United Way when I was young, because my mother was very active in it; she would talk about the campaigns she was running and how the money was being divided up among different organizations. We talked about the tension between local social services and things like disease research. We talked about how much of our allowances we should be giving to the church, to the Salvation Army.

From the very earliest days at Microsoft, we used our United Way campaign to draw employees together and help them to see outside our world — to see the entire community and understand the needs of the most vulnerable people in it. We wanted to make this outward-looking worldview a part of our culture.

In the last few years, we've developed a tool that helps our employees look for volunteer opportunities and instituted a program that matches their philanthropic giving. Last year, with these matching funds, the people at Microsoft donated more than $ 68 million and more than 100,000 hours of their own time. Many of the people who have volunteered and made donations have taken on major roles with charitable organizations. In the end, these experiences make them better employees.

Still, for many years, I thought of myself as focused exclusively on work that would help the business. But one day my wife, Melinda, and I were reading an article about millions of children in poor countries who

善。 其中一件事是与美国联合慈善总会的合作。 我小时候就听说过这个组织,因为我母亲是其中的积极分子。 她总是谈起她组织的那些活动,谈起善款是如何在不同机构之间分配的。 我们谈起过地方社会服务机构和疾病调查之类的事情之间的矛盾。 我们还谈起过我们应该从津贴中拿出多少钱来捐给教会,捐给救世军。

微软公司创立之初,我们就借助美国联合慈善总会的活动将雇员聚集到一起,帮助他们观察微软之外的世界,即看一看整个社会,了解其中最弱势人群的需求。 我们想把这种放眼世界的胸怀变成企业文化的一部分。

在过去几年里,我们开发了一种工具,可以帮助雇员寻找参加志愿者活动的机会,并建立了一个项目,协调他们的慈善捐款。 去年,微软的员工用这些协调基金捐出了 6 800 多万美元,做了 10 万多个小时的义工。 许多当过志愿者和捐过善款的人在慈善机构里都发挥了重要的作用。 最终,这些经历使他们成为更加出色的员工。

尽管如此,我多年来一直觉得自己应该全力以赴去做有利于企业的工作。 可是有一天,妻子梅琳达和我读到一篇文章,说的是穷国有数百万孩子死于在我国已经绝迹的疾病。 其中有一种我从未听说过的病,叫做轮状病毒感染。 那篇文章还说,轮状病毒每年会夺去 50 万儿童的生命。 我当时想,这不会是真的。 我一向关心时事。 我阅读过飞机失事和各种匪夷所思的意外事件,为什么没见过报道这 50 万生命垂危孩子的新闻?

die from diseases that have been eliminated in this country. These included a disease I'd never even heard of — rotavirus — and the article said rotavirus was killing half a million kids each year. I thought, that can't be right. I read the news all the time. I read about plane crashes and freak accidents. Where is the news about these half-million kids dying?

It's hard to escape the conclusion that in our world, some lives are seen as worth saving, but others are not. And that realization really forced us not only to start our philanthropy earlier but also to make reducing inequity the central priority of our giving.

We want the world to allocate its resources knowing that the death of a child in a poor country is every bit as tragic as that of a child in a rich country. The principle that every human life has equal worth guides us to look for the most effective ways to reduce the suffering that comes as a result of inequality. To us, that means improving economic opportunity and health in developing countries, as well as education in the United States.

Public health is amazing. It's not just about saving lives. As health improves, life improves by every measure. Every other problem you're dealing with — education, transportation — becomes far easier to manage. As you improve health, literacy goes up dramatically, people have smaller families, and all of the factors that drive a stable, prosperous society come together.

When it comes to health, technology is the key to getting us from where we are to where we want to be. Discovery, development,

我们回报社会的方式

由此只能得出这样一个结论：在我们这个世界上，人们认为有些人的生命值得去挽救，而有些人的命却一文不值。说实话，正是这次觉醒，使我们不仅提前开始了慈善工作，并且把消除不平等确定为我们捐赠的头等大事。

我们想让世界在分配资源时心照不宣，穷国孩子的死完全与富国孩子的死一样悲惨。每个人的生命具有同等的价值，这个原则指导着我们去寻找最有效的方法，以减少由不平等造成的苦难。在我们看来，这就意味着改善发展中国家的经济机遇和医疗水平，同时在美国开展这方面的教育。

公共卫生是一项了不起的工作，它不仅仅是为了挽救生命。随着健康状态的改善，生活的各个方面都会改善，我们面临的教育、交通等所有其他问题，应对起来都要容易得多。人们的健康改善了，读写能力会大幅度上升，家庭规模会越来越小，促进社会稳定、繁荣的一切因素都会不谋而合。

说起健康状况，技术是带领我们从现状走向理想社会的关键。发现、开发、应用，这些事情都离不开技术。但有的时候，尽管我们有着最好的意图，光靠应用技术也无法解决问题。

1997年，我去南非索韦托地区的一个社区中心做捐赠工作。索韦托是南非最贫穷的地区之一。微软公司向这个社区中心赠送了一台电脑。我到了那儿之后，他们想对我表达感激之情。但他们最终却在无意间向我展示了另外一个事实：这个社区中心里没有电，

107

delivery: All of those things take technology. But sometimes, despite our best intentions, just applying technology to problems doesn't fix them.

In 1997, I went to South Africa to dedicate a community center in Soweto, one of the poorest parts of the country. Microsoft had given a computer to this community center, and when I was out there they wanted to show me their appreciation. But in the end they unintentionally showed me something else. The community center didn't have electricity, so they had run an extension cord more than 200 yards to a noisy diesel generator. And sure enough, the computer was up and running.

But I knew that the minute the press left and I left, the generator would be used for some more urgent task, the computer would be largely irrelevant to the people who used the community center, and they'd go back to worrying about the very basic challenges they face in their lives — problems that a computer was not going to solve.

So even though PCs and technology can often be part of a solution, we need to remember to put technology in the service of humanity. It's not just taking what we do in the rich world and subsidizing① its use in the developing world. Doing that elevates technology as if it were the end goal, but we're just trying to use technology to meet human needs.

Meeting human needs, of course, is the starting point for all philanthropy. The challenge is to do the most you can with your time and money, to take advances in science and learning and make sure they get

---

① subsidize ['sʌbsidaiz] vt. 补助

于是他们把电线连接到 200 多码开外的一台噪音很大的柴油发电机上。 当然，电脑接通电源后能够运行了。

但是我知道，等媒体一走、我也离开之后，发电机立刻会被用于某种更要紧的工作。 在大部分时间里，那台电脑与使用社区中心的人毫不相干，他们回去后仍然要为生活中遇到的最基本问题操心——这些问题是电脑无法解决的。

所以，电脑和技术虽然经常充当部分解决方案，但我们必须记住，要让技术为人类服务。 这不仅仅是把我们在富国生产的东西送给发展中国家的人使用。 这样做提高了技术，仿佛是最终目的，但我们就是要设法用技术来满足人类的需求。

当然，满足人们的需求是一切慈善工作的出发点。 面临的挑战是利用你的时间和金钱、利用科学和知识的进步最大限度地做慈善，并确保他们得以应用到最紧急的需求之中。

当你发现一个已经错过的问题，并且可以集中专门的知识去设想出独特的解决方法之时，善款最有可能产生重大的影响力。

慈善事业可以在市场力量无法介入时参与进来。 它可以聘请专家，它可以颁发奖项，它可以与私人公司做出新的安排，它可以与大学合作。 我们赖之于行善的科学平台一年比一年完善。

技术之所以成为我们基金会的重中之重，部分原因是技术能够帮助我们看到当今世界的现实情况。 眼下，我们尚未关注正在受苦的发展中国家的人民。

The Way We Give

applied to the most urgent needs.

Philanthropic dollars have the best chance to make a big impact when you find a problem that's been missed and you can gather together unique expertise to formulate a unique approach.

Philanthropy can step in when market forces aren't doing the job. It can draw in experts. It can give awards, it can make novel arrangements with private companies, it can partner with universities. Every year the platform of science that we have to do this on gets better.

Technology is a central focus of our foundation partly because it can help us see what's really going on in the world. Right now we don't make eye contact with the people who are suffering in developing countries.

If you took the world and you randomly resorted it so that rich people lived next to people in developing-world conditions, you'd walk down your block and say, "Those people are starving. Did you meet that mother over there? Her child just died. Do you see that guy suffering from malaria? He can't go to work." Basic human instinct would kick in and we would change our priorities.

Thank you.

(1,155 words)

110

假如你掌控世界，可以随意安排它，让富人与发展中国家的人比邻而居，那时，你会走在你居住的小区里说："这些人正在挨饿，你见过住在那边的那位母亲吗？ 她的孩子刚刚死掉。 你看到了那个患疟疾的人吗？ 他丧失了工作能力。"这时，人类最基本的恻隐之心就会爆发，我们就会改变轻重缓急的顺序。

谢谢大家。

知识链接 🔍

Bill & Melinda Gates Foundation 比尔和梅琳达·盖茨基金会。比尔和梅琳达·盖茨基金会是由比尔·盖茨与梅琳达·盖茨夫妇资助的全球最大的慈善基金会。该基金会以美国华盛顿州西雅图市为基地，于 2000 年 1 月，通过盖茨学习基金会和威廉·盖茨基金会的合并而创立。该基金会现有资金约 270 亿美元，而每年必须捐赠其全部财产的 5%，也就是多于 10 亿美元。该基金主要在全球人的健康、教育、图书馆和美国西北部的建设等方面提供援助。

题　记

国际互联网由个别国家一统天下的局面将有可能在未来 10 年内终结，取而代之的是一个分裂的态势，形成多体系共存竞争的数字虚拟世界内的多极化格局。但互联网分裂的同时也创造了一些特殊机遇，它给世界各国带来的战略机遇更是百年一见。著名商界女强人帕特里夏·鲁索在数码首脑会议上就此发表了精彩的演讲，表达了作为一名 IT 行业工作者的职业荣誉感。她指出了当今用户控制的互联网时代的特征，分析了协调虚拟世界和现实世界的交集路线，阐明了创新推动的价值革命在新一代互联网全部潜力的关键，提出了构建全球宽带网络覆盖的历史使命。宽带网络各个领域下一阶段的创新和生产率增长正在以乘数效应向前推进，人们正在见证这一发展谱写的崭新序曲。

The Beginnings of
Broadband Network

— A Speech by Patricia Russo at the DigiWorld
Summit IDATE in Montpellier, France

Good afternoon.

I would like first to thank Francis Lorentz and Yves Gassot for the invitation to speak to this important conference. It is a wonderful opportunity to meet colleagues and to talk about the challenges and opportunities that lie ahead — for us as technology and business leaders, and as people who care passionately about creating a better future for everyone.

We are in a very honorable profession. There has never been a better or more challenging time to be in our industry. The innovations that carry much of the world's commerce, its entertainment and, ultimately, its knowledge are our responsibility. And this becomes more the case every day.

We live in a time of tremendous innovation and rapid change. Sometimes it may even seem as if our machines, which seem to have a momentum of their own, are driving us. It is important to remember,

宽带网络的序曲

——帕特里夏·鲁索在法国
蒙彼利埃数码首脑会议上的演讲

下午好。

首先，我要感谢弗拉西斯·洛伦茨和耶夫·高特邀请我到一个这么重要的会议上发言。 这是一个极好的机会，会见同僚并探讨摆在我们面前的机遇和挑战，因为我们是技术和商界的领袖，因为我们是充满激情、要为每一个人创造更美好未来的群体。

我们从事着一个非常光荣的职业。 我们的行业从来没有碰到过如此多的挑战。 创新在全球的商界被广泛运用，它的娱乐和它的知识最终是我们的责任。 这一点日渐重要。

我们生活在一个巨大创新和快速变化的时代。 有时看上去仿佛是我们的机器在推动着我们，这些机器本身似乎具有动力。 然而，重要的是要记住，正是需要交流和分享知识的人类实际上推动着技术创新。 网络的扩散起源于亚历山大·格雷厄姆·贝尔对电话的创新，现在已经延伸到我们的孩子们生活的在线社交世界，它继而创造性地提高了生产率，扩充了知识，并推动了进一步的创新。 只有当更多的人

however, that it is the very human need to communicate and share knowledge that is actually driving innovation. The proliferation① of networks, which began with Alexander Graham Bell's invention of the telephone and which now extends to the online social worlds our children inhabit, is in turn creating productivity gains, extending knowledge and fueling further innovations, a cycle which only speeds up as more people, devices and processes get connected.

We see the beginnings of the multiplier effect of the next phase of innovation and productivity growth all around. It is in things like Nicholas Negroponte's $ 100 computer to leave no child behind in the developing world. It is in the efforts of the people I am fortunate to call colleagues at Alcatel-Lucent labs around the world. We are intent on making communications — faster, smarter, easier to use and maintain, more versatile, and more available to everyone regardless of their means.

Phase 1 of the Internet opened what had previously been private data networks to public consumption at low cost. It smashed traditional notions of value. It disrupted business models based on proprietary② environments, and ones where the dominating interests were those of sellers rather than buyers.

It established a platform that insured an increased pace of change would be a constant in our lives. And, for the first time, users are in control in fact, and not just rhetorically. We live in an era of user control. Those who don't accommodate this new reality will fail.

---

① proliferation [prəuˌlifəˈreiʃən] *n.* 扩散
② proprietary [prəˈpraiətəri] *adj.* 私有的

力、设备和工艺联系到一起，这个循环才能加速。

各个领域下一阶段的创新和生产率增长正在以乘数效应向前推进，我们见证了这一发展的序曲。 这就像尼古拉斯·尼葛洛庞帝倡导的项目一样，即开发 100 美元一台的电脑，不让发展中国家的任何一个孩子落后。 这正是阿尔卡特朗讯世界各地的实验室努力的结果，我幸运地称呼他们为同事。 不管采用什么手段，我们都在设法组建更快、更智能化、更易于使用和维护、功能更多以及更便捷的通讯系统。

互联网的第一阶段就以低成本向公共消费者打开了原来的私人数据网络。 它打破了传统的价值观。 它扰乱了基于私人环境的商业模式，在这些商业模式中，是卖家而不是买家决定着利润。

它设立了一个平台，确保加速改革的步伐在我们的生活中延续下去。 并且，用户第一次事实上占据了统治地位，而不仅仅是口头上的。 我们生活在一个用户控制的新纪元。 那些适应不了这一新现实的人将会一败涂地。

创造力拒绝垄断。 获取知识的壁垒正在消退。 易趣、谷歌、亚马逊、苹果播放器和其他公司的业绩表明，从事商务活动和快速创造新商机的能力并不受任何限制。

分裂市场的能力也不受限制。 新的竞争者可以迅速在全球形成规模。 他们的目标可以锁定越来越小的市场，考虑市场细分、定制产品和针对个人的服务。 适应这种变化和风险管理是我们时代的口号。

There is no monopoly on creativity. Barriers to knowledge acquisition are falling away. eBay, Google, Amazon, Apple's iTunes and others show there are no limits on the ability to conduct commerce and rapidly create new businesses.

There are also no limits on the ability to disrupt markets. New competitors can scale globally in a hurry. They can target smaller and smaller markets, allowing for micro-segmentation and customized products and services to individuals. Adaptability for change and risk management are the watchwords of our times.

Already, our virtual world personas, especially those of our children, whether on social networks such as MySpace or game worlds, such as World of Warcraft, are as much if not more important than our physical ones. The proper care and feeding of the intersection of the physical and virtual worlds is key to the realization of the full potential of the next generations of the Internet. Providing security, along with dynamic content and context mediation according to users needs and desires is an important role. It is critical that we ensure that users interact appropriately and safely and that those creating value are properly compensated for their efforts.

We are not living through a technology revolution. We are living through a value revolution that is being driven by the inexorable① march of innovation. We supply what I would call "infostructure". While challenging, it is nice work being one of the key, trusted architects of the network in the information age. However, while we have educated

---

① inexorable [in'eksərəbl] *adj.* 不可阻挡的

　　和现实世界相比，我们虚拟世界的角色，尤其是我们的那些孩子们，不论是"我的空间"这种社交网络，还是"魔兽争霸"之类的游戏世界，即使不是更重要也是同等重要。 适当关心和协调现实世界与虚拟世界的交汇点是实现下一代互联网全部潜力的关键。 根据用户的需求和意愿提供安全、动态内容和语境调解在此扮演着极重要的角色。 确保用户适当和安全地相互配合、并给予那些为创造价值而努力的人适当的奖赏是十分必要的。

　　我们并不是生活在一个技术革命的时代。 我们生活在一个价值革命的时代，它被不可阻挡的创新推动着前行。 我们提供我称之为"信息结构"的模式。 虽然具有挑战性，但在信息时代，值得信任的网络建筑师的出色工作才是关键。 然而，尽管我们已经深思熟虑，但是我们没有水晶球，无法预测下一个成功的网络与通讯中心商业是什么样的模式。 我们与客户和战略伙伴紧密合作，并小心翼翼地投资，以确保我们与市场机会合理地对接。

　　我们确实应该拥有的就是责任感，对任何人或实体来说，确保我们是可信和有效的价值创造的推动者。 厂商利用专利技术作为锁定客户战略的时代已经谢幕。 我们接受这个挑战。

　　我们还必须负责任地保证，无论新的商业模式是什么，他们依赖的信息基础设施环境必须使所有的参与者从中获利。

　　我们还具有成为倡导者的强烈责任感，为无处不在的通讯在改善人类环境的过程中发挥中心作用。 这就是我们为什么这么积极参与标准机构的原因。 这就是为什么阿尔卡特朗讯坚决支持联合国千

guesses, we have no crystal ball on what will be the next successful network and communication centric business models. We are working closely with our customers and strategic partners and investing carefully to insure we are properly aligned with market opportunities.

What we do have is the responsibility to insure we are a trusted and efficient enabler of value creation by anyone or any entity. The days of proprietary technology being used by suppliers as customer lock-in strategies are over. We embrace that challenge.

We must also be accountable for assuring that whatever the new business models turn out to be, the information infrastructure environment upon which they rely must be rewarding for all players involved. Otherwise innovation dies. Risk must be rewarded.

We also feel a strong obligation to be advocates for the central role ubiquitous① communications plays in enhancing the human condition. It is why we are so active in standards bodies. It is why Alcatel-Lucent is firmly behind the efforts announced in the UN Millennium report which targeted connecting every community in the world with broadband by 2015.

This will not be easy. We just passed the mark where 1/2 of the world's population had yet to make a basic phone call. And the fact is that tele-densities remain low in less-developed countries. Even in places that are developing quickly like India and China, tele-densities tend to be high in selected urban areas, creating a digital divide that is counter-productive to both cultural diversity and economic vitality.

We all know the benefits of education. The old saying is that if you

---

① ubiquitous [juˈbikwitəs] *adj.* 无处不在的

宽带网络的序曲

年报告中的目标，努力争取在 2015 年利用宽带网络连接全球。

这不是一件容易的事。 我们刚刚使 1/2 的世界人口用上基本的电话。 事实上，电话密度在不发达国家仍然很低。 但在快速发展的印度和中国，电话密度在选定的城市地区很高，创造了一个既不利于文化多样性、又不利于经济活力的数字鸿沟。

我们都知道教育的好处。 古语有云：如果你给人一条鱼，只能给他提供一顿饭；但是如果你教给他捕鱼的技术，他就会一辈子衣食无忧。 这个例子说明，我们要给予无处不在的宽带传播国际优先权，并把它扩展到无人关注和缺医少药的地区。

个人拥有基本权利的概念似乎并非在世界所有地方都得到支持。 但是，我们必须坚持，宽带接入被全球视为一项基本权利，而不是一种特权。

我们将钱用在我们关心的地方。 上个月，我们在马达加斯加首都的五个较贫困的地区使用 DSL 和 WiMax 软件，开办了宽带接入中心。 接下来的一月份，我们将见证海地首个宽带网络开幕式。 而且，我们正在与印度政府合作，实施国家第一个 3G 村计划。

这不仅仅是为当地提供基础设施，它同时也确保了国家的骨干网络具有必要的能力，并连通了全球的光纤网络。 我们知道，兴趣各方的目标融资可以战胜挑战本身。 此外，在各个项目中，我们不仅提供技术，而且与当地政府合作，创建了可持续发展的教育和经济生态系统。

我将从我开始的地方结束我的讲话。 我们从事着非常光荣的职

121

give a man a fish you feed him for a meal, but if you teach him to fish he can feed himself for a lifetime. That is the case for making the ubiquitous spread of broadband an international priority and extending it to the unserved and the underserved.

The notion of individuals having fundamental rights may not have adherents① in all parts of the world. Yet, we should insist that access to broadband be viewed globally as a fundamental right and not a privilege.

We've put our money where our hearts are. Last month we opened broadband access centers using both DSL and WiMax in five of the more deprived areas of the capital of Madagascar. This coming January will see the inauguration of the first broadband network in Haiti. And we are working with the Indian government on the country's first 3G village.

This is not just about supplying local infrastructure. It is also about insuring national backbone networks have the needed capacity and are connected to the worldwide fiber network. A challenge in itself that we know can be overcome by targeted financing from interested parties. In addition, in each case we are not only providing technology, but we are working with the local government on creating a sustainable educational and economic ecosystem.

I'll finish where I began. We are in a very honorable profession with an awesome responsibility. We are enablers of new business models, and are architecting the future so we are part of the solution and not creating more challenges.

Thank you for this opportunity. I look forward to your questions.

(1,172 words)

---

① adherent [ədˈhiərənt] *n.* 支持者

业，肩负着令人钦佩的责任。 我们是新商业模式的推动者，我们正在设计未来，所以，我们的职责是解决部分问题，而不是创造更多的挑战。

感谢大家给我这次机会。 我期待你们的提问。

知识链接

Patricia Russo 帕特里夏·鲁索。帕特里夏·鲁索有着拉丁血统，曾担任全球最大的通信设备制造商朗讯科技的董事长兼首席执行官、美国国家电信安全顾问委员会成员。她的权力曾一度达到电信业的顶峰，被称作"全球电信第一女强人"，全球收入最高的女掌门。鲁索先后三次进入《财富》杂志全美最具影响力的 50 位女性排行榜。

题　记

地球由 21% 的陆地和 79% 的海洋共同组成。随着社会经济的不断发展，人类早晚会将陆地资源开发殆尽，并转而向海洋索取生存的各种资源，但是由于人类对海洋的不合理开发，如过度捕捞海洋鱼类，向海洋排放各种废弃物等种种不良举措，从而严重破坏了海洋环境。英国王储查尔斯在海洋环境保护协会上的演讲直陈海洋环境威胁：过度捕捞和海滩垃圾。与整个不列颠群岛相比，英国海洋现在有 7 倍以上的脊椎动物物种濒临灭绝；信天翁的胃中几乎塞满了各种塑料垃圾；超过 90% 的海鸟塘鹅的鸟窝包含塑料碎片，它们与鸟的脚、翅膀、有时是幼鸟的鸟嘴缠在一起；塑料袋阻滞了庞大的海洋爬行动物棱皮龟的肠道。在英国本土，查尔斯王子的观点被批评为保守、过时和精英主义。不论争议如何，查尔斯已经成为保护海洋环境事业的领军人物，海滩监管代表了查尔斯王子的所有环保哲学。

Beach Watch

— A Speech by the Prince of Wales
at the Marine Conservation Society

Ladies and gentlemen,

I am so delighted to welcome you all here today for this landmark in the history of the Marine Conservation Society.

I can only imagine that this silver jubilee must be a source of particular pride to the two visionary① people who, all those years ago, recognized the crucial need for an organization to protect and champion Britain's marine environment. Bernard Eaton and Professor David Bellamy are certainly owed an incalculable debt of gratitude from many of us. And, if I may say so, I am proud to have been involved almost from the beginning — if I remember, I was Patron of the Underwater Conservation Year, which eventually evolved into the Marine Conservation Society, of which I am delighted to be President and which has worked tirelessly for cleaner seas, sustainable fisheries and protection for our remarkable

---

① visionary ['viʒənəri] *adj.* 有远见的

海 滩 监 管
——威尔士王子殿下在海洋
环境保护协会上的讲话

女士们，先生们，

我非常高兴地欢迎大家今天来见证"海洋环境保护协会"这一具有里程碑意义的历史时刻。

我只能想象，这个25周年纪念日必须归功于令人特别感到自豪的两位有远见的人，多年以前，他们认识到了问题的紧迫性：需要建立一个组织来保护和捍卫英国的海洋环境。 贝尔纳·伊顿和大卫·贝拉米教授理所当然地受到我们许多人无以表达的感激。 而且，如果我可以这样说的话，我为从一开始参与了这项工作而感到自豪，如果我没有记错的话，我是"水下环保年"的赞助人，"水下环保年"最终发展成"海洋环境保护协会"。 我很高兴成为协会的会长，协会为清洁海洋、可持续渔业发展和对罕见的海洋生物的保护做出了不懈的努力。

有必要为这个了不起的成就好好庆祝一番。

海洋保护协会的"优质海滩指南"已经施加了大量的压力，

Beach Watch

marine wildlife.

And what a record of achievement it has to celebrate.

The MCS Good Beach Guide has applied the unstinting① pressure needed to ensure that sewage pollution on our beaches is relegated to history. The basking shark — one of the most impressive native animals in our seas — was protected because the Society presented the evidence for its decline. And, more recently, the Good Fish Guide has changed the basis on which many major retailers and consumers source their seafood, driving the market to support sustainably managed fisheries. Indeed, you will be glad to hear the seafood you have been served tonight was Marine Stewardship Council-certified!

It is little wonder that the MCS is one of the most respected environmental champions.

So there is much to celebrate but, dare I say it, there is still much to be done.

That is why the Society is launching a new report which will highlight one of the greatest environmental threats of this century — the systematic decline in the state of our seas. Overfished and awash with rubbish, there are now seven times more vertebrate② species facing extinction in UK seas than in the entire British Isles.

Entitled "Silent Seas", deliberately echoing Rachel Carson's "Silent

---

① unstinting [ʌnˈstintiŋ] adj. 无限制的
② vertebrate [ˈvɜːtibreit] n. 脊椎动物

128

海滩监管

需要确保海滩污水污染成为历史。 在我们海洋中最令人印象深刻的本地动物之一——姥鲨，由于协会出具了其减少的证据而受到保护。 最近，"优质鱼指南"已经改变了许多主要零售商和消费者获得海鲜来源的基地，并推动市场支持可持续的渔业管理。 的确，你将高兴地听到，你今晚享用的海鲜曾经过海洋管理理事会认证！

难怪海洋保护协会是最受尊重的环境拥护者之一。

所以，值得庆祝的事有很多，但是我必须说，还有很多工作要做。

这就是协会为什么要推出一份新的报告，其中将突出本世纪最大的环境威胁之一，即我们的海洋状态在系统性地下降。 由于捕捞过度和垃圾充斥，与整个不列颠群岛相比，英国海洋现在有 7 倍以上的脊椎动物物种濒临灭绝。

报告题为"寂静的海洋"，有意与雷切尔·卡森的"寂静的春天"相呼应。 报告将敲响警钟：我们的海洋需要紧急援助，以确保它们不会沦落到寂静或者沉默的地步。 报告具有真正的海洋保护协会的风格，它将提出问题和解决方案。 我已经事先查看了这份报告，我在此对绘制如此美妙插图的艺术家和每一位为这份报告做出贡献的人表示祝贺。

还有更令人鼓舞的消息，特别是关于海洋保护区的消息，我始

129

Spring", the report will be a wake-up call that our seas need urgent help to ensure that they do not fall silent or still. In true MCS style, it will present the solutions as well as the problems and, having had a sneak preview of the report, I can only congratulate everyone who has contributed, not least the artists who have illustrated it so remarkably.

And there is more encouraging news, particularly with regard to marine reserves which I have always believed can make a vital contribution to the health of our seas. Recent research has shown that reserves not only afford marine wildlife the protection that it so desperately requires, but also that they have a key role to play in helping our fisheries recover. The only current marine reserve at Lundy in Devon has seen lobster numbers increase seven-fold in just four years and, not surprisingly, local fishermen are very supportive. This is why I am so delighted by the UK and Scottish Governments' proposals for Marine Acts that will establish a comprehensive network of marine protected areas. And I am particularly keen on their proposals for "Highly Protected Marine Reserves", where no damaging activities will be allowed and for which I know the MCS has been a powerful proponent. Of course, time is of the essence and so I am delighted that the Government seems to be making the creation of Marine Protected Areas such a priority.

That is the good news, but there is yet another threat that will cross the boundaries of even the strictest of marine reserves and that is litter. It is an eyesore on the beaches, but at sea, largely out of sight and thus out of

海 滩 监 管

终相信，海洋保护区能对我们海洋的健康做出重大贡献。 最近的研究表明，保护区不仅为迫切需要保护的海洋野生动物提供保护，而且对帮助我们的渔业复苏起到了关键的作用。 德文郡伦迪岛目前唯一的海洋保护区仅在四年之内龙虾的数量就增加了 7 倍，这并不奇怪，因为当地渔民都非常支持海洋保护行动。 这就是为什么我对英国和苏格兰政府关于《海洋法》的倡议感到高兴，《海洋法》将建立一个全面的海洋保护区网。 我对他们的"高度保护海洋保护区"特别感兴趣，保护区不允许有任何破坏活动，我知道海洋保护协会是该提案的强大支持者。 当然，时间是至关重要的，所以我感到高兴的是，政府似乎正在优先考虑建立海洋保护区的相关事项。

这是个好消息，但还有另外的威胁，它将跨越最严格的海洋保护区的边界，那就是垃圾。 它是海滩上让人看了难受的东西，但我们大多数时候是眼不见、心不烦，而我们这个社会充斥着"用过即丢"的概念，残留物漂浮在海上，对海龟、鲸和海鸟造成了无法估量的痛苦。

人们发现那些华美而神奇的信天翁已经死亡，这些鸟儿的胃中几乎塞满了各种塑料垃圾。 实际上，长线捕鱼钩都无法将他们拖住淹死。 就在英国这儿，我们本地饲养的最大海鸟塘鹅，也同样受到威胁。 在草霍尔姆岛屿，超过 90% 的鸟窝包含塑料碎片，它们与鸟

131

Beach Watch

mind, the remnants① of our throwaway society are causing incalculable suffering to turtles, whales and seabirds.

Albatrosses, those magnificent and magical birds, are being found dead with their stomachs almost full to bursting with plastic litter of all kinds — and that is when they haven't actually been drowned by long-line fishing hooks. Here, in Britain, our largest native breeding seabird, the gannet, is equally threatened — over 90 per cent of the nests at Grass Holm Island contain plastic debris which entangles the feet, wings and sometimes the beak of the chicks. And our largest marine reptile, the magnificent leatherback turtle is particularly susceptible — their favourite food is jellyfish, which bears a striking similarity to a floating plastic bag — a bag that can block their gut and so they starve to death. If you are in any doubt, just take a look at the model next door showing the sort of debris that is found in the stomach of a dead turtle.

We simply cannot continue to treat the oceans in this way. How can we talk about sustainability and stewardship② when we are allowing this to happen?

That is why the Marine Conservation Society is so vital. Its annual "Beach watch" event involves thousands of volunteers who not only clear our beaches of litter, but painstakingly identify what each item of litter is so that the MCS can target the sources. I am so delighted that there

① remnant ['remnənt] *n.* 残余
② stewardship ['stjuədʃip] *n.* 管理工作

的脚、翅膀、有时是幼鸟的鸟嘴缠在一起。 我们最大的海洋爬行动物庞大的棱皮龟特别易受影响。 他们最喜欢的食物是水母，而水母与漂浮的塑料袋惊人地相似。 塑料袋可以阻滞他们的肠道，使他们饿死。 如果你有任何疑问，就请到隔壁看一看样本，它展示了从死海龟的腹部发现的一些碎片。

我们绝不能继续用这种方式来治理海洋。 当我们眼睁睁地看着这件事发生的时候，我们还谈什么可持续性和管理工作呢？

这就是为什么海洋环境保护协会是如此的重要。 一年一度的"海滩监管"活动吸引了成千上万的志愿者，他们不仅清理了我们的海滩垃圾，而且煞费苦心地将垃圾分类，以便海洋环境保护协会可以锁定目标源。 我很高兴今天与会代表中有一群勇敢的志愿者，你们为了更好的未来做出了如此与众不同的贡献。

事实上，有太多的人今天在此支持海洋环境保护协会的工作，他们都值得我们千恩万谢。 我希望你们中的每个人为过去 25 年的成就感到真正的自豪。 我特别要感谢新的企业赞助商尼斯·杜阿尔特、威特罗丝、尼斯·法伊夫和龙源，他们都参加了这场活动。 我谨希望有更多的企业追随这项事业。

女士们，先生们，随着气候变化危机的出现和食品成本的上升，立即采取行动保护海洋生物，确保我们的海洋提供给我们所有人的大量资源和环境效益的可持续管理，这些都从来没有这么重要

Beach Watch

are representatives here today from that brave band of volunteers who are making such a difference for the better.

Indeed, there are so many people here today to whom huge thanks are owed for their support of the Marine Conservation Society and I hope that each and every one of you is feeling a real sense of pride in the achievements of the last twenty five years. I particularly want to thank the new corporate supporters — Loch Duarte, Waitrose, Loch Fyfe and Dragon Feeds — who have joined the campaign. I can only hope that many more businesses will follow the lead.

Ladies and gentlemen, with the crisis of climate change and the rising cost of food, never has it been so important to take immediate action to protect marine life and ensure the sustainable management of the many resources and benefits that our seas provide to us all. The Marine Conservation Society is at the very heart of this fight. For all our sakes, let us hope that it is as successful in the next quarter of a century as it has been in the last, and I can only end by congratulating the members, staff — led so ably by Samantha Fanshawe — together with the volunteers and the supporters for your unstinting commitment and dedication.

(1,079 words)

海滩监管

过。 海洋环境保护协会是这场斗争的中心。 为了我们所有人，让我们希望，在未来四分之一个世纪它将同过去一样成功。 结束之际，我谨祝萨曼莎·范肖带领的成员和工作人员，还有志愿者和支持者，感谢你们慷慨的承诺和奉献。

知识链接 🔍

Charles Philip Arthur George 英国王储查尔斯王子。全名查尔斯·菲利普·阿瑟·乔治，1948 年 11 月 14 日出生，是英国女王伊丽莎白二世和爱丁堡公爵菲利浦亲王的长子。1952 年被封为康沃尔公爵、卡里克伯爵、伦弗鲁男爵、苏格兰诸岛和大斯图尔德勋爵。1958 年，被封为威尔士亲王（英国王位继承人在储位期间的专用封号）和切斯特伯爵。

题 记

　　英国借贷银行受金融危机的影响先后告急，近乎破产。连续增长了16年的英国经济急剧下滑，其衰退程度远远大于任何其他的主要经济区。英国财政部大臣在记者招待会上坦承，虽说这些银行均受美国次贷危机的连累，但今日的恶果与工党政府执政以来着重走完全自由的市场路线、放宽政府对金融的监管密切相关。英国政府为稳定银行系统采取了三个步骤，即解决银行之间的资金流动，支持银行筹集追加资本和允许银行在市场上自筹资金。这些方案旨在恢复大众对金融系统的信心和信任，使英国的银行体系建立在更加健全的基础之上，为未来的发展蓄积力量，以便使它能够在英国经济中支持就业，促进经济的繁荣发展。

Stabilizing the Banking System

— A Speech by Alistair Darling, Chancellor of the Exchequer① of UK at the Press Conference

Prime Minister:

Good Morning. Up and down the country families and small businesses are worried and anxious about their futures, and I know and understand this. Good strong banks are essential for every family and for every business in the country and extraordinary times call for the bold and far-reaching solutions that the Treasury has announced today.

The problems that started in America have now hurt every banking system in every continent of the world. The global financial market has ceased to function, putting in danger the necessary flow of money to businesses and families on which all of us depend in our daily lives.

So our stability and restructuring programme is comprehensive, it is specific and it breaks new ground. The programme is designed to restore confidence and trust in the financial system and, more than that, to put the British banking system on a sounder footing and to build strength for

---

① Exchequer [iks'tʃekə] n. [英]财政部

稳定银行系统

——英国财政大臣阿利斯泰尔·达林
在记者招待会上的演讲

首相：

早上好。 举国上下的家庭和小企业都对未来感到不安和焦虑，我对此表示同情和理解。 强大优质的银行对国家的每个家庭和每个企业意义非凡，非常时期呼唤大胆而影响长远的解决方案，财政部今天宣布了这种方案。

始于美国的问题现在已经伤害到世界每一块大陆的每一家银行系统。 全球金融市场已经停止运作，在这一发千钧之际将我们所有人日常生活必需的流动资金输入企业和家庭。

因此，我们的金融稳定和重组计划是全面的、具体的、突破性的。 该方案旨在恢复大众对金融系统的信心和信任，更重要的是，它使英国的银行体系建立在一个更加健全的基础之上，为未来的发展蓄积力量，以便使它能够在我们的经济中支持就业，促进经济的繁荣发展。

在过去的一年中，我们一直在采取行动，以稳定银行系统。 几个星期以前，我们开始与英格兰银行的行长和金融服务管理局一起

the future so that it can support jobs and prosperity right across our economy.

While over the last year we have consistently acted to stabilise the system, some weeks ago we started working with the Governor of the Bank of England and the Financial Services Authority on a programme that delivers a comprehensive restructuring of our banking system. We decided we had do more than provide liquidity or buy up assets, as in the American programme, and when we have to meet immediate and long term challenges no one measure alone will be sufficient. So we have taken a comprehensive approach.

This is not a time for conventional thinking or out-dated dogma, but for the fresh and innovative intervention that gets to the heart of the problem.

We are taking three steps. First, to address the immediate issue of flows of money between banks, the Governor of the Bank of England is extending and he is widening the provision of short term liquidity. Loans under the special liquidity scheme will be increased from £ 100 billion to at least £ 200 billion, and the Bank will also now bring forward proposals for a permanent facility.

Secondly, to ensure the long term health of the British banking system we are today offering to support banks in raising additional capital by investing directly through preference shares, or at their request by assisting them by raising ordinary shares. The largest banks have committed that they will increase their capital by £ 25 billion, which we will make available to them if they so wish. In addition we will provide at

合作，制定全面的重组我们银行系统的方案。 我们决定像美国方案那样，不仅仅只是提供流动资金或收购资产。 当我们必须满足即时和长期挑战的时候，单一的措施远远不够，所以，我们已经采取了一种全面的方法。

这不是一个采取常规思维或过时教条的时刻，而是一个崭新和创新的干预时刻，这样才能触及核心问题。

我们正在采取三个步骤。 首先，解决银行之间资金流动的紧急问题，英格兰银行的行长正在竭尽全力扩大提供短期流动资金的范围。 特别流动资金计划下的贷款将由 1 000 亿英镑增加至少 2 000 亿英镑，英格兰银行现在还准备推出永久性附加服务的建议。

其次，为确保长期健康的英国银行体系，我们目前将会通过对优先股进行直接投资的方式，或者根据他们的需求通过筹集普通股帮助他们的方式，支持银行筹集追加资本。 最大的几家银行已经承诺，他们将会增加 250 亿英镑的资金，如果他们愿意，我们将向他们发放资金。 此外，我们将至少再提供 250 亿英镑的资金。 我们、英格兰银行和英国金融服务管理局坚信，英国的银行应该是牢固和安全的。

最后，我们将为充足的商业费用提供担保，允许银行在市场上自筹资金，恢复正常借贷。 我们预计至少提供 250 亿英镑的担保。

所有的这些都是政府做的投资，但他们会使纳税人获得适当的回报。 这套建立在稳定、结构调整和筹措资金基础上的综合决策是必不可少的构建模块，它使银行恢复了自己的基本职能，为家庭和企业提供现金和投资，进而推动经济向前发展。

这些决策是为存款人和储蓄者提供长期安全的最好方法。 正如

least another £ 25 billion. We, the Bank and the FSA are determined that UK banking should be strong and secure.

And thirdly, for a fully commercial fee we will provide guarantees to allow banks to raise their own money in the markets and to resume normal lending. We expect to provide at least £ 250 billion of guarantees.

All these are investments being made by the Government which will earn a proper return for the taxpayer. And this comprehensive set of decisions on stability, on restructuring and on financing are the necessary building blocks to allow banks to return to their basic function of providing cash and investment for families and businesses and thus help the economy move forward.

These decisions are the best way of providing long term security for depositors and savers. And as people will now know, we are taking legal action against the Icelandic authorities to recover the money lost to people who deposited in UK branches of this bank. The Chancellor is saying today that he will stand behind the deposits of these customers.

We are showing by our actions that we stand by people who save in Britain. At all times we will ensure taxpayers' money is protected. As the people of Britain will expect, there will be strings① attached and conditions to be met. The Treasury has made clear today that it will need to be satisfied about the banks lending to home owners and businesses, including small businesses. We will insist on bank credit lines to small businesses being maintained on a normal commercial basis.

---

① strings [striŋz] n. 附带条件

人们现在知道的那样，我们正在对冰岛当局采取法律行动，恢复人们存在当地英国支行损失的资金。 财政大臣今天声称，他将为这些客户的存款做后盾。

我们正在用行动显示，我们将和在英国存款的客户站在同一战线。 无论什么时候我们都将确保纳税人的钱受到保护。 正如英国人民所期望的那样，将会有附加条件和需要满足的条件。 财政部今天已经明确宣布，银行必须满足业主和企业、包括小企业在内的贷款。 我们一定坚持将中小企业的银行信贷额度维持在正常的商业基础之上。

因为我们的经济应该围绕工作道德规范、利润丰厚的企业和责任来建设，而不是不负责任的冒险精神，所以我们还必须满足银行的行政报酬、股息支付和监管改善等各项条款。 我们将保证纳税人分享适当的收益。

由于这种支持基于商业条款，所以我们期望能从我们提供的支持中获得回报。 通过这次调整，我相信，我们可以期待一个更公平、更公正和更可靠的金融体系。

由于以上情况也是全球性的问题，所以需要全球性的行动。 这是一个漫长的过程，我们已经邀请欧洲其他国家考虑我们今天上午向他们提出的中期资金建议，并正在积极协商我们如何采纳一项欧洲范围的资金计划，我今天上午已经向萨科齐总统通报了此事。

与此同时，我们正在与所有七国集团领导人和 20 国集团领导人商谈各国正要聚首的事宜，我们准备在这样的会议上提出英国的建议。

各个国家都在经历困难时期的考验。 当然，这些问题开始于美

And because our economy should be built around the work ethic, rewarding enterprise and responsibility, rather than irresponsible risk-taking, we must also be satisfied in the terms of our agreements with the banks about executive remuneration, about dividend payments and about improvements in supervision, and we will insist that the taxpayer gets an appropriate share of the upside.

This support is therefore on commercial terms, we expect to be rewarded for the support we provide. Out of this restructuring I believe we can look forward to a fairer, more equitable and reliable financial system.

Because these are also global problems, global action is required. This is a long haul and we have invited other European countries to consider proposals we have put to them this morning on medium term funding, and are in active consultation about how we can adopt a European-wide funding plan, and I have spoken to President Sarkozy this morning about this.

At the same time we are in conversations with all the G7 leaders and G20 leaders about a gathering of Heads of Government and we are ready to put British proposals to such a meeting.

Countries are tested in difficult times. These problems certainly started in the United States of America, but they are having a big impact on our and on other financial systems. But I believe that the decisions we have taken today, with the conditions we have set, are the right decisions to allow us to come through this and help build financial security.

(931 words)

144

稳定银行系统

国，但它们对我们国家以及其他国家的金融系统具有强大的冲击力。 不过，我相信我们今天所做的决策以及我们制定的条款都是正确的抉择，它能够使我们成功地渡过这次难关，并帮助我们建立金融安全体系。

知识链接 🔍

Chancellor of the Exchequer 财政大臣是英国内阁中主管经济与金融事务的官员职称，负责管理女皇陛下财政部，通常简称财相(The Chancellor)，职位相当于其他国家的财政部长。在英国的四大国务大臣首相(首席总理大臣)、财政大臣(财相)、外交大臣(外相)和内政大臣中，财政大臣的地位仅次于首相。

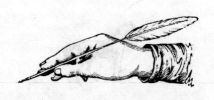

题 记

人类在 21 世纪加速了走向信息社会、踏入网络时代的步伐。超高速信息公路建设取得了实质性进展，计算机正朝着巨型化、微型化、智能化、网络化等方向进入应用的年代。计算新纪元的到来让人们目不暇接：今天清晰可见的市场规则似乎隔天已经陈旧过时，产品的生命周期从几年、到几个月、进而再到几周不断萎缩，计算从小规模的本地网络扩展到全球规模的互联网。康柏电脑决意在这个划时代的时刻，利用产业标准平台、强大的伙伴关系、实用的创新和用户反馈等使其成功的诸多特点再次创造奇迹，并将他们应用到掌上型电脑和数据中心的所有计算环境之中，满足客户快捷而轻松地接通所需的信息、随时随地有效使用任何计算装置的期望值，以更低廉的价格提供更强大的功能，使购买操作集成和产品服务更加容易。

Welcome to the New World
of Computing

— A Speech by CEO of Compaq
at World PC Expo

Thank you, and good morning.

It is this point that is really at the heart of what I want to talk about today — how Compaq is evolving to meet your rapidly changing needs. I want to discuss our vision of a new world of computing, our decision to acquire Digital and what the combined company will be able to do for you.

Success in our industry is a constant process of invention and reinvention. How could it be any other way in a world that is changing so rapidly — where the market rules that seemed clear one day appear to be out of date the next? Where product lifecycles continue to shrink from years to months and even to weeks? Where computing has moved from the small scale of local area networks to the planetary scale of the Internet? In this interconnected world, customer expectations have never been higher. You expect to be able to access the information you need quickly and easily, from any place at any time using virtually any computing device. You expect vendors to deliver more power at a lower

欢迎大家进入计算新纪元

——康柏电脑执行总裁在世界电脑出口交易会上的演讲

谢谢大家。 早上好!

我今天将要重点谈论的问题集中在一点,即康柏将如何发展以满足你们快速变化的需求。 我想与你们探讨一下计算新纪元的蓝图,康柏收购美国数字设备公司的决策,以及合并后的公司可以为你们做些什么。

在我们的行业里,成功是一个不断创造、再创造的过程。 在这个变化如此之快的世界里,还有别的成功方式吗? 今天清晰可见的市场规则似乎隔天已经陈旧过时。 产品的生命周期在什么领域从几年、到几个月、进而再到几周不断萎缩? 计算在什么领域从小规模的本地网络扩展到全球规模的互联网? 在这个相互连接的世界里,客户的期望值比以往任何时候都要高。 你们希望能够快捷而轻松地接通所需要的信息,随时随地有效使用任何计算装置。 你们希望厂商以更低廉的价格提供更强大的功能,使购买操作集成和产品服务更加容易。 无论你们谈论的是网络本身,还是支持在线银行、在线书店或在线商店的系统,你们都希望信息基础设施一年 365 天、一

cost and to make it easier to buy operate integrate and service their products. You expect the information infrastructure to be reliable and available 24 hours a day, 365 days a year — whether you're talking about the network itself or the systems that support your online bank online bookstore or online grocery. In this environment, Compaq determined that we needed to do more for our customers. We wanted to take the attributes that had made us successful — industry standard platforms, strong partnerships, useful innovation and customer responsiveness — and apply them to the full range of computing — from the palmtop① to the data center.

Compaq has developed significant enterprise strengths over the past few years. But we also needed capabilities that we could not build easily or quickly. So earlier this year, Compaq announced its intention to acquire Digital Equipment Corporation — one of the premier suppliers of enterprise solutions and services and one of the pioneers of internetworked computing. As most of you probably know, Compaq completed the acquisition last week after Digital shareholders voted overwhelmingly to approve the merger agreement. This is an historic moment for Compaq as well as for our customers and the industry. It brings together two companies with proud traditions of technology innovation and industry leadership. With its minicomputers, DIGITAL defined the computing paradigm of the 1970s and much of the 1980s. With its industry standard personal computers — including the first PC server — Compaq defined the computing paradigm of the 1980s and 1990s. We now see an opportunity

---

① palmtop ['paːmtɔp] *n.* 掌上型电脑

天 24 小时保持可靠和方便。 在这种环境里,康柏认为,我们要为客户做更多的事情。 我们要利用产业标准平台、强大的伙伴关系、实用的创新和用户反馈等使我们成功的诸多特点,并将他们应用到掌上型电脑和数据中心的所有计算环境之中。

康柏在过去几年中已经积累了强大的企业实力。 但我们仍然需要建立在短期内无法轻易或快速获得的能力。 所以在今年早些时候,康柏宣布了收购美国数字设备公司的意向。 这家公司是提供企业解决方案和服务的主要供应商之一,同时也是网络互联计算解决方案的业界先锋之一。 也许大多数人已经知道,美国数字设备公司的股东们上周以压倒多数票通过合并协议之后,康柏已经完成了收购。 这场收购对于康柏、对于我们的客户和整个业界,无疑是一个划时代的时刻。 它使两家在技术创新和业界领先方面享有盛誉的厂商合并在一起。 美国数字设备公司以其微型计算机在 20 世纪 70 年代和 80 年代的大部分时间里领导着计算发展的潮流。 而康柏则通过其工业标准个人电脑(包括第一台个人电脑服务器)在 20 世纪 80 年代和 90 年代领导着计算发展的潮流。 我们现在见证了一个建立计算新纪元标准的机会。 它将极大地拓宽我们在标准计算领域的视野,它将汇聚康柏、美国数字设备公司、天腾公司以及康柏诸多战略合作伙伴的强大力量,它将承诺为你带来比以往任何时候都更广泛的选择、更多的功能和更大的自由度。 我们的目标其实非常简单,那就是通过使计算获得更高的灵活性、简单性和高效率,赋予客户强大的功能。 收购美国数字设备公司之后,康柏增强了其为金融、制造和通讯等重要市场提供定制解决方案的能力。

目前,我们已经完成了对美国数字设备公司的收购,我们将合

to set the standard for a new world of computing. One that expands on our vision of standards-based computing; One that builds on the combined strengths of Compaq, Digital, Tandem and our strategic partners and one that promises you more choice, more power and more freedom than ever before. Our goal is really very simple: to empower customers by taking computing to new levels of flexibility, simplicity and efficiency. With the acquisition of Digital, we have enhanced our ability to provide customized solutions for key markets like finance, manufacturing and communications.

Now that we have completed the acquisition of Digital, we will merge the two companies' PC product lines. This will give Compaq the most extensive and competitive line of desktop and networked PCs in the industry. According to first quarter numbers from International Data Corporation, Compaq remains the #1 desktop PC company in the world. I am particularly pleased that Compaq regained the #1 position in portable PCs in North America — in both the commercial and consumer segments. What that should tell you is that we are determined to maintain our position as the number one PC company worldwide. And we will do it by continuing to offer standards-based, innovative and easily managed desktops and portables that integrate seamlessly into your enterprise environment. To those in the audience who are Digital customers, I want to assure you that we are not taking your business for granted. We intend to earn your trust and confidence. Although we will move the Digital PC line to Compaq-branded products, we will do so over a period of time that allows you to make the transition at your own pace. I believe our customers will be well-served by this combination. Our desktop businesses

并两家公司的个人电脑生产线。 这将使康柏拥有业界台式机和联网电脑产品最广泛、最具竞争力的生产线。 根据国际数据公司第一季度的统计数字，康柏仍然是全球最大的台式电脑生产厂商。 让我感到特别欣慰的是，康柏重新赢得了北美地区商用市场和家用市场笔记本电脑的首席位置。 我们希望让大家知道，我们已经下定决心继续保持康柏全球第一的个人电脑公司的位置。 为了达到这一目标，我们将会继续提供符合工业标准、具有创新功能和易于操作的台式机和手提电脑，实现与你们的企业环境无缝对接。 在座的美国数字设备公司的客户们，我向你们保证，我们并不是理所当然地和你们做生意，我们决意赢得你们的信任和信心。 尽管我们将把美国数字设备公司的电脑系列产品转为康柏品牌的产品，但我们的这一目标将会在一段时间内逐步实现，以便你们能够按照自己的节奏过渡。我相信，通过这次合并，我们的客户将会享受优异的服务。 我们的台式机业务十分兼容，两家公司在提供最好的可操作电脑降低经营成本方面均是业界的领导者。 我们在这个业务领域引领着世界的潮流。

今天我已经在这里谈了很多，现在我来概括一下我们对于电脑新纪元的展望，并以此来结束这次演讲。 首先，我相信未来的计算新纪元将基于开放的工业标准技术。 康柏希望成为所有标准计算领域中的佼佼者，无论是在你的家中、你的公司，还是在你的车里。其次，我们会不断加强康柏在关键业务计算领域的领先地位。 这使我们可以加速发展新的和现有的技术，并将他们运用于符合工业标准的平台，同时提供伸缩性更高和可靠性更强的系统。 第三点，我们将继续占据提供全球服务支持的领先地位。 这使我们的客户只需

153

are very compatible. Both companies lead the industry in reducing cost of ownership by providing the best managed PCs. We are leading the trends of the world in this business area.

I have covered a lot of ground today, so let me conclude by summarizing our vision for the new world of computing. First, we believe that this new world will be built on open, industry-standard technology. Anywhere there is standards-based computing, Compaq wants to be the driver — whether it's in your home your business or your car. Second, we will build on our leadership in business-critical computing. This will enable us to accelerate both new and existing technologies into industry standard platforms and to deliver even more scalable and reliable systems. Third, we will lead in delivering global service and support. This will give our customers a single point of accountability as well as a lower total cost of ownership and reduced risk. Fourth, we will focus on solutions that build on our leadership in enterprise platforms, our expertise in key markets, our service capabilities and our partnerships with industry-leading companies. And finally, we will build even stronger relationships with you, our customers. I hope you will look at Compaq not only as a computing company, but as a strategic partner whose mission is to give you what you need when you need it and how you want it, at the lowest total cost.

Welcome to the new world of computing.

Thank you.

(971 words)

要承担单一的经营责任、较低的总拥有成本和降低的风险。 第四点，我们将高度重视有助于巩固康柏在企业平台领导地位的解决方案、我们在主要市场的专长、我们的服务能力以及我们与业界领先厂商的合作关系。 最后，我们会与你——我们的客户——建立更加稳固的关系。 我希望康柏在你们的心目中不仅仅是一个计算机厂商，而且还是一个战略合作伙伴，它的任务就是在你需要的时候以任何你喜欢的方式、以最低的总体拥有成本来满足你的需求。

欢迎大家进入计算新纪元。

谢谢大家。

知识链接

Compaq　康柏电脑公司。美国电脑公司，是由罗德·肯尼恩(Rod Canion)、吉米·哈里斯(Jim Harris)和比利·默顿(Bill Murto)三位来自德州仪器公司的高级经理于 1982 年分别投资 1000 美元共同创建的。康柏电脑 2002 年被惠普收购，现为惠普/康柏电脑。

题　记

　　在 Legend(传奇)走向 Lenovo(创新)品牌标识更迭的过程中，联想已经发展成为一家在信息产业内得到多元化发展的大型企业集团。它秉承自主创新与追求卓越的传统，将最新的研发成果从实验室带到市场，转化为生产力并改善人们的工作和生活，为全球 PC 技术的进步做出了重要贡献。联想执行总裁杨元庆在演讲中总结了联想今天所取得的骄人成绩，并特别提出了公司的宏伟愿景：为企业和个人提供最好的客户体验，实现业界领先的股东回报，实现利润翻番和营业额增长，运用长线投资的方式提高市场地位，以及创造注重职业道德、业绩导向、团队精神和职业发展的企业文化。这些美好的愿景不仅秉承了联想自主创新与追求卓越的传统，而且清晰地描绘了指导联想决策和行为的价值观。

The Commitments of Lenovo

— A speech by Yang Yuanqing, CEO of Lenovo

Good morning, good afternoon, good evening.

Today, you and all our colleagues around the world are making history. The new Lenovo has become the worlds third largest PC Company. And this makes us the 5th largest IT company in the world. And the largest IT company in China. In fact, the new Lenovo ranks among one of the largest 200 companies of any type in the world. In a very important Asia market, we are the PC market leader, both profitable, and with more market share than any other company in Asia according to IDC. We are the ONLY Company who manufactures our own notebooks — with 95% of our ThinkPad built by our own plants — under the Lenovo flag. I'm very proud of what you've accomplished. Congratulations.

Now let's discuss who we are to become — our aspirations as a company — and our 3-phase plan to achieve these aspirations. To become all that we can be. First, satisfying our customers: Lenovo will deliver the highest customer satisfaction to both businesses and individuals. Second, shareholder value: Lenovo will be the company people want to

联想的承诺

——联想执行总裁杨元庆的演讲

早上好,下午好,晚上好!

今天是你们和我们全球的同事共同创造历史的一天。 新联想已经成为全球第三大个人电脑厂商,这使我们成为全球排名第五的信息技术企业,也是中国最大的信息技术企业。 事实上,新联想已经跻身全球此类公司的200强。 根据国际数据公司的统计,无论是盈利还是市场份额,在举足轻重的亚洲市场上,我们已经成为个人电脑市场的领导者。 我们是唯一自主生产笔记本电脑的公司,95%的ThinkPad笔记本电脑是在联想旗下的工厂生产的。 我对你们已经取得的成就感到无比的自豪。 祝贺你们。

现在,我们谈一下公司的未来,我们对公司的愿景以及实现这些愿景的三个阶段的规划。 我们要实现我们能够做到的一切。 第一,满足客户:联想将为企业和个人提供最好的客户体验。 第二,股东利益:联想将成为投资人的选择,我们将在未来的 2 年、5 年以及 10 年内实现业界领先的股东回报。 第三,财务目标:联想将在三年内实现利润翻番,使营业额增长超出业界水平。 第四,市场地位:联想决心每年不断地提高我们的市场地位,根据市场状况运用

invest in by leading our industry in shareholder returns over the next 2, 5, and 10 years. Third, financial targets: Lenovo will double our profit within 3 years, and grow revenue faster than our industry. Fourth, market position: Lenovo is committed to improve our market position every year by applying long term investments where we can become #1 or #2 in share or profit, depending on the market. Fifth is my aspirations for each of us, the people who chose to work at Lenovo. We at Lenovo will create an inspiring culture of ethics, performance, teamwork and professional development.

Some of these might appear to be big aspirations. I want you to know that we're committed to them, and that while I expect progress every day, every week, these aspirations will take years to fully achieve. Now to get this done we have a broad 3-phase plan. Phase one began on December 8th, and will continue well into the beginning of the next year. Our second phase has also begun. And each project in phase 2 will be at least 12 to 24 months in length. Our third phase will launch when we stand before the world as the IT sponsor of the Olympics.

So let me speak about phase one: Deliver on the promise of Lenovo and on our commitments. By this I mean we must delight our current customers and retain their business. We must maintain product leadership, sales momentum and market share. We must ensure effective business operations, and positively introduce the position of new Lenovo and of our brands. And very importantly, develop our employees and reward excellence and performance. So that's phase one. Execute and hug

长线投资的方式，在份额和利润方面占据数一或数二的位置。 第五是我对我们每一个人、选择来联想工作的人的愿景：我们要在联想创造一个注重职业道德、业绩导向、团队精神和职业发展的企业文化。

其中的一些似乎是非常宏伟的愿景。 我希望你们知道，我们一定要努力达到这些目标，虽然我期待每天、每周都要进步，但这些愿景需要多年的努力才能实现。 为了达成这些愿景，我们现在制订了三个阶段的规划。 第一阶段于去年12月8日开始，并将持续到明年初。 第二阶段也已经开始。 第二阶段的每个项目将至少历时12~24个月。 我们的第三阶段将以奥运会信息技术赞助商的身份面向世界启动。

下面先谈一下第一阶段：履行联想的承诺和义务。 谈到这一点，我指的是我们必须取悦于我们目前的客户，并保留他们的业务。 我们必须保持产品的领先地位、销售势头和市场份额。 我们必须确保有效的业务营运，并积极地宣传新联想和我们品牌的地位。 非常重要的是，发挥我们员工的才能，奖励出类拔萃和业绩出色的员工。 这就是第一阶段。 采取行动并拥抱那些对我们重要的人：我们的客户、我们的业务伙伴、我们的供应商以及我们的员工。

在第二阶段，我们将通过卓越运作、不断创新和品牌管理增强我们的竞争力。 我们必须一如既往地专注卓越运营、速度和效率，提高我们 Think 的品牌价值，并将联想打造成全球品牌。 我们必须建立全球范围内的创新和以绩效为导向的文化和声誉。 在这个阶段，我们将对新产品和新市场发起目标投资。

those that are important to us: our customers, our business partners, our suppliers, and our employees.

In phase two we increase our competitiveness through operational excellence, innovation, and branding. We must continue our focus on operational excellence, speed and efficiency, increase our Think brand equity and grow Lenovo into a worldwide brand. We must build a global innovation and performance culture and reputation. During this phase we will initiate targeted investments in new products and in new markets.

And then we are ready for the third phase: To drive aggressive①, profitable growth. To do this we will invest to lead in selected market segments. In each of these three phases we will build on these areas of competitive advantage. This starts with:

§ Our obsession② with understanding our customers,

§ Our brands — especially Think and Lenovo,

§ Our innovation in products, services and software,

§ Our operational excellence and efficiency,

§ Our leading position in China and Asia,

§ Our partnership with IBM in services, financing and sales,

§ Finally, and perhaps most importantly, the dedication and skills of our people.

Finally, I want to wrap up by speaking about the values of Lenovo. Those of us who came from IBM created "new" values only 18 months

---

① aggressive [əˈgresiv] *adj.* 有进取心的

② obsession [əbˈseʃən] *n.* 痴迷

然后，我们将为第三阶段做好准备：达到迅猛、盈利的业务增长。 我们将为此投资，引导选定的细分市场。 在三个阶段每一时期，我们都将打造在这些领域的竞争优势。 从下列步骤开始：

§ 孜孜以求地了解我们的客户；

§ 我们的品牌，特别是 Think 和联想品牌；

§ 我们在产品、服务和软件方面的创新；

§ 我们的卓越运营和效率；

§ 我们在中国和亚洲的领导地位；

§ 我们在服务、融资和销售领域与美国国际商用机器公司的合作；

§ 最后，也许是最重要的，我们员工的奉献和技能。

最后我想集中谈一下联想的价值观。 18 个月前，美国国际商用机器公司的全体员工参与了"价值观大讨论"的部分活动，我们那些来自美国国际商用机器公司的员工创造了"新的价值观"。 在过去的几年中，四个核心价值观一直指导着我们联想的同仁。 联想的价值观与美国国际商用机器公司主张的价值观是如此的相似，这绝对不是一种巧合。 第一，服务客户：我们致力于实现每一个客户的满意和成功。 第二，创新和企业精神：这意味着事关我们客户和我们公司的创新以高效的方式创造科技和发布产品。 第三，精准和追求真理：这表示我们根据仔细斟酌的事实管理业务和制定决策。 第四，信用和诚实：这表示在所有的合作关系中取得他人的信任和承担个人责任。

我已经亲身见证了你们每个人对自己的期待和你们可以做些什么。 这不能不令人啧啧称奇。 我们正面临一个非凡的机遇，在这

ago — as part of a "Values Jam" that all IBM employees participated in. Our Lenovo colleagues have been guided for the last several years by four key values. Its no coincidence that the values Lenovo has worked by are so similar to the values held by IBM. First, Serving customers: we are dedicated to the satisfaction and success of every customer. Second, innovative and entrepreneurial spirit: this means innovation that matters to our customers and our company created and delivered with speed and efficiency. Third, accuracy and truth-seeking: this means we manage our business and make decisions based on carefully understood facts. And Fourth: trustworthiness and integrity: meaning trust and personal responsibility in all relationships.

I've seen first hand what each you expect of yourselves and what you can do. It's nothing short of amazing. We have before us an extraordinary opportunity to make a difference for our customers and to succeed at this exciting new venture. So that's it, a short list of difficult but achievable aspirations. A 3-phase plan of how well go from a new company to one that uses its competitiveness to aggressively grow. And four clear values punctuated① with the word integrity that will guide our decisions and our behavior.

This is our opportunity and our time. Let's go make the most of it.

Thank you and congratulations.

(900 words)

---

① punctuate['pʌŋktjueit] vt. 强调

联想的承诺

个令人兴奋的新的风险企业，为我们的客户提供价值并取得成功。这就是我要谈的愿景，虽然有一系列简短的困难，但仍然是可以实现的愿景。三个阶段的规划描绘了一个新公司如何运用竞争力迅猛地增长；四个明确的价值观强调了诚信是指导我们决策和行为的准则。

这是属于我们的机会和我们的时代。我们将全力以赴。

谢谢大家。再次表示祝贺。

知识链接

Lenovo 联想集团有限公司。"Lenovo"寓意为"创新的联想"。联想集团有限公司成立于1984年，由中国科学院计算所投资20万元人民币、11名科技人员创办，到今天已经发展成为一家在信息产业内多元化发展的大型企业集团。联想公司主要生产台式电脑、服务器、笔记本电脑、打印机、掌上电脑、主机板、手机等商品。2004年，联想收购IBM个人电脑事业部，成为全球第三大个人电脑厂商。联想在全球有19 000多名员工。

题　记

　　随着社会的快速发展，人们的生活水平得到了显著的提高，但与此同时，人类赖以生存的环境却遭受到了前所未有的破坏，而全球变暖问题也逐渐成为人类关注的焦点。著名的可口可乐公司主席兼首席执行官内维尔·伊斯戴尔在绿色和平中国商业论坛上发表了令人振奋的演讲，论证了拯救人类共同的家园——地球这一环保话题。他以可口可乐公司采用绿色环保系统进行生产、从而减少碳排放量为例，号召全世界的人们共同努力，回归社会，回归自然。他呼吁世界领导人建立一个强有力的国际框架，控制全球的碳排放，以应对气候的变化。他鼓励更多的企业加入这一行动，与绿色和平组织合作，实现一个更为绿色、和平和可持续发展的未来。

The Virtuous Cycle: Kick-Starting
a Climate-Friendly Future
— Remarks by Neville Isdell, Chairman
and CEO of the Coca-Cola Company

Thank you, SzePing, for that introduction. I'm actually very deeply honored to be part of this inaugural Greenpeace Business Lecture Series in China, and to join with Mr. Zhang, with Gerd Leipold, and with you — leaders of industry, government, and just as importantly, civil society.

We recognize that there's a long road ahead, and of course, we at The Coca-Cola Company will continue to support the relief efforts, as we have, in the weeks and the months to come.

I want to thank Greenpeace for creating this forum. For many years now, we've been working with Greenpeace, and I've come to know and really respect their organization, and to respect Gerd, in particular. Greenpeace, and other NGOs, play a critical role in raising the world's awareness and fighting for a better, more sustainable future. Not only does society need Greenpeace and other NGOs, but we — our business — need you, as well. If we're going to deliver the solutions that are required

良性循环：开创环境友好的未来
——可口可乐公司主席兼首席执行官
内维尔·伊斯戴尔的演讲

　　谢谢卢思骋先生的介绍。 我非常荣幸能在"绿色和平中国商业论坛"上发表演讲，能和张先生、葛德·莱堡先生以及在座的工业界和政界的领袖们一起参加这个盛会，我感到非常荣幸。

　　当然我们还有很长的路要走。 可口可乐公司将在未来的日子里——一周一周、一月一月，一如既往地支持环境救助行动。

　　感谢绿色和平组织创办了这个论坛。 这么多年以来，我们和绿色和平组织一直在合作，我逐渐了解了这个组织，并实实在在地尊敬这个组织，我尤其敬重葛德先生。 绿色和平组织和其他一些非政府组织在唤起世人的意识、争取更加美好的未来方面起到了重要的作用。 不仅社会需要绿色和平组织和其他一些非政府组织，我们商界同样也需要你们。 如果我们想在 21 世纪推行绿色和平解决方案的话，我们需要商业界、政府和民间社团的共同努力。

　　所以，葛德先生，我们很乐意接受你到目前为止给我们的挑战，也欣然接受你在未来给予我们的挑战。 因为这些挑战最终将会推动我们的星球、我们的工商业更好地可持续发展。 我们认识到，

in the 21st Century, we need new partnerships, among businesses, government, and civil society.

So, Gerd, we welcome the challenges that you've given us, so far, and the challenges that you're going to give us in the future. Because, ultimately, they help make our planet and our business, more sustainable. And that really captures our approach to sustainability. We recognize if the communities that we serve are not sustainable, that we do not have a sustainable business for ourselves. We recognize that we need to be part of the solution on global issues that threaten the communities we serve, and that are relevant to our business, and therefore we've made a number of commitments.

We've set the aspirational goal of returning to communities and to nature, an amount of water equivalent to what we use in all of our beverages① , and in their production. We call it water neutrality② . We're expanding our efforts to recycle and to reuse PET③ plastic bottles, and today we're building the world's largest PET bottle to bottle recycling facility in the United States. We also engage in significant work to understand our climate footprint, and to set goals in this area, and I'll talk more about that in a few minutes.

You can see some of these commitments coming to life, here in

---

① beverage ['bevəridʒ] *n.* 饮料
② neutrality [njuː'træliti] *n.* 平衡
③ PET 聚对苯二甲酸乙二醇酯,简称:聚酯

如果我们共同服务的社会不能够持续发展，那么我们就不可能为我们自己建造一个可持续发展的商业。 我们认识到，我们需要成为解决全球化问题的一部分，这些问题正在威胁我们为之服务的社会，这些问题与我们从事的商务活动相关，所以我们已经做出了若干承诺。

我们已经制定了鼓励性的目标：回归社会，回归自然，我们饮料中的用水量相当于他们的生产量。 我们称之为水平衡。 我们正努力扩大聚酯塑料瓶的回收利用，我们目前正在美国建造世界最大的聚酯瓶回收设施。 我们正在从事一项意义重大的工作，即了解我们气候的轨迹，并在这个领域设定目标。 我将在几分钟后更详细地谈论这个问题。

在中国，你可以看到一些承诺已经走进了人们的生活。 比如说，我们在回收瓶子的同时，提高了我们瓶装水厂中水的利用效率。 在中国，仅去年一年，我们就在生产成品饮料时节水 8%。 从全球来看，我们正和另一个非政府组织合作，建立进一步提高我们用水效率的目标，以帮助、保存和保护全球的水域。 在中国，我们关注长江流域的项目。 我们还在全球投资了雨水收集和存储系统的项目。 在宁夏，我们为 3 000 居民改善了供水系统。

这只是眼下一个微不足道的例子，我要谈谈社区——成功基于社区。 我们正在与联合国开发计划署和中国政府合作，解决中国很多农村地区的饮水难和饮水卫生问题。 我们和北京奥组委（BOCOG）合作，发起了一个环境教育项目，超过 25 万人参与了此项活动，鼓励他们"节约一桶水"。 总体来说，这将在未来使中国

China. For example, together with our bottlers, we're improving our water efficiency at our bottling plants. In China, we reduced the amount of water it takes to create our finished beverages by 8 percent, last year alone. And globally, we're working with another NGO to set targets for improvement in our water use efficiency, and to help, and conserve, and protect, watersheds globally. And here in China, we're focusing on projects around the Yangtze River. We've also invested globally in rainwater harvesting and storage systems. In Ningxia, we've improved the water supply for 3,000 residents.

Now, this is a small example, but I talked about communities — success is community-based. We're working with the United Nations Development Program and the Chinese government, to enhance water access and sanitation① in many parts of rural China. And we've partnered with the Beijing Organizing Committee for the Olympic Games, BOCOG, on an environmental education program that has encouraged more than 250,000 people to "Save a Barrel of Water." In the aggregate, this will benefit millions of people in China in the future. Each one I've talked about is a small step, but every drop counts.

When it comes to global warming, given the expertise in this room, I don't need to make the case that global climate change is occurring; that man-made gas emissions are a crucial factor; and that the implications for our planet are profound — from biodiversity to public

①　sanitation [ˌsæniˈteiʃən] n. 公共卫生

数百万人受益。 我所说的每一点也许都微不足道,但每一滴水都异常珍贵。

谈到全球变暖的问题,考虑到在座的各位专家的意见,我不需要列举全球气候正在发生变化的例子。 人为排放的气体是一个决定性的因素。 这些气体对我们的星球造成了深远的影响——从生物多样性到公众健康、从农业到耗水量几乎无所不包。 当然这种影响也与可口可乐之类的公司密切相关。 我给大家举一个例子,看看如果我们不采取任何行动,将会发生些什么。 一项研究表明,气候变化在 50 年之后会迫使 10 亿人离开他们的家园。 这就意味着这个星球上每 9 个人中有一个人离开家园,而每 9 个人中有一个人是我们的客户。

来自联合国政府间气候变化专门委员会的科学家告诉我们,本世纪全球需要减少 50% 到 80% 的温室气体排放才能够阻止环境的进一步恶化。 如果我们要迎接这一挑战,那么社会的每一个部门都必须参与这项工作。 所以,今天我想强调商界和非政府组织可以合作做些什么。 但我还想指出,政府也必须采取行动。 这也就是为什么在去年 11 月份巴厘岛会议之前,可口可乐公司和许多其他公司共同签署了一份公告。 我们呼吁世界领导人建立一个强有力的国际框架,控制全球的碳排放,以应对气候变化。 我认为我们处于一个独特的重要时刻,我们面前打开了一扇窗,我们仍然可以做出改变,以防止发生最恶劣的气候变化形式。

可口可乐公司和气候变化之间有什么联系吗? 我们已经检查了我们的碳排量,它涉及四个领域:我们的包装、我们的制造业务、

health, and from agriculture to water usage, generally — which makes it, of course, very relevant for a business like Coca-Cola. So, let me just share one example of what's at stake if we do not act. One study projects that climate change could force 1 billion people to leave their homes over the next 50 years. That is 1 in every 9 people on this planet, 1 in every 9 of our consumers.

Scientists from the Intergovernmental Panel on Climate Change tell us our global society needs to reduce greenhouse gas emissions between 50 and 80 percent in this century. If we are going to meet this challenge, then every sector of society will have to be part of that solution. So, today I'm focusing on what business and NGOs can do together. But I also want to acknowledge that political systems must also act. That's why, last November, Coca-Cola and many other companies signed a communiqué , prior to the Bali meeting. We asked world leaders to work towards a strong international framework, to govern global carbon emissions, and to combat climate change. I believe that we stand at a unique moment in time, a window when we can still make changes that will prevent the worst forms of climate change from happening.

So what is Coca-Cola's connection to climate change? We've examined our carbon footprint, and it touches on four areas: our packaging, our manufacturing operations and those of our bottling partners, transportation, and our focus today — cold drink equipment. We, of course, are working to reduce our impact in all of these areas. For example, on packaging, we are making bottles that have less

174

我们的装瓶合作伙伴、运输，以及我们目前关注的重点——冷饮设备。 当然，我们正在致力于减少所有这些领域的气体排放。 比如说，在包装方面，我们正在通过一项名为"减轻重量"的工序，制造含塑料较少或含玻璃较少的瓶子。 可能你们已经听说了，我们正在全球范围内投资回收再利用领域。 在我们的制造过程中，我们的目的是增加业务，而不是增加碳排放。 我们在全世界有 1 000 个左右的瓶装厂，每一家工厂都有能源利用效率方面的投资。 我们的一些瓶装厂早已采用了混合动力卡车，其他厂正在实施绿色分销系统，减少了卡车的行驶里程和碳排放。

我们也许只能解决百分之一的问题，但我们知道，由于我们的品牌效应，由于我们的全球影响力，我们有机会扮演领导者的角色，正如我们公司内部的通用语："舍我其谁？"

为了拯救我们的星球，我们正在与绿色和平之类的组织合作，在自己的行业内部尽力而为，推动更快的变革。

谢谢大家！

知识链接 🔍

Greenpeace "绿色和平"是绿色和平组织的简称，属于国际性的非政府组织，以环保工作为主，总部设在荷兰的阿姆斯特丹。绿色和平的前身是 1971 年 9 月 15 日成立于加拿大的"不以举手表决委员会"，1979 年改为现名，并迁至荷兰。绿色和平组织的创始人为工程师戴维·麦格塔格，捐款的人数已经累积到 280 万，在全球 41 个国家设有办事处。绿色和平组织开始时以使用非暴力方式阻止大气和地下核试以及公海捕鲸著称，后来转为关注其他的

plastic, or less glass in them, through a process known as "light-weighting." And as you've already heard, we are making investments in recycling around the world. In our manufacturing operations, our intention is to grow the business, and not the carbon, and we are making investments in energy efficiency at every single one of our nearly 1,000 plants with our bottlers around the world. Already, some of our bottlers have adopted hybrid trucks, and others are implementing green distribution systems, to reduce miles and emissions.

We may only make one percent of the problem, but we understand that because of our brand awareness, because of our global reach, we have an opportunity to play a leadership role. And as we say, within our company, "If not us, who? "

To help our planet, we're doing what we can do inside our own business — and working with organizations like Greenpeace, — to drive change faster.

Thank you.

(1,048 words)

良性循环:开创环境友好的未来

环境问题，包括水底拖网捕鱼、全球变暖和基因工程。绿色和平组织宣称自己的使命是："保护地球、环境及其各种生物的安全及持续性发展，并以行动做出积极的改变。"

题 记

　　作为全球性的医药化工企业，德国默克公司在分析化学、合成化学、微生物、水质检测等领域提供一系列高品质产品和服务，为全球经济的发展做出了巨大的贡献。默克公司以自己的方式回馈社会，成立了默克公司基金会，并支持了许多项目，默克科学教育研究所就是其中之一。默克集团董事会主席兼首席执行官柯禄唯博士在演讲中阐述了默克科学教育研究所的教育理念：在这里，每个孩子无论过去的经验、现有的知识、文化和语言有何差异，都可以学习科学知识；在这里，教师有着极大的热情，他们像学生学科学一样去教科学；在这里，默克的各位员工是将使命传达到学生的大使，他们带领学生走在科学发展的前沿。默克坚守着支持学校科学教育的承诺，并秉承了培养下一代科学家领袖的宗旨。

Merck Institute for
Science Education
— Remarks by Dr. Karl-Ludwig Kley,
Chairman and CEO of Merck

It's an honor to be here tonight to mark the 15th anniversary of The Merck Institute for Science Education with the very people who make MISE what it is — a learning community of teachers, principals and superintendents dedicated to improving science education in our schools.

When I came to Merck a few years ago and began to learn about the many programs that the Company and The Merck Company Foundation support I was particularly impressed by the work of this Institute. I was inspired by its vision — or, I should say, Carlo Parravano's vision — that every child can learn science, regardless of past experience, existing knowledge, or cultural and linguistic differences.

It was this vision that the Company had when it created MISE. Today, the first students who benefited from the workshops MISE conducted in the late 1990s are entering college. Some have already graduated. One student, whose success in science enriched her high school experience, is now a junior at Boston University, majoring in

默克的科学教育

——德国默克集团董事会主席兼
首席执行官柯禄唯博士的演讲

今晚我很荣幸能在这里与各位创建者一起参加默克科学教育研究所 15 周年的纪念活动。 对于所有致力于提高我们教育机构科教水平的教师、校长、所长而言，默克科学教育研究所是一个大家共同学习的社区。

几年前，当我来到默克、开始了解公司和默克公司基金会支持的很多项目时，研究所的工作给我留下了深刻的印象。 它的前景——或者，我应该说，卡罗·帕拉瓦罗的远见——令我备受鼓舞，即无论过去的经历、已有的知识或文化和语言差异如何，每个孩子都可以在这里学习科学知识。

公司创建默克科学教育研究所之初就是基于这种愿景。 今天，20 世纪 90 年代末第一批受益于默克科学教育研究所讲习班指导的学员正在进入大学，有些已经毕业。 有一个学员现在是波士顿大学化学专业的大三学生，正是在科学上的成功丰富了她的高中经历。 还有一个学员，他以班级第一名的成绩从林登高中毕业，目前在麻省理工学院电子工程专业读三年级。 另外一个拉威高中毕业生已经获

chemistry. Another who graduated at the top of his class at Linden High School is now a third year electrical engineering student at MIT. And a Rahway High School graduate earned her doctorate at the University of Rhode Island and is now a Marine Biologist.

I think it is only fitting that 15 years later, not only are we celebrating the accomplishments of MISE and the impact the Partnership has had on students, but we are also kicking off an innovative new initiative: the Academy for Leadership in Science Instruction. We hope that the Academy will provide you with new experiences and professional relationships that will ultimately help to improve student performance and sustain science education as a priority in your schools and districts.

Working with our partners in Elizabeth, Hillside, Linden, Rahway, Readington Township and North Penn during the past 15 years, MISE has provided vital resources to help students develop a passion for science at a young age. Since MISE was instituted 15 years ago:

More than 5,000 educators have attended 350 MISE-sponsored workshops.

Some 500 principals, superintendents and supervisors have attended The Administrators' Institute, an annual retreat that assists principals in supporting high-quality science instruction.

Time spent teaching science in some schools has almost doubled.

Enrollment in AP classes has increased so dramatically that some schools have had to create additional classes to serve student needs.

In elementary schools the expectation now is that science will not only be taught, but it will be taught well.

MISE has gone global. In 2006, MISE launched its first international

得了罗德岛州立大学的博士学位，现在是一名海洋生物学家。

我认为，经过 15 年的努力，我们不仅要庆祝默克科学研究所取得的成就和合作企业对学员的影响，而且我们还在启动一项创新举措，即建立科教所领导学院。这是一项非常合适的配套工程。我们希望，这个学院将为大家提供全新的体验和职业的人际关系，这些将成为学校和地区的优势，最终有助于改善学员的表现并支撑科学教育。

在过去的 15 年中，默克科学教育研究所与伊丽莎白、希尔赛德、林登、拉威、雷丁顿乡和北宾的合伙人共同努力，为帮助学生从小建立对科学的热情，提供了至关重要的资源。默克科学教育研究所 15 年来的主要工作如下：

超过 5 000 个教育工作者参加了默克科学教育研究所发起的 350 个研讨会。

大约有 500 名校长、院长和督学参加了行政管理者协会，这是一个帮助校长支持高品质科学教育指导的年度会议。

有些学校的科学教育时间几乎翻了一倍。

选修科学课程的学生越来越多，引人瞩目，以至于有些学校不得不增加课时，以满足学生的需要。

在小学里，人们现在不仅期待科学课程的教学，而且希望取得良好的教学效果。

默克科学教育研究所已经走向全球。2006 年，默克科学教育研究所在泰国海啸灾区推出首个国际项目。我知道你们中间有些人参与了这个重要的项目。

默克科学教育研究所的团队成员还在修订新泽西州科学课核心

program in the tsunami① -ravaged② areas of Thailand. I know some of you here have joined MISE on this important project.

Members of the MISE team have also played a leadership role in the revision of the New Jersey Core Curriculum Content Standards in Science, and were instrumental in the development of the State of New Jersey's Professional Development for Teachers Initiative.

Thanks to the efforts of the people in this room, the partnership is making a difference. Today, in our partner district classrooms, science is carried out much the same way scientists work at Merck. Students are asking questions, gathering data and testing hypotheses, and they are interested in and excited about expanding the frontiers of knowledge.

And teachers are generating that enthusiasm③ . They are as engaged in teaching science as students are about learning science. And, we at Merck are inspired to see these great changes. MISE would not be a success without the people here tonight who devote their time and energy to realizing the vision of the Merck Institute for Science Education. I would like to acknowledge the educators here tonight:

The 119 teachers and principals from 22 schools from our six partner school districts. You are the real heroes here tonight, planting the seeds of inquiry in the minds of our students and inspiring a passion for science as they grow.

The 22 superintendents and assistant superintendents. Your support has

---

① tsunami [tsju:ˈnɑːmi] *n.* 海啸
② ravage [ˈrævidʒ] *vt.* 破坏
③ enthusiasm [inˈθjuːziæzəm] *n.* 热情

 默克的科学教育

课程内容标准，他们在新泽西州教师主动性的职业发展过程中发挥了领导作用。

谢谢在座的各位，合作正在产生重大的影响力。今天，在我们合作伙伴地区的教室里，教授科学的方式与科学家在默克公司工作的方式大致相同。学生们提出问题，收集数据，测试假设，他们对扩展知识前沿感兴趣并为之兴奋。

教师们对此产生了极大的热情。他们像学生学科学一样去教授科学。我们在默克欣喜地看到这些变化。如果没有今晚在座的各位，把时间和精力都投入到默克科学教育研究所，实现美好的愿景，默克很难有今天的成功。今晚，我要在这里谢谢我们的教育工作者们：

他们是来自6个合作伙伴学校地区的22所学校中的119名教师和校长。你们今晚在这里是真正的英雄，你们在我们学生的头脑中撒下求知的种子，激发出的科学热情伴随着他们成长。

他们是22位所长或助理所长。你们的支持使默克科学教育研究所具有可持续性，并将这种可持续的工作带入了课堂。

还有来自特伦顿的新泽西州教育专员露西·戴维。你在州一级的工作十分重要。能与这样强大的伙伴一道进行学校改革，我们感到非常荣幸。

我还要谢谢默克的各位员工。虽然他们今晚并不在场，但7 000多员工自愿地把时间投入到我们伙伴学校的工作之中。他们是大使，将使命传达到教育领域的中心——学生。他们在很多领域指导学生，无论是通过立体星像馆进行的虚拟月球之旅，还是写给科学笔友的信件。他们的时间和精力是这个项目最强大的资产。

Merck Institute for Science Education

enabled MISE to be sustainable and to translate its work into the classrooms.

From Trenton, Lucille Davy, Commissioner of Education in the State of New Jersey. The work you are doing at the state level is so important. We're privileged to have such a tremendous partner to work with on school reform.

I'd also like to acknowledge the work of Merck employees. Although not represented here tonight, more than 7,000 of our employees have volunteered their time to work in our partner schools. They are ambassadors who carry the mission to the center of education's universe — the students. And they engage students on many frontiers, whether it's through a virtual trip to the moon in STARLAB, or on a letter written to a science pen pal. Their time and energy are powerful assets to this program.

And finally, I want to applaud the MISE staff. Each member works thoughtfully and diligently to provide our partner schools with current, high-caliber resources and to provide high-quality professional development.

To everyone, thank you. It is moving to consider how much the people in this room care about students, and how hard you are willing to work to make sure every child in your schools has access to the highest-quality education.

Merck remains committed to supporting science education in our schools. This is the key to fostering the next generation of scientific leaders — which is essential for the sustainability of our business and for the economic development and well-being of our communities.

Thank you.

(912 words)

默克的科学教育

最后，我要为默克科学教育研究所的所有同仁们拍手喝彩。 每一个成员都用心地勤奋工作，从而为我们的合作学校提供现代的、宽口径的资源，提供高质量的职业发展。

谢谢，谢谢所有的人！ 想到这个房间里的人们是多么的关心学生，想到你们为了学生能接受最高水平的教育而付出的辛苦工作，真的很令人感动。

默克在我们的学校坚守支持科学教育的承诺。 这是培养下一代科学家领袖的关键，它对于我们事业的可持续性，对于经济的发展和我们集团的福利都是至关重要的。

谢谢大家！

知识链接 🔍

Merck 默克集团成立于 1668 年，总部位于德国的达姆施塔特，是国际著名的化学及制药公司。默克以对产品品质的严格要求而著称于世，它不仅是全球首家合成维生素 C、B、E 及 K 的公司，而且在液晶制造、Irio din 珠光颜料、实验室产品及半导体工业超纯化学制品等方面，也居于世界领导地位。默克集团已在全世界 56 个主要国家设立了分公司。其中在 28 个国家建有 80 个生产基地，员工数达 28 300 人。

题　记

　　全球能源体系目前已经渗透到世界各国的经济领域。石油工业必须应对日益增长的能源需求、日趋严格的环保要求和能源供应及安全等方面的巨大挑战，以满足现在和将来能够获得经济、可靠而清洁的能源供应。美国最大的石油公司埃克森美孚首席执行官雷克斯·W·泰勒森用广阔的视角阐述了技术进步在促进能源发展和应对挑战方面所扮演的重要角色。技术进步使人类能够到世界上更多的地方开采能源，从而使能源供应来源多元化。技术进步增强了能源供应的安全性，如致密地层天然气和深水等技术，可以开发以前人类无法开发的能源，将能源进口国与出口国通过分散的国际供应渠道连接起来。技术进步在某种意义上开辟了能源革新的新纪元。

A New Era of Energy Innovation

—A Speech by Rex W. Tillerson,

Chairman and CEO of Exxon Mobil

I appreciate the opportunity to speak today about the role technology plays in meeting the world's growing energy needs.

The theme of this year's seminar, "OPEC in a New Energy Era," speaks to the new challenges and opportunities in the years ahead, from expanding production capacity, to stabilizing markets, to meeting environmental expectations, and to supporting development.

ExxonMobil is proud to participate in the energy sectors of many OPEC member nations, acting as a partner in meeting these challenges and advancing opportunities. However, when it comes to the development of petroleum technologies, I would suggest that OPEC and the world energy community as a whole are not entering a new era.

With all due respect to many who have said otherwise, the era of "easy oil" is not over. Why? Because there never has been an era of "easy oil." Our industry has constantly operated at the technological frontier. Oil only seems easy after it has been discovered, developed and produced.

能源革新的新纪元
——埃克森美孚公司董事长兼
首席执行官雷克斯·W. 泰勒森的演讲

今天我非常荣幸，能够站在这里谈论技术在满足世界对能源不断增长的需求中发挥的重要作用。

今年研讨会的专题是"能源新时代的石油输出国家组织"，从扩大生产能力、稳定市场、实现保护环境目标以及支持可持续发展等方面讨论未来数年里我们将要面临的机遇与挑战。

埃克森美孚公司很荣幸以合作者的身份参与很多石油输出国家组织成员国的能源业，共同面对这些挑战和机遇。 然而，在石油技术的发展方面，我不得不说石油输出国家组织和世界能源共同体整体上并没有进入一个新时代。

我非常尊重那些持相反意见的人，但我要说，"廉价石油时代"并没有结束。 为什么呢？ 因为 "粗制石油"的时代根本没有存在过。 我们的工业一直走在技术的前沿，石油只是在被发现、开采和生产之后才显得 "廉价"。

Understanding this fundamental fact is essential to creating and sustaining the conditions for future technological progress. As has been noted by other speakers, by 2030, the world's energy needs will be 50 percent greater than they are today. Growing populations, especially in developing countries, will require more energy to attain higher standards of living, to address social pressures, and to achieve greater security.

OPEC is destined to play an important and growing role in meeting this future demand. Within the next decade, crude production from non-OPEC sources is expected to plateau① , while world oil demand continues to increase. The result will be a call on OPEC of nearly 50 million barrels a day by 2030 — an increase of over 50 percent above OPEC's current levels. To reach the needed levels of production worldwide, we must continue to innovate. And fostering innovation will require free trade and investment, open access, and international partnerships. Oil producers need consumers, and oil consumers need producers.

Under these conditions of energy interdependence, industry can continue to develop, transfer and apply the energy technologies needed to support economic growth and social progress in OPEC's member countries and beyond.

The history of our industry shows when these conditions are consistently met, energy technology advances, and it advances in some truly remarkable ways.

---

① plateau [ˈplætəu] n. 平稳时期

理解这个基本事实对创造和维持有利于未来技术进步的各种条件非常关键。 很多发言人都引用过的观点是，到2030年，世界能源需求将较目前增长50%。 不断增长的人口，特别是在发展中国家，将需要更多的能源来达到更高的生活水平，控制社会压力，并获得更好的保障。

石油输出国家组织一定会在满足未来需求上扮演越来越重要的角色。 在未来十年，非石油输出国家组织的原油生产应该趋于平稳，而世界石油需求仍将持续增长。 结果就是到2030年，对石油输出国家组织石油的需求将达到每天5 000万桶，这个数字比石油输出国家组织现在的生产水平高了50%。 为了达到满足世界需要的生产水平，我们必须继续革新。 而鼓励革新需要自由贸易和投资、开放通路和国际合作关系。 石油生产者离不开消费者，同样，消费者也离不开生产者。

在这种能源相互依存的关系下，石油产业可以持续发展，转换和应用所需的能源技术，支持石油输出国家组织成员国和非成员国的经济增长和社会进步。

我们行业的历史证明，当这些条件被持续满足的时候，能源技术会进步，并且在很多方面真正实现了跨越式的进步。

如果有人问，未来石油技术的进步是以渐进的方式还是以革命性的方式发展，回答是肯定的。

然而，技术进步在我们这个行业从来不会发生在一夜之间，也

The question whether petroleum technologies in the future will be evolutionary or revolutionary can be answered "yes."

Technological progress in our industry is never an overnight phenomenon, however, and it rarely makes headlines. It results from an incremental① process involving consistent investment and the application of scientific, engineering and managerial expertise over sustained periods of time. And in the end, this evolutionary process can have revolutionary results that dramatically improve our energy future.

ExxonMobil is proud to be a technology leader. It is reflected in our consistent R&D investment, over $700 million in one year alone, our ongoing technical training, representing 25,000 employee training days last year, our integrated functional organizations and associated research departments that enable us to rapidly and globally apply technology, and our many Technology Assistance Agreements with host governments, including several OPEC countries.

To make my point, I would like to highlight several revolutionary technologies spanning the supply chain that have evolved over time, before turning to the conditions required to sustain such innovation in the future.

Let me begin with advances in the area of reservoir simulation, which have been instrumental in improving reservoir management and recovery worldwide.

Nearly fifty years ago, Exxon engineers applied a new mathematical

---

① incremental [inkri'mentəl] *adj.* 增长的

很少成为报纸头条。它源于一个渐进的过程，是很长一段时间内持续投资，以及应用科学、工程和管理专业知识的结果。最后，这种进化过程可以产生革命性的结果，并戏剧性地改进我们能源的未来。

埃克森美孚公司很荣幸地成为了技术革新的领头人。这主要反映在如下方面：我们每年的持续研发投入超过 7 亿美元；我们从未间断过技术培训，仅在去年就培训了 25 000 名员工；我们综合性的功能组织和相关研发部门使我们能够迅速在全球范围内应用技术；我们与东道国政府签订了技术援助协议，其中包括几个石油输出国家组织的成员国。

为了证明我的观点，在阐述维持未来技术革新需要满足的条件之前，我想先强调几个贯穿供应链的创新技术，它们会随着时间的推移不断改进。

请允许我从油库模拟领域的进步说起，它们有助于提高全球的油藏管理和复苏。

大约 50 年以前，埃克森的工程师运用一项新的数学方法求解多相流体运动方程，即依靠最新的计算机技术模拟油库行为。

我们与沙特和其他风险投资合作伙伴一起，率先在沙特阿拉伯把这项技术成功运用于阿布扎克的全部油田。

这个创新工艺利用新模型技术和计算机信息处理技术的进步，帮助我们更好地理解多相流体流动的全部物理意义。这是一个逐渐

technique for solving multiphase flow equations using the latest computer technology to simulate reservoir behavior.

Working with our Saudi and other venture partners, we first applied this technology on a full-field scale to the Abqaiq field in Saudi Arabia with success.

That revolutionary technology has been built upon, capitalizing on new modeling techniques and computing advances to better understand the full physics of multiphase fluid flow. It has been an evolutionary process in which ExxonMobil has dedicated more than 900 work years over the past 30 years.

And it has had revolutionary results. Our latest generation and industry leading reservoir simulator — EMpower — is currently being applied to over 150 reservoirs in 20 countries worldwide, including 8 OPEC partner countries.

Application of Empower to two major developments in Nigeria underpinned[①] $ 5 billion of investments resulting in new production supply this year that will reach 350,000 barrels per day.

Advances in deepwater production provide other examples of evolutionary technologies.

Since building our first steel pile platform in the Gulf of Mexico 50 years ago, we have upgraded our capabilities through the application of a succession of new technologies.

From fixed platforms we have graduated to tension leg platforms,

---

① underpin [ˌʌndəˈpin] vt. 为打下基础,巩固,支持

改良的过程，它让埃克森美孚公司在过去 30 年中投入了总计为 900 多个人工作一年的时间。

它也带来了飞跃性的结果。 我们的最新一代和行业领先的油库模拟器"授权"目前正被用于世界 20 个国家的 150 多座油库，其中包括 8 个石油输出国家组织成员国。

我们将"授权"模拟器运用于尼日利亚的两个基础开发项目，并投资 50 亿美元，结果是今年的产量将达到每天 35 万桶。

技术革新的另外一个例子是深水生产的进步。

自从 50 年前墨西哥湾建立第一个钢管平台以来，我们已经通过一系列新技术的应用提升了我们的能力。

我们已经从固定平台升级到张力腿平台和海底完井，再到最近的浮式采油平台和储运卸载货轮，这些技术使我们达到超过 1 800 米的深海。

我们最近与尼日利亚石油公司合作，在尔哈油田部署了这些深海技术，从超过 1 200 米的水下开采石油。

创新给液化天然气运输也带来了类似的好处。 我们与卡塔尔石油公司合作，不久将开始用货轮运载洁净液态天然气，其载荷量将比传统的液化天然气船高出 80%。 获得这种航运能力将对世界能源版图的连接产生戏剧性的冲击。

技术沿着这条供应链帮助我们提升了能力，有效地增加了我们的炼油能力和开发出更洁净的燃料。

subsea completions and most recently to floating production, storage and offloading vessels, enabling us to reach water depths of over 1,800 meters.

We recently deployed these deepwater technologies in the Erha fields, where we are partnering with the Nigerian National Petroleum Corporation to produce at water depths of over 1,200 meters.

Innovations in liquefied natural gas shipping have similar benefits. Working with our partner Qatar Petroleum, we will soon begin safely transporting clean-burning natural gas in liquefied form on vessels with 80 percent more capacity than conventional LNG ships. Such gains in shipping capacity will have a dramatic impact in connecting the world energy map.

Moving along the supply chain, technology has contributed to our ability to efficiently increase our refining capacity and develop ever cleaner fuels. Nanotechnology① has enabled us to tailor our refining catalysts② to accelerate reactions, increase product volumes, and remove impurities. Such "nanocatalysis" is an important part of our molecule management systems that have enabled ExxonMobil to increase refining capacity at a rate equivalent to building a new grassroots③ refinery every three years worldwide.

(950 words)

---

① nanotechnology [ˌænɔtek'nɔlədʒi] n. 纳米技术
② catalyst ['kætəlist] n. 催化剂
③ grassroots ['grɑːsruːts] n. 基层

纳米技术使我们能够调整炼油催化剂，从而加速反应、增加产品容量和减少杂质。这种"纳米催化剂"是我们分子管理系统的重要组成部分，它们帮助埃克森美孚公司提高的精炼能力，相当于在世界范围内每三年多建造一座新的基层精炼厂。

知识链接

Exxon Mobil 艾克森美孚是全世界第一大型石油企业，其总部设于德克萨斯州爱文市。艾克森美孚公司的前身是 1882 年约翰·洛克菲勒创立的标准石油公司，该公司建立了世界上的第一个托拉斯组织。进入 20 世纪，美国通过的《反托拉斯法案》，将标准石油分拆为"新泽西标准"（Jersey Standard）、美孚（Socony）和"真空石油"（Vacuum oil）。1966 年美孚和真空石油合并，改名为 Mobil Oil Corporation。1972 年新泽西标准改名为 Exxon Corporation（Esso 为其子公司），1999 年 Mobil 和 Exxon 合并，成立艾克森美孚，埃克森、美孚及埃索分别为其旗下的分公司。埃克森美孚与壳牌、英国石油（BP）及 Total 同为全球四大原油公司。

题　记

　　坐落在明尼苏达州的嘉吉公司，是一个超级庞大、以农产品为基础的帝国。嘉吉公司在谷物、肉类、家禽和农业融资等行业拥有巨额投资，他们采用"连通性"策略加强与其他行业之间的联系，关注能源、环境、土地利用、贸易政策等所有问题，开拓基于信任的贸易。嘉吉公司支持农场主自由选择植物种植，这使他们应对变化更加得心应手。嘉吉公司崇尚食品创新，既推出了广受欢迎的纤维食品，也对大众做了有益健康的承诺。嘉吉公司竭尽全力规避生物能源对粮食安全产生的风险，实行灵活的农业政策，精心调配作物的选择，并且进行合理的能量使用，从而促进了新能源与人类基本的饮食需求之间的平衡。这一切说明了嘉吉总裁格雷戈里·佩奇高度关注食品价格和环境的预期并非天方夜谭。

Facing Challenges to
Ride Herd over Businesses
—A Speech by Cargill CEO Gregory Page
on Food Prices and the Environment

Good morning.

For a private company, we put out a lot of financial information. Why shall we decide to become so transparent? In the early 1990s, we instituted an employee stock-ownership program. We had about 25,000 eligible employees, and by law we had to communicate with them about the financials. But I think the bigger idea was that if you don't go out and explain yourself, you'll be defined by your mistakes, whether you have a fire or an employee sues you, some negative event. We do too many good things and there are too many ideas that benefit mankind that are originated by thoughtful employees. Cargill now publishes its earnings, and we have a call with the media once a quarter to talk through a lot of issues.

Cargill remains huge in grain, meat, poultry and agricultural finance, but we've also made an effort to move up the food chain a bit.

从容应对行业挑战

——嘉吉总裁格雷戈里·佩奇对
食品价格和环境问题的演讲

早上好。

我们作为私营企业公布了大量的财务信息。 我们为什么决定如此公开透明呢？ 20 世纪 90 年代初，我们制订了员工持股计划。 我们有 25 000 名左右符合条件的员工，我们必须依据法律与他们进行财务交流。 但是我认为还有更深层次的原因，如果你没有坦率地解释清楚，无论是裁员还是员工起诉等负面事件，你都将为自己的错误付出代价。 我们做了太多的好事，有太多造福人类的创意，但他们都源自善于思考的员工。 嘉吉现在公布它的盈利状况，并且我们会在每个季度给媒体打一次电话，交流大量的问题。

嘉吉公司在谷物、肉类、家禽和农业融资等行业仍然拥有巨额投资，但我们也已经努力向食品产业链迈进了一小步。 我们采用什么样的策略呢？ 我们用"连通性"来描述我们如何设法使我们

What kind of strategies do we adopt? We use "connectivity" to describe how we try to make businesses we've elected to stay in matter to each other. Take our cocoa business, in which we deal with confectioners① . We ask, "What can we build out of that cocoa-based relationship with confectioners? " We can sell products like erythritol for sugar-free chocolates. At its root, it's not about being a conglomerate② in the sense of "Let's just get this disparate③ basket of businesses and hopefully, we'll have uncorrelated returns."

With rising food costs, changing energy needs, increased demands from developing countries and the push into biofuels, the food business has become fairly dramatic. I think people's understanding of the impact of food, energy, land utilization and the environment will probably keep us more in the news than we've been in the past, but probably not to the degree we've been in the last 18 months.

Of all these issues — energy, the environment, land use, trade policy — our top focus is trust-based trade. A lot of the volatility of the past year wasn't because the food wasn't there. It was because the people that had it closed their border, and those who had trusted them, who had come to depend on them, were sorely mistreated.

I don't feel the same pull to be engaged in the dialogue about

_____

① confectioner [cənˈfekʃənə] *n.* 糖果店
② conglomerate [cɔnˈglɔmrəit] *n.* 聚结
③ disparate [ˈdispərit] *adj.* 全异的

选择的各个行业之间相联系。 拿我们的可可豆业务来说，我们在这个产业中会和糖果厂打交道。 我们会问："我们除了可可豆之外还能和糖果厂做什么生意呢"？ 我们能销售无糖巧克力所需的赤藻糖醇等更多的产品。 归根结底，这样做并不是要成为某种意义上的"让我们得到迥然不同的一揽子交易，并期待获取彼此不相关回报"的企业集团。

随着持续上升的食品成本、不断变化的能源需求、发展中国家日益增长的需求以及转向生物燃料的压力，食品行业的竞争已经相当激烈。 我认为，人们对食物、能源、土地利用和环境影响的理解可能会使我们比过去更多地受新闻报道的影响，但也可能不会达到我们过去 18 个月的程度。

在能源、环境、土地利用、贸易政策等所有问题中，基于信任的贸易是我们最关注的问题。 过去一年的很多波动并不是因为食物匮乏。 而是因为那些拥有食物的国家关闭了他们的边境，以及那些信任他们的人、依赖他们的人受到了非常不公正的待遇。

我认为与政府磋商补贴的类似需求不再存在。 农民过去为了保护自己的土地，必须按政策要求种植作物。 现在农场主对种什么有相对自由的选择，这使我们应对变化更加得心应手。 在我的家乡北达科他州，人们过去被迫种植小麦，现在他们种起了油菜子和向日葵，将来也许会种植大麦这样反复来回地变化。 所以，15 年前实际

government subsidies. In the past, in order to secure your acreage allotments, you had to grow the crops mandated by the policy. Today we have relatively free choice in what a farmer plants, and with that has come a more robust ability to respond to changes. In my home state of North Dakota, where a person was in the past compelled to grow wheat, today they're growing canola① and sunflower, and they'll switch back and forth to barley. So a farmer that 15 years ago had really only one choice today has seven or eight reactions he can make to the price of fertilizer, to the price of crops and to the input that people like Cargill give him about what the world needs.

What does Cargill mean when it talks about food innovation? An array of things. In some cases it's fiber you enjoy eating. In other cases it's the sensation of sweetness that comes without a calorie burden. In some cases it's a healthfulness promise: phytosterols from soybeans, antioxidants that people are concerned about. In some cases, they're high-performance sports drinks that have a glycemic response that coincides with an athlete's needs. These are probably things that a lot of people don't think about, but there are sports beverages where our role is to understand metabolism② to the level that we understand how the energy is released into the bloodstream.

As for the view on biofuels, we have one very strong principle,

① canola [kəˈnəuna] n. 菜籽油
② metabolism [meˈtæbəlizənm] n. 新陈代谢

上只能有一种选择的农场主，现在有七种或八种应变机制，他可以根据肥料价格、农产品价格以及嘉吉等公司的建议者给出的世界需要什么的信息，确定自己的选择。

嘉吉提及的食品创新是什么意思呢？它涉及好多好多的内容。在某些情况下，它是你喜欢吃的纤维食品；在另一些情况下，它只是没有热量的甜点感觉。有时候，它是一种有益健康的承诺，如大豆中的植物甾醇类和人们关注的抗氧化剂；有时候，它是高性能的运动饮料，含有运动员需要的血糖反应。这些也许是很多人还没有想到的东西，但对于有些运动型的饮料，我们的角色是了解能量如何被释放到血液循环的层面，从而理解新陈代谢。

至于生物燃料的观点，我们有一个十分坚定的原则，认为强制使用从本质上来说有害无益。农业是一项户外生产活动，很难让人坐在世界上的任何一个房间里，推断来年的天气情况，从而规定种植任何特定的作物。从另一个方面来说，我们并不是农业补贴的坚定支持者，但这种做法至少会带来可计量的损失。如果你认为你打算付45美分一加仑来生产乙醇，你可以计算你的费用。但是在强制作用下，这是不可计算的。

作为嘉吉公司的首席执行官，从容应对如此广泛的行业总会面临挑战。我认为，任何决定涉猎广泛行业的人都会危害到公司和员工前景。在某种程度上，嘉吉是个相对宽松的企业集团公司，

which is that mandates are inherently bad. Agriculture is an outdoor sport, and it's very difficult for somebody to sit in any chamber in the world and determine what next year's weather's going to be, and therefore to mandate some specific level of any crop. And on the other side of it, we're not big supporters of subsidization, but at least it's a quantifiable set of damage. If you say you're going to pay 45 cents a gallon to have ethanol produced, you can calculate what the burden is. But with a mandate, it's incalculable.

As the CEO of Cargill, you always face challenges to ride herd over such a wide range of businesses. And I think anybody that set out to do that would disserve the organization and the employment promise. Cargill is, at one level, a relatively loose confederation of entrepreneurial businesses, and I think it's why a lot of people work here a long time and enjoy it. At the same time, we share one balance sheet and one reputation, and so we have other principles about which we're fairly intolerant. There is this dual reality at Cargill.

(820 words)

并且我认为这就是很多人在这里工作很长时间、并且喜欢在这里工作的原因。 与此同时，我们享有同一张资产负债表和同一种声誉，所以我们还有很不能容忍的其他原则。 这就是嘉吉的双重现实。

知识链接

Cargill 嘉吉公司是美国的食品企业。嘉吉公司 1865 年创立以来，85％以上的股权一直由创始人家族——嘉吉和麦克米伦家族所有。现在嘉吉年营业额高达 900 亿美元，年获利达 25 亿美元以上，是美国第二大私有资本公司，法国第三大粮产输出公司，美国最大的玉米饲料制造商，美国第三大面粉加工企业和屠宰、肉类包装加工厂、最大的养猪和禽类（如肉鸡、火鸡）养殖场。公司业务横跨五大洲 66 个国家，还拥有超过 100 亿美元资产的避险基金——黑河资产管理（Black River Asset Management）和从事高科技及高回报（包括基因工程等）的生物工程研发计划。

题　记

　　欧盟的扩大提供了结束欧洲被人为分割、与美国相抗衡的唯一契机。欧盟成员国的增加和经济的发展不仅使欧洲人可以跨边境自由往来、学习和工作，而且中欧和东欧的商业和经济也将因实行市场经济而兴旺昌盛。无论是在布拉格或布达佩斯的主干道，还是在布鲁塞尔的会议室，欧洲重新团聚宣布了第二次世界大战和冷战遗产的消失。而欧洲复兴开发银行在欧盟的扩张过程中一直充当着举足轻重的角色。这家银行通过国际间的协作，已经帮助巴尔干半岛实现了稳定和重建，成为俄罗斯改革努力中越来越重要的伙伴，与欧洲地区处于过渡初期阶段的国家齐心协力，在减轻贫困、促进增长、打击腐败和犯罪以及防治艾滋病方面进行了大量的工作。得之不易的欧盟需要彼此共同珍惜与维系。

Treasuring an Asset to the EU

— Speech on EU Enlargement and the European
Bank for Reconstruction and Development

Development was set up in 1991, there was a unique opportunity to develop a new wider Europe, based on plural democracy and market-based economies.

Today, only twelve days before the accession to the EU of 10 new member states, we can say with pride that the opportunity has been successfully seized. It is a credit to the Governments of the region, and a credit to the EBRD, which has played a vital role in the process thanks to its unique mandate.

The extent and speed of change has been impressive. It may have been slower than some optimists hoped for at the start. And it has sometimes been painful for those losing the security and certainty of an old system and not seeing the early benefits of a new one. But the completion of the Europe's biggest ever enlargement, with the prospect of more countries joining in the years ahead, is the clearest sign that the reform journey has been worthwhile.

珍惜欧盟的财富

——关于扩大欧盟和欧洲复兴开发银行的演讲

欧洲复兴开发银行成立于 1991 年，恰逢基于多元民主和立足于市场经济的欧洲迎来新一轮更广泛发展的独特机遇。

今天，距加入欧盟的 10 个新成员国仅有 12 天，我们可以骄傲地声称，我们已经成功地抓住了这次机遇。 这是地区政府的荣誉，是欧洲复兴开发银行的荣誉。 欧洲复兴开发银行的独立授权在这个进程中起了至关重要的作用。

欧洲的变化程度和速度给人印象深刻。 它可能在开始时比有些乐观主义者期待的要慢一点。 那些对旧体制失去安全感和确定性、看不到新体制初期利益的人有时又感到痛苦。 但是，欧洲有史以来最大的扩张已经完成，未来将会有更多的国家加入欧盟，这种前景释放出最清晰的信号：这是值得一做的改革征程。

5 月 1 日将会真正成为一个具有历史意义的日子。 第二次世界大战和冷战的遗产——欧洲分裂将会在这一天消失。 它将是欧洲重新团聚、欧盟 25 个成员首次相逢的日子。 无论是在布拉格或布达佩斯的主干道，还是在布鲁塞尔的会议室，这是我们可以亲眼见证

The 1st May will be a genuinely historic day. The day that the division of Europe — the legacy of the Second World War and the Cold War — will be erased. The first day for new reunited Europe, for an EU of 25. It is a transformation which we can see for ourselves, whether in the high streets of Prague or Budapest, or in the conference rooms of Brussels. Europe has changed in a thousand ways, and for the better.

From the outset, there has been no stronger supporter of the enlargement process than Britain. It has been a rather rare point of cross-party consensus in Britain, where Europe is concerned. This government has championed it energetically. We are proud of the part we have played — both up front and behind the scenes — to help the accession countries along the path to membership. You, the members and the staff of the EBRD also deserve to be proud. But the real achievement belongs to the ten countries which themselves have managed this transition. Enlargement will increase stability, security and prosperity in our region. It will help prevent conflict in Europe ever reoccurring. It will entrench and help spread democracy, the rule of law and human rights. It will widen our co-operation to face new threats — from environmental degradation to terrorism — together. It will create a vast free trade market of 450 million consumers, with immense potential for the future. Increased trade, investment, and competition will benefit us all — in the new EU countries and the existing members alike.

In Britain, the Treasury estimates that 100,000 British jobs are already linked to the export of goods and services to the new EU member

的转变。 欧洲一直以千种方式寻求着改变，并且会越变越好。

从扩张过程开始，就没有比英国更加强大的支持者。 就欧洲而言，这一直是英国相当罕见的跨党共识的角度。 这个政府为此殚精竭虑。 无论是在幕前还是在幕后，我们都为自己扮演的角色感到骄傲，即帮助各国加入欧盟，成为成员国。 你们作为欧洲复兴开发银行的成员和全体员工，也同样值得骄傲。 但是，真正的成就属于设法完成这个转变的 10 个国家。 扩张将会增进我们地区的稳定、安全和繁荣。 它将有助于防止欧洲曾经复发的冲突。 它将巩固和帮助传播民主、法治和人权。 它将拓宽我们的合作，使我们共同面对从环境退化到恐怖主义的新威胁。 它将创造一个庞大的自由贸易市场，拥有 4.5 亿消费者，并对未来拥有巨大的潜力。 贸易、投资和竞争的增加将会让我们所有人获益，包括新欧盟国家和目前的成员国。

据英国财政部估计，10 万英国人的工作已经与新欧洲成员国的出口商品和服务相关。 我们与 8 个最大盟国的贸易在上个 10 年已经增长了 200% 左右。 研究预测，这样的贸易将会继续扩大，在未来创造更多的工作。

当然，扩张也会带来新的挑战。 它将迫使欧盟重新审视它的流程、制度和观念。 这意味着欧盟有了新邻居，我们必须和他们一道巩固我们的关系。 我们必须适应会员国的扩大，以及改变我们生活的世界。

特别的是，欧洲必须推进经济改革的进程。 我确信，新增加的

states. Our trade with the eight largest accession states has grown by almost 200% in the last decade. Studies predict that this trade will continue to expand, creating more jobs in the future.

Of course enlargement also bring new challenges. It will force the EU to review its processes, institutions and ideas. It means that the EU has new neighbors, with whom we must strengthen our relationships. We must adapt to reflect our expanded membership, as well as the changing world in which we live.

In particular, Europe must press ahead with the process of economic reform. I am convinced that the entry of ten new members will be a boost for this agenda. The record of modernization which the new members have demonstrated in the last decade and a half is an inspiring example to all of us. Their proven determination and commitment to reform will be an asset to the whole of the EU.

Ten years ago, few of us would have envisaged[①] the shape of Europe we now live in. But few could deny that Europe is today a more secure, stable and prosperous place.

This enlargement has undoubtedly been one of the European project's greatest success stories. Now we must sustain the process so future generations can continue to reap the benefits.

We hope to complete negotiations with Bulgaria and Romania by end of this year. Then we have a crucial decision on Turkey in December, with the chance to anchor Turkey's place in Europe. And we have the

---

① envisage [in'vizidʒ] vt. 设想,想像

珍惜欧盟的财富

10 个成员将会大力推动这一议程。 新成员在过去 10 年半中已经展现的现代化记录对我们所有人来说都是一个鼓舞人心的例子。 他们坚定的决心和改革的承诺是整个欧盟的一笔财富。

10 年前，几乎没有人设想过我们现在的欧洲生活模式。 但是，几乎没有人能够否认，欧洲现在是一个更加安全、稳定和繁荣的地方。

这种扩张无疑是欧洲计划最成功的案例之一。 我们现在必须维持这种进程，以使后代能继续受益。

我们希望在今年年底完成与保加利亚和罗马尼亚的谈判。 然后，我们会在 12 月对土耳其做出关键性的裁决，看是否有机会保住土耳其在欧洲的位置。 我们看好西巴尔干半岛未来成员国的前景。

这就是欧洲复兴开发银行为什么在这些年里一直充当着举足轻重的角色。

欧洲复兴开发银行是这场转变进程中的核心，它在过去的 13 年间支持着许多国家的经济和政治改革。

这家银行并不是为了永远存在而设立。 它的存在是为了帮助各国完成过渡搭建一个平台，使他们自己的国内金融机构、投资者和国际业务提供其经济增长的依据。

这些国家的转变并没有因为加入欧盟而结束。 欧洲复兴开发银行仍然在帮助他们完成这个过程。 但是，他们获得了欧盟成员国的新的支持构架，随着国际投资者的兴趣增长，欧洲复兴开发银行的作用应该在随后的多年中自然消失。

217

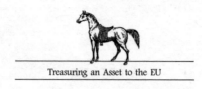
prospect of future membership for the Western Balkans.

That is why the EBRD will still have a very important role in the years ahead.

The EBRD has been at the heart of the process of transition, supporting the economic and political transformation of many nations over the last thirteen years.

The Bank was not set up to exist for ever. It is there to help countries make the transition, to a point where their own domestic institutions and investors and international business provide the basis for their economic growth.

The transition is not yet finished in the countries which are about to join the EU. The EBRD will still help them complete this process. But as they gain a new framework of support as EU members, and as the interest of international investors grows, the EBRD's role should naturally fall away over the years to come.

Nevertheless, there is still a major role for the Bank in countries further east and south. It is already playing a key role in Bulgaria and Romania. The Bank has assisted international efforts for stabilization and reconstruction in the Balkans. It has become an increasingly important partner in Russia's reform efforts. This vital work must continue.

The Bank needs to make a more concerted effort in those countries of the region which are at an early stage of transition. These countries require substantial help to reduce poverty, to promote growth and tackle corruption, organised crime and HIV/AIDS.

The EBRD can bring its unique mix of private sector expertise,

珍惜欧盟的财富

　　然而，这家银行在更远的东部和南部仍然扮演着重要角色。 它已经在保加利亚和罗马尼亚发挥了重要的作用。 这家银行通过国际间的协作，已经帮助巴尔干半岛实现了稳定和重建。 它已经成为俄罗斯改革努力中越来越重要的伙伴。 这种至关重要的工作必须持续下去。

　　这家银行需要与这个地区正处于过渡初期阶段的那些国家进一步齐心协力。 这些国家需要大量的帮助，以减轻贫困、促进增长和打击腐败、组织犯罪和艾滋病。

　　欧洲复兴开发银行可以对其私营部门专业知识、机构经验和财政这一独特的混合体施加影响力。 但是，它需要这些国家亲自承诺，来自国内和国际投资者的新兴趣，以及国际社会和赠款资助的有效协调。

　　我们十分欢迎这家银行的新倡议，支持处于初期转变的国家，英国准备与欧洲复兴开发银行接洽，共同构建这一倡议的框架，并给予新的财政支持。 这个议程需要在银行内部提升为核心的优先事项。

　　银行必须继续寻找办法，建设性地参与问题国家的政治改革。这不是强加给来自外部民主的特殊形式，相反，它反映了这家银行创始人的信仰，并在实践中得到证实，即政治改革和经济发展之间的联系剪不断、理还乱。

　　欧洲复兴开发银行有许多值得骄傲的地方，我们有可能在欧盟扩张的前夕，没有较好地安排时间来认识这一点。 欧洲复兴开发银

219

institutional experience and finance to bear. But it needs the commitment of the countries themselves, new interest from domestic and international investors, effective coordination with the international community and grant support.

We strongly welcome the Bank's new initiative to support the early transition countries. The UK is ready to engage with the Bank in shaping this initiative and in giving new financial support. Within the Bank this agenda needs to be promoted as a core priority.

The Bank must continue to search for ways to engage constructively in countries where problems exist over political reform. This is not about imposing a particular form of democracy from outside. Rather, it reflects the beliefs of the Bank's founders, confirmed in practice, that political reform and economic progress are inextricably① linked.

The EBRD has much to be proud of — and there could be no better time to recognise that than the eve of the EU's enlargement. It is also well positioned to meet the new challenges. Its location in the City of London enables it to benefit from a huge range of expertise and experience close to hand. Its leadership and its staff have shown themselves ready to take on the next set of challenges with vigour.

(1,164 words)

---

① inextricably [in'ikstrikebli] *adv.* 解不开地,解决不了地

珍惜欧盟的财富

行也整装待发，随时准备迎接新的挑战。 它在伦敦金融城的位置使之能够从近在咫尺的大量专业知识和经验中获益。 它的领导能力和全体工作人员已经证明，他们正在精神抖擞地准备迎接下一轮挑战。

知识链接 🔍

European Bank for Reconstruction and Development 欧洲复兴开发银行（简称 EBRD）。欧洲复兴开发银行成立于 1991 年，最初的设想由法国总统密特朗于 1989 年提出，并得到欧洲共同体各国和其他一些国家的积极响应。欧洲复兴开发银行的宗旨是：在考虑加强民主、尊重人权、保护环境等因素下，帮助和支持东欧、中欧国家向市场经济转变，以调动上述国家中个人及企业的积极性，促使他们向民主政体和市场经济过渡。投资的主要目标是中东欧国家的私营企业和这些国家的基础设施。

题 记

　　在知识经济时代，除了金融和实物资本之外，知识分子和人力资本在经济发展中扮演着不可或缺的角色。出色的商界领袖以扭转乾坤之势震撼着这个世界。史蒂夫·乔布斯一手打造了全球最具价值的公司，山姆·沃尔顿创立的沃尔玛曾在 12 个月中创造了 4 500 亿美元的销售神话。商业领导原则因此成为人们顶礼膜拜的业界圭臬。雅虎董事会主席和首席执行官卡罗尔·巴茨在此呼吁商界领袖们首先要坚持建立成功企业文化的原则；其次要充满激情地点燃公司内部的增长引擎，培植并发展新兴市场；第三条原则是开发多元化的思想和多元化的创造性。毕竟，乔布斯是加州反主流文化的商业代表，而沃尔顿则是美国心脏地带的保守派，但作为商界领袖，他们在企业经营和社会变革方面都做出了重要贡献。

The Principles of
Business Leadership

— Remarks by Carol Bartz,
Chairman and CEO of Yahoo

Thank you. Good morning, everyone.

As the world moves toward a knowledge economy the mandate for leadership changes. There are three key leadership imperatives that are at work, and must be mastered, for all of us as leaders to operate and succeed going forward.

Imperative number one is the principle of leadership and the mandate to build a winning culture. This first leadership imperative starts within the walls of your company — in the vision you set, and in the culture you build. In this context, as leaders, we must answer the question for our employees: in a world where know-how and insight and intelligence and inventive spirit are the keys to success, what role will our company play in fostering it — and what role will we play in harnessing it? Once we answer this, we then have to foster a culture that can deliver on that vision. It's important to remember that top leaders can set a vision, set a

商业领导原则

——雅虎董事会主席和首席
执行官卡罗尔·巴茨的演讲

谢谢。 大家早上好！

全球进入知识经济时代之时，对领导能力的要求也随之改变。对我们所有人来说，有三个势在必行的关键领导规则，作为操控和成功推动企业前进的领导者，我们必须掌握这些原则。

规则一是领导的原则和建立成功文化的需求。 这个首要的领导规则始于公司内部，即在你的视线范围内，在你建立的文化之中。 作为领导者，我们必须在这个背景下为员工解答下列问题：在知识、洞察力、智慧和创造精神代表成功核心含义的当今世界，我们公司在培育它时会扮演什么角色，即在驾驭它时我们将扮演什么角色？ 回答这个问题之时，我们就必须培养一种可以实现这一愿景的文化。 重要的是记住：优秀的领导者能够设置愿景，制定策略，建立奖励和指标体系，这些机制可以鼓励、奖赏和培训员工，但是余下的工作取决于公司的个人和团队。这是非常个人的行为，也是很多人的日常行为，他们使公司的整

strategy, set a system of rewards and metrics that encourage people, reward people, train people — but the rest is ultimately up to the individuals and teams in our companies. It is very much acts of individuals, the every day acts of many that make the biggest difference in the overall performance of a company.

I think that's something that Bill Hewlett and Dave Packard understood when they started HP sixty-two years ago. Bill and Dave didn't create HP in 1939 to build an empire or a fortune. These two young Stanford guys with $538 between them simply wanted to invent what they called the useful and the significant — useful in people's lives, and contributing to the world in a significant way. And they wanted to create a meritocracy — where personal, every day acts of leadership counted. Which is why they were devoutly egalitarian and progressive in the way they designed employee programs such as employee stock ownership — all employees would become leaders, in a sense. They rewarded people based on performance and contribution, rather than on rank or title or size of organization or time in job.

Today, you can see the foundations of that culture magnified in initiatives like HP's World E-Inclusion effort, designed to spread the benefits of the digital world into areas that have been excluded until now — to nations across the globe, to towns and villages and businesses everywhere, into the lives of billions who have up to now not had the tools to share their invention with the rest of the world, and who have every right to participate in a knowledge economy. It's not about recycling

体表现焕然一新。

我认为，这就是比尔·休利特和戴维·帕卡德 62 年前创建惠普时心照不宣的思想。 比尔和戴维 1939 年创建惠普时并不是为了缔造一个王国或者一笔财富。 这两个斯坦福的年轻小伙子共有 538 美元，只是想发明他们称之为有用和有意义的东西，即在人们生活中有用的东西，并以一种有意义的方式为世界做出贡献。 他们想创建一种精英管理模式，个人和领导的日常行为都可在其中凸显价值。这就是为什么他们虔诚地主张以平等和渐进的方式设置员工股份所有制等员工项目，即在某种意义上，所有员工都可以成为领导者。他们根据业绩和贡献奖励员工，而不考虑他们在工作中的等级、头衔、机构规模或时间。

今天，你们可以看到这种文化的根基，惠普的"世界 E 家"活动等举措充分展示了这种文化，"世界 E 家"旨在将数字世界的成果传播到目前还没有达到的地区，传播到全球的每个国家，传播到各地的城镇、乡村和企业，传播到目前还没有工具与世界其他地方分享他们发明的数以亿计的人们当中，这些人有权参与到知识经济中来。 这不是在发展中国家回收电脑或者将西方的技术强加给他们。它是一种发自内心的创造，是从基层开始、与本地文化相关的可持续解决方案。 它是对技术如何授权、持续和释放，而不是排斥、腐蚀和限制的重新思考。

PCs or imposing Western technology on developing nations. It's inherently about creating, from the ground up, locally sustainable solutions that are culturally relevant. It's about rethinking how technology can empower and sustain and liberate, rather than exclude and erode and restrain.

It's ultimately about technology as means, not end itself. So that's imperative number one.

Imperative number two is about leadership and the need for sustainability. In these challenging economic times, we are all trying to ignite the growth engines inside our companies and to help re-ignite the economy as a whole. Most of us have taken the necessary steps to boost efficiency, eliminate redundancy and reduce costs. But it's not possible to cost-cut our way to growth. Growth is dependent on new revenues. And so the next leadership imperative is focused on creating sustainability through the simultaneous pursuit of growth opportunities in existing businesses — as well as in wholly new markets. Pursuing growth in existing businesses means avoiding complacency and postponing short-term gains for medium term rewards. But let me underscore the importance of emerging markets — and the distinctively different approach that must be taken in discovering them, nurturing them, and growing them.

Obviously, most of these markets are located in the developing world. The potential for growth in the emerging market economies has never been greater. As an example, recent OECD statistics show that spending on information technologies in these economies is growing at twice the rate of the industrialized world, although off a lower base. It

技术最终是一种手段，而不是自我终结。这就是规则一。

规则二是关于领导能力和可持续性需求。在这个充满竞争经济的时代，我们都尝试着点燃公司内部的增长引擎，并且重新点燃整个经济的引擎。我们中的许多人已经采取了必要的步骤来提高效率、消除冗余和削减成本。但这并不是减缓成本增长的方式。增长依赖于新的收入。所以接下来的领导规则就集中于通过同时追求整个新兴市场的已有业务增长机会创造可持续性发展。追求已有业务的增长意味着避免自满，为中期利益推迟短期收益回报。但是我还要强调新兴市场的重要性，我们要采取与众不同的方法去发现新兴市场，培植新兴市场，并发展新兴市场。

显然，大部分这样的市场存在于发展中国家。新兴市场经济的增长潜能从未达到如此之大。例如，近来经济合作与发展组织的统计数据显示，在这些经济中花费在信息技术上的成本以工业化世界两倍的速度增长，尽管他们的基数较低。这就表明，有必要重点考虑将新兴市场作为公司增长战略的核心部分。在这些新兴市场，稳定持续的体制是你获得长期增长的唯一途径。"可持续性"指解决方案在经济上具有可行性，如果没有外部干扰可以维持多年。"可持续性"指解决方案不会恶化当地环境。"可持续性"指解决方案尊重社会和文化习俗，事实上，他们对这些习俗给予了优化、赞美和回报。这些市场特别真实地

illustrates the importance of thinking about developing markets as a central part of a company's growth strategy. And in these developing markets, sustainable systems are the only way you can derive long-term growth. "Sustainable" in that the solutions are economically viable①, and can remain so for years without outside interference. "Sustainable" in that the solutions do not degrade the local environment. "Sustainable" in that the solutions respect social and cultural mores — in fact, they optimize, celebrate, and reward them. In these markets, it's especially true that it's not just what you do — but also the character with which you do it. We will lose customers, shareowners, and ultimately employees if we do not demonstrate leadership and develop new metrics for gauging② our performance on a world stage: Leadership — both at the highest level and at the personal level — is what causes the pendulum to swing in one direction or the other. The system needs to find balance. Humankind is the catalyst that forces the balance to swing one way or the other.

That leads us to imperative number three. This imperative is about leadership and diversity. If we are truly going to continue to lead our companies through periods of growth, and broaden our role as stewards of a new global economy that nurtures (rather than destroys) every culture in its path, we need to take an approach that embraces ideas and

---

① viable ['vaiəbl] *adj.* 可行的
② gaug [geidʒ] *vt.* 测量,估计

反映了两方面的情况，他们不仅关注你做的事，而且关注你做事的特点。 如果我们不能证明自己的领导能力，开发新标准测量我们在世界舞台上的表现，最终会导致顾客、股东和员工的流失。 不管是最高层次还是个人层次的领导能力，都会引起事态在两个方向之间来回摇摆。 这个系统需要找到平衡点。 人类就是促进两点间摇摆平衡的催化剂。

这就引导我们走向第三条规则。 该规则解释了领导能力和多元化。 如果我们真想继续带领公司维持增长期，拓展我们作为新的全球经济管理者的角色，培育而不是损毁各种发展中的文化，我们需要采取一种方法，获取我们无法模仿的思想和方法。 为了成功，我们必须驾驭各种各样的思想。 确实，多元化的人就会有多元化的背景、多元化的经历和多元化的技术，但最重要的是多元化的思想和多元化的创造性。

我们生活在一个被定义为思想的力量、知识和信息连接的力量的时代。 聪明的人住在世界的各个地方——各种各样的人和聪明的人充满了不为人知的想法。 这是一个多元化的新定义，它不仅仅与国籍、种族和宗教相关，还通过向市场输入新模型、新思想和新方法，保持市场的活力。

领导者的工作不应该仅仅局限于短期结果。 领导者必须在未来的数年中为股东、客户和员工服务，致力于机构长期健康的发展，

approaches we have no model for. To be successful, we must harness diversity of thought. Yes, diversity of people, diversity of background, diversity of experience, diversity of skills. But most important, diversity of ideas. Diversity of inventiveness.

We're living in an era that's defined by the power of ideas, the power of connections to knowledge, to information. Smart people reside everywhere in the world — all kinds of people and smart people brimming[①] with ideas that have yet to be heard. This is about a new definition of diversity that has to do with more than national origin or race or creed — it has to do with keeping the market in motion by feeding it new models, new ideas, new approaches.

A leader's job can't focus solely on short-term results. A leader must focus on the long-term health of the franchise and the creation of business value for shareowners, customers and employees over years to come. This means, as leaders, we must be bold in our actions — ahead of the market, using the courage of our convictions and our judgment, experience and instincts as our guide.

Thank you!

(1,104 words)

---

① brimm[brim] *vi.* 满溢,溢出

创造商业价值。 作为领导者，这就意味着我们必须勇敢地运用我们的信心，以及我们的判断能力、经验和直觉做指导，在市场面前大胆施展拳脚。

谢谢！

知识链接

Carol Bartz 卡罗尔·巴茨 2009 年 1 月接替杨致远出任雅虎首席执行官，2011 年 6 月结束任期。在这之前，巴茨担任过美国电脑软件公司欧特克、美国计算机公司——太阳微系统公司的首席执行官等职。她还曾出任布什总统科技顾问委员会委员。作为行业领袖，她在塑造和设置从研发资助到新的宽带激励等政府高科技议程方面发挥了关键作用。

题 记

资本主义利用了人性中自利的力量，取得了经济进步和社会发展，但这种制度只服务于有钱人，而穷人则只能依靠政府援助和慈善。世界首富、著名慈善家比尔·盖茨在面对社会发展和科技进步导致的巨大社会分化之时，提出了创造性资本主义这一理念，即政府、企业和非营利机构共同作用，拓宽市场力量运行的范围，从而让更多的人获利，或得到认可，缓和世界不公平的现象。这种体制具有双重使命：赚钱盈利和让那些无法充分享受市场好处的人群生活也得到改善，让全人类都能享受到资本主义发展带来的福利。怀揣着创造性资本主义的理念，比尔·盖茨一边泪眼婆娑地宣布从一手创建的微软退休，一边慷慨大方地把自己平生积累的580亿美元财产全部捐出。

Creative Capitalism

— A Speech by Bill Gates at Davos

As you all may know, in July I'll make a big career change. I'm not worried; I believe I'm still marketable. I'm a self-starter; I'm proficient in Microsoft Office. I guess that's it. Also I'm learning how to give money away. So, this is the last time I'll attend Davos as a full-time employee of Microsoft.

Some of us are lucky enough to arrive at moments in life when we can pause, reflect on our work, and say: "This is great. It's fun, exciting, and useful; I could do this forever." But the passing of time forces each of us to take stock and ask: What have I accomplished so far? What do I still want to accomplish?

Thirty years ago, 20 years ago, 10 years ago, my focus was totally on how the magic of software could change the world. I saw that breakthroughs in technology could solve key problems. And they do, increasingly, for billions of people. But breakthroughs change lives primarily where people can afford to buy them, only where there is economic demand, and economic demand is not the same as economic need. There are billions of people who need the great inventions of the

创造性资本主义

——比尔·盖茨在达沃斯论坛的演讲

众所周知，我的职业生涯在 7 月将发生重大改变。 我并不担心。 我相信我仍然会受到公众的欢迎。 我是个创业者。 我精通微软办公软件。 我想是的。 我也要学习如何花钱。 因此，这是我作为一名全职微软员工最后一次参加达沃斯论坛。

我们有些人够走运，能够在生活中暂停一刻，并反思我们的工作，然后说："这真了不起。 这是一件有趣、令人兴奋和有益的事。 我愿为此奋斗终生。"但是时间的流逝迫使我们每个人仔细思考并扪心自问：我到目前为止做了些什么？ 我还想做些什么？

30 年前，20 年前，10 年前，我的注意力全部集中在神奇的软件上，看它如何改变世界。 我见证了技术突破能够解决关键问题。 他们逐渐地为数以亿计的人服务。 但是这些突破性的进展主要是改变了具有购买能力的人们的生活，而且仅仅是在有经济需求的地方，当然经济需求并不等同于经济需要。 还有数以亿计的人，他们需要计算机时代的伟大发明，以及许多更基本的需要，但是他们没有途径把自己的需要传递给市场，所以他们一无所获。 如果我们有机会改变他们的生活，我们需要另一种层次的创新。 不仅是技术创

computer age, and many more basic needs as well, but they have no way of expressing their needs in ways that matter to the market, so they go without. If we are going to have a chance of changing their lives, we need another level of innovation. Not just technology innovation, we need system innovation, and that's what I want to discuss with you here in Davos today.

Let me begin by expressing a view that some do not share: The world is getting better, a lot better. In significant and far-reaching ways, the world is a better place to live than it has ever been. Consider the status of women and minorities in society — virtually any society — compared to any time in the past. Consider that life expectancy has nearly doubled during the last 100 years.

Consider governance, the number of people today who vote in elections, express their views, and enjoy economic freedom compared to any time in the past. In many crucial areas, the world is getting better. These improvements have been triggered by advances in science, technology, and medicine. They have brought us to a high point in human welfare. We're really just at the becoming of this technology-driven revolution in what people can do for one another. In the coming decades, we'll have astonishing new abilities: better software, better diagnosis for illness, better cures, better education, better opportunities and more brilliant minds coming up with ideas that solve tough problems.

This is how I see the world, and it should make one thing clear: I am an optimist. But I am an impatient optimist. The world is getting better, but it's not getting better fast enough, and it's not getting better for everyone.

238

新，我们还需要制度创新，这就是我今天在达沃斯这里与大家一起探讨的话题。

让我们从一个有些人并不赞同的观点说起：世界正在变得越来越好，好很多。 从重要性和广泛性方面来说，世界比以往任何时候都更适于人类生活。 与过去的任何时代、任何社会相比，女性和少数民族的社会地位已经发生了变化。 想想在过去的 100 年中，人类的平均寿命几乎增长了一倍。

在今天的政治生活中，参与选举投票的人数比过去任何时候都要多，人们可以畅所欲言，并享受经济自由。 在许多至关重要的领域，世界正在变得越来越好。 科学、技术和医疗的进步是引发这些改进的原因。 他们已经带我们进入人类福祉的制高点。 我们已经真正遭遇技术驱动的革命，人们将因此可以互相帮助。 在接下来的几十年里，我们将拥有令人惊奇的新能力：更好的软件，更好的疾病诊断，更好的治疗手段，更好的教育，更好的机会，以及更杰出的人才，他们能够提出创意，解决难题。

这就是我看待世界的方式，它应该清楚地说明了一件事：我是一个乐观主义者。 但是，我是一个急躁的乐观主义者。 世界正在变得越来越好，但它变好得不够快，而且并不是每个人都感觉到世界正在变得更好。

社会的巨大进步往往加剧了社会的不平等。 最不需要的人享受了社会进步带来的最大好处，最需要的人得到的是社会的最低待遇，特别是还有近 10 亿的人，他们每天的生活不足 1 美元。 全世界大约有 10 亿人得不到足够的食物，喝不上纯净的饮用水，他们没有电，而我们认为这些都是理所当然的事。 每年死于疟疾等疾病的人

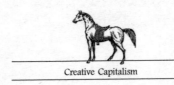

Creative Capitalism

The great advances in the world have often aggravated the inequities in the world. The least needy see the most improvement, and the most needy get the least — in particular the billion people who live on less than a dollar a day. There are roughly a billion people in the world who don't get enough food, who don't have clean drinking water, who don't have electricity, the things that we take for granted. Diseases like malaria that kill over a million people a year get far less attention than drugs to help with baldness. So, the bottom billion misses the benefits of the global economy, and yet they'll suffer from the negative effects of economic growth they missed out on. Climate change will have the biggest effect on people who have done the least to cause it.

Why do people benefit in inverse proportion to their need? Well, market incentives make that happen. In a system of capitalism, as people's wealth rises, the financial incentive to serve them rises. As their wealth falls, the financial incentive to serve them falls, until it becomes zero. We have to find a way to make the aspects of capitalism that serve wealthier people serve poorer people as well. The genius of capitalism lies in its ability to make self-interest serve the wider interest. The potential of a big financial return for innovation unleashes① a broad set of talented people in pursuit of many different discoveries. This system, driven by self-interest, is responsible for the incredible innovations that have improved so many lives. But to harness this power so it benefits everyone, we need to refine the system.

As I see it, there are two great forces of human nature: self-

---

① unleash [ˌʌn'liːʃ] vt. 解除……的束缚

超过 100 万，而它受到的关注远不如治疗秃顶的药物。 因此，成千上万的社会底层的人们无法享受全球经济带来的好处，而且他们还要承受错失经济发展带来的负面影响。 气候变化将给那些最少引起环境问题的人施加最大的影响。

为什么人们的受益与他们的需求相反呢？ 这是市场激励机制在起作用。 在资本主义体制下，随着人们的财富增长，为他们服务的经济刺激也在增强。 经济刺激随着财富的减少而消退，直到降为零。 我们需要找到一种办法，使服务于富人的资本主义也服务于穷人。 资本主义的真谛在于使自身利益服务于更广泛利益的能力。创新带来的巨额回报的潜力解除了大量天才的束缚，使他们追求各种各样的新发现。 这种受自身利益驱动的体制催生了许多令人难以置信的创新，这些创新改善了很多人的生活。 但是，要让这种能力惠及所有人，我们还需要重新定义这一体制。

在我看来，人生来有两种伟大的力量：利己主义和关心他人。资本主义在有用和可承受的方式上运用利己主义，但这只对那些有支付能力的人有益。 政府援助和慈善事业为那些没有支付能力的人提供帮助。 但为了迅速改善穷人的生活条件，我们需要有一个远比我们今天更好的创新和商业体制。

这种体制具有双重使命：赚钱盈利和让那些无法充分享受市场好处的人群生活也得到改善。 为了持续发展，我们需要充分发挥利润的激励作用。 同时，当企业设法服务的对象非常贫困时，就不大可能产生利润。 在这种情况下，我们就需要另外一种激励手段，这就是认可。 认可提高了公司的声誉并招揽客户，最重要的是，它将优秀的人组织到一起。 这样，认可就激发了市场对良好行为的嘉

241

Creative Capitalism

interest, and caring for others. Capitalism harnesses self-interest in a helpful and sustainable way, but only on behalf of those who can pay. Government aid and philanthropy channel our caring for those who can't pay. But to provide rapid improvement for the poor we need a system that draws in innovators and businesses in a far better way than we do today.

Such a system would have a twin mission: making profits and also improving lives of those who don't fully benefit from today's market forces. For sustainability we need to use profit incentives wherever we can. At the same time, profits are not always possible when business tries to serve the very poor. In such cases there needs to be another incentive, and that incentive is recognition. Recognition enhances a company's reputation and appeals to customers; above all, it attracts good people to an organization. As such, recognition triggers a market-based reward for good behavior. In markets where profits are not possible, recognition is a proxy①; where profits are possible, recognition is an added incentive.

This week's Economist had a section on corporate responsibility, and it put the problem very nicely. It said it's the interaction between a company's principles and its commercial competence that shape the kind of business it will be. The challenge here is to design a system where market incentives, including profits and recognition, drive those principles to do more for the poor.

I like to call this idea creative capitalism, an approach where governments, businesses, and nonprofits work together to stretch the reach of market forces so that more people can make a profit, or gain

---

① proxy [ˈprɔksi] n. 代理品

奖。 当市场上无利可图时，认可是一种代理品；当市场上有利可图时，认可也是一种额外的激励。

本周的《经济学家》杂志有一部分讨论了公司的责任问题，它非常清楚地提出了这一问题。 它声称，公司的原则和商业能力之间的相互作用决定了公司的类型。 这里的挑战是设计一个市场激励体制，包括利润和认可，这种体制驱动这些原则更多地为穷人服务。

我喜欢将这种理念称之为创造性资本主义，它是一种方法，即政府、企业和非营利机构共同作用，拓宽市场力量运行的范围，从而让更多的人获利，或得到认可，缓和世界不公平的现象。

我想问在场的各位，你是否打算来年在企业、政府和非营利组织中从事创造性的资本主义项目，查看在何处拓宽市场力量触及的范围，从而推动事情向前发展。 无论是国外援助，还是慈善捐助或新产品，你能够找到一种应用这种项目的方式、以利用市场的力量帮助穷人吗？

我希望，企业会奉献一定比例的顶级创新者的时间来应对这些问题，从而帮助那些被排除在全球经济之外的人。 这种贡献甚至比提供现金或给员工提供时间做志愿者更有影响力。 它集中使用了你们公司做得最好的方面。 这是一种创造性资本主义了不起的形式，因为它需要智慧，让富人生活得更好，也能在一定程度上改善其他所有人的生活。

我们生活在一个非凡的时代。 如果我们可以在 21 世纪早期花几十年的时间，按照为企业创造利润和认可的方式，寻找满足穷人需要的方法，我们将会发现减少世界贫穷的可持续性方法。 这是一个没有尽头的任务。 它永远也不会结束。 但是，满腔热忱地迎接

recognition, doing work that eases the world's inequities.

I'd like to ask everyone here, whether you're in business, government or the non-profit world, to take on a project of creative capitalism in the coming year, and see where you can stretch the reach of market forces to help push things forward. Whether it's foreign aid or charitable gifts or new products, can you find a way to apply this so that the power of the marketplace helps the poor?

I hope corporations will dedicate a percentage of their top innovators' time to issues that could help people left out of the global economy. This kind of contribution is even more powerful than giving cash or offering employees' time off to volunteer. It is a focused use of what your company does best. It is a great form of creative capitalism, because it takes the brainpower and makes life better for the richest, and dedicates some of it to improving the lives of everyone else.

We are living in a phenomenal age. If we can spend the early decades of the 21st century finding approaches that meet the needs of the poor in ways that generate profits and recognition for business, we will have found a sustainable way to reduce poverty in the world. The task is open-ended. It will never be finished. But a passionate effort to answer this challenge will help change the world.

I'm excited to be part of it.

Thank you.

(1,289 words)

创造性资本主义

这场挑战将有助于改变世界。

　　能够成为其中的一员，我感到非常激动。

　　谢谢大家。

知识链接 🔍

Davos 　达沃斯论坛。达沃斯论坛又称世界经济论坛，是瑞士一个独立的非官方机构。其前身是 1971 年由瑞士日内瓦大学教授克劳斯·施瓦布创建的"欧洲管理论坛"。1987 年，更名为"世界经济论坛"，宗旨是探讨世界经济领域存在的问题并促进国际经济合作和交流。因为论坛为期一周的年会于 1 月底至 2 月初在瑞士风光旖旎的小城达沃斯举行，故又称达沃斯论坛。迄今为止，论坛已举办了 40 多届，拥有 1000 多个"世界经济论坛"。论坛的参加者主要是各国的高层政治和经济界领导人、知名企业首脑。

题　记

　　全球化和信息技术的传播正在掀起一场知识驱动世界经济的高潮。资本和劳动力曾经为人类创造价值，而设计与创新的能力在现代为社会创造了大量的财富。印度作为亚洲第二大发展中国家，蕴藏的巨大创新潜力赋予设计神奇而美妙的内涵：设计被视作一种强大的战略工具，它通过设计思维构成了满足客户需求的商业模式；设计传承着传统意义上的协作与整合，用户生成内容与用户聚焦组织相结合的社会网络的兴起已经成为当今商业文化中新型设计中心体制的主要驱动力；设计也是凤凰涅槃，从崭新的视角推动陈旧的事物趋于价值最大化。设计思维在模棱两可中蓬勃发展，帮助人们迂回地看待问题，将形式赋予理论、可能性和选择项的能力同时也允许设计加速决策过程。这就是设计创新的魅力所在。

Wonder and Beauty in the
Realm of Design Thinking
— A Speech at the Indian CII-NID
Design Summit by Bruce Nussbaum

Thank you Gita. I am honored to be here in India, the country which has designed some of the most innovative business models in the world for super-efficient eye care hospitals, inexpensive cell phone service and small-size consumer goods. They were designed specifically to provide services and products to people at the Bottom of the Pyramid, but these innovative models created in India are being copied as we speak around the world.

As we proceed over the next two days to discuss design, design theory and innovation, we might keep in mind that globalization and the spread of information technologies are giving rise to a world economy driven by knowledge. Where once capital and labor gave us value, now talent is most precious commodity on the planet. Where once efficiencies in production gave us profits, jobs and taxes, now the ability to design and innovate increasingly generate wealth in society. And where once

设计思维领域的神奇和美妙

——布鲁斯·努斯鲍姆在印度工业联盟全国设计研究协会峰会上的演讲

　　谢谢你，吉塔。我很荣幸能来到印度，这个国家设计了一些世界上最具有创新意义的商业模式，包括超高效的眼部护理医院、价格低廉的移动电话服务以及小型消费商品。这些特定设计的模式为金字塔底部的人们提供了服务和产品，但是这些在印度创造的具有创新精神的模式正在我们所说的全世界范围内被复制。

　　因为我们在接下来的两天中即将讨论设计、设计理论和创新，所以我们也许要记住，全球化和信息技术的传播正在掀起一场知识驱动世界经济的高潮。资本和劳动力曾经为我们创造价值，才能如今成为了这个行星上最宝贵的商品。生产效率曾经为我们提供利润、工作和税收，设计与创新能力如今日益为社会创造财富。研发和最先进的高校曾经集中于西方，如今他们均匀地向全球发展——创新也是如此。这是一件好事情，因为我们必须相互学习，而且，聪明的商业人士和政府领导者也正在如此行动着。实际上，这就是我们在这场设计峰会上所做的事情。

research & development, and the most advanced universities were concentrated in the West, they are now spread more evenly around the world-and so is innovation. This is a good thing, for we must learn from each other-and smart business people and government leaders are doing just that. That is, in fact, what we are doing here at this design summit.

This is a perfect time for India to be launching a new National Design Policy, some 50 years after the Eames White Paper on design to Prime Minister Nehru. The field of design has evolved much since that time and the power of design to change our lives for the better has risen sharply. I would argue that in recent decades, the secrets of the design process have been revealed, deconstructed and reformulated as a powerful methodology of creativity. Many people call this design thinking. Others prefer the term "innovation." Call it what you will but we are seeing design shift from its traditional-and still vibrant-role of form giver to a significantly more important role as organizational strategist. Everywhere in the US and Europe, you hear corporations and, increasingly, educators, health care managers, transportation officials and even mayors of big cities asking for people trained in design thinking. The power of design has exploded and design has become transformative. I believe this new formulation of design has major implications for Indian economic and business policy. It could form the basis of what I call a High-Low Design Strategy for India.

Let us take a moment to do our own deconstruction of design and see why it is becoming such a powerful strategic tool. Design has always been

距尼赫鲁总理将关于设计的埃姆斯白皮书颁布大约 50 年之后，这是一个在印度制定新的国家设计政策的绝好时机。 从那时起，设计领域已经逐渐发生了许多变化，设计的力量急剧上升，让我们的生活变得更美好。 我认为，在最近几十年，设计流程的秘密已经作为创造力的强大方法论而被公开、解构和重组。 许多人将此称为设计思维。 而其他人则更乐意称之为"创新"。 如何称呼它是你自己的意愿，但是我们正在见证设计从传统角色中的给予者——尽管仍然富有活力——过渡到值得注目的、更重要的组织策略者的角色。 在美国和欧洲的任何地方，你都可以听到越来越多的公司、教育者、健康护理经理、交通部门的官员，乃至大城市的市长呼吁人们进行设计思维的训练。设计的力量已被打破，设计已经具有改革能力。 我相信，这种新的设计形式对印度的经济和商业政策有着主要的含意。 它可能形成被我称为印度的高-低端设计战略。

让我们来花点时间对设计进行自己的解构分析，看看它为什么会成为一种如此强大的战略工具。 设计通常要考虑用户，无论他是消费者、患者、学生、读者，还是媒体观察家。 当今，了解用户的需求和欲望也许是最重要的一种商业驱动力。 公司发明新产品并将他们投入市场供客户选择的时代快速地进入穷途末路的困境。 当各地的一家家公司要求自己的产品具有高水平的全球标准时，这一点尤为真实。 人们还在苛求对自己的产品和服务拥有更多的控制。 他们希望具备定制自己的手机和调整

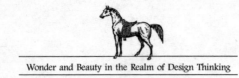

about the user-be it the consumer, the patient, the student, the reader, the media watcher. Today, understanding the wants and needs of the user is perhaps the most important driving force in business. The era when companies invented new things and threw them into the market at consumers is fast ending. This is especially true as individuals everywhere demand high global standards for their products. People are also demanding more control of their products and services. They want the ability to customize their cell phones and adjust their tractors. C. K. Prahalad coined the term "co-creation" some time ago and while CK is not a trained designer, his conceptualization is pure design thinking. When Cavin Kare looked at consumers in rural Indian villages, it saw their need for shampoo and other products in the context of their limited incomes. It then designed small sachets① at low prices to satisfy them. This is design thinking. It's not about designing the color of the sachets but about designing the model of the business.

Design is also traditionally about collaboration and integration. Working with other people across what we call silos② these days and integrating information to solve problems has always been a strong suit of design. Now, with the growth of social networks and collaborative innovation, design is ever more powerful. I would argue that the rise of social networks, which combine both user-generated content and user-

---

① sachet ['sæʃei] *n.* 小袋洗发剂
② silo ['sailəu] *n.* 筒仓

自己的拖拉机的能力。 战略学家普拉哈拉德不久前首创了"共同创造"这一术语,而他并不是一名受过训练的设计者,他的概念化是纯正的设计思维。 当卡文凯尔公司对印度乡村的消费者进行观察的时候,它发现了他们在自己有限的收入背景下对洗发香波和其他产品的需求。 于是,它设计了小包装的洗发水,以低价来满足他们的需求。 这就是设计思维。 它并没有设计这种小袋洗发水的颜色,而是构思了一种商业模式。

设计也是指在传统意义上的协作与整合。 在近来被我们称之为"简仓"的企业结构中与他人一起工作,并整合相关信息以解决问题通常是设计的一种强大的套装的设计。 现在,随着社会网络和协作创新的发展,设计变得更具感染力。 我认为,用户生成内容与用户聚焦组织相结合的社会网络的兴起是当今商业文化中新型设计中心体制的主要驱动力。

设计也是凤凰涅槃,它并不只是在现存的事物中进行选择,而是创建新的事物。 设计不是效率的最大化,尽管它理所当然地可以这么做,它只不过使可能性达到最大值。 设计从新鲜的视角看待老问题。 成千上万收入微薄的人希望得到电话服务,你们不是有很多这种客户吗? 为这些客户寻找一种按分钟少量计费的方式,同时设计一个廉价、优质且功能简单的手机。

设计过程同样允许我们在模棱两可的状态中进行操作。 它帮助我们迂回地看待问题。 全球化、科学技术进步、恐怖主义、全球变暖——这些都是在我们生活中造成巨大变化的强劲驱动力。 事实

focused organization, is a major force today for the new centrality of design in business culture.

Design is also about being generative — it doesn't just choose among the existing, it creates the new. Design isn't about maximizing efficiency although it certainly can do that, but about maximizing possibilities. It is about seeing old problems with fresh eyes. You have millions of people who want phone service but have little income? Find a way to charge them small amounts by the minute — and a cheap, quality cell phone with simple functions needed by these consumers.

The design process also allows us to operate in ambiguity. It helps us see around corners. Globalization, technological change, terrorism, global warming — there are huge forces causing immense change in our lives. In fact, there is so much change that many of us live life in constant beta. Look around you in India. The change is startling. Design thrives in ambiguity. It has the tools to explore unknown places, not simply make the known better or more efficient. Again, this is another reason why design is in such demand today.

And finally, the power of design resides in its unique ability to give form to concept — you make stuff, sometimes incredibly beautiful, wonderful stuff that we all passionately want. But in the realm of design thinking, the ability to give form to theories, possibilities, options, also allows design to speed up the decision-making process. Seeing something, whether it is a model of a product or a video of a service, enables managers to make better choices faster. It gives them more information to take manage risk.

上，生活中有如此多的变化，以至于我们很多人生活在常态的变数之中。 看看你周围的印度，变化令人吃惊。 设计在模棱两可中蓬勃发展。 它拥有探索未知区域的工具，不仅使已知的部分变得更好或者更有效率。 此外，这也是为何当今人们对设计拥有如此大需求的另一个原因。

最后，设计的力量在于其为概念赋予形式的独特能力。 我们所有人都热切地期盼你设计的产品，他们有时竟那么令人难以置信地美丽，那么奇妙。 但是在设计思维领域，将形式赋予理论、可能性和选择项的能力同时也允许设计加速决策过程。 无论它是一个产品的模型，还是一种服务的视频，观看某物都会使管理者更快地做出更好的选择。 它给他们带来了接受管理风险的更多信息。

基于以上原因，设计在美国和欧洲是一种有溶解力的淡入淡出教育。 为了使具有设计思维的人跟上不断增长的需求，设计学校，或 D 类学校，以及商业学校，或 B 类学校，都在迅速改变他们的课程和教学方法。 你可以选择丹麦 180 之类的新学校，也可以选择芝加哥设计学院之类的年代较久的学校，抑或斯坦福 D 类学校，或者多伦多的罗特曼管理学院，他们都从根本上改变了教授的内容和方法。 而其他大多数设计和商业学校也在快速跟进。

此刻，设计的巨大变化及时为印度提供了极大的机会。 举例来说，它表明国家设计策略不仅包含指定的设计学校，也包含顶级工程和商业学校的设计思维教学。 设计作为策略即使不比设计作为美学更重要，也与它一样重要。 让学生、教授、顾问和设计的习艺者

For all these reasons, design is a solvent dissolving education in theUS and Europe. To keep up with the growing demand from business for people who can do design thinking, both design schools, or D-Schools, and business schools, B-Schools are quickly changing their curricula and their methods of teaching. You have new schools like the 180 in Denmark and older schools like the Institute of Design in Chicago, the D-School at Stanford or the Rotman School of Management in Toronto radically altering what they teach and they way they teach it. Most other design and business schools are fast following them.

This huge change in design at this moment in time offers enormous opportunities forIndia. For one, it suggests that a National Design Policy include the teaching of design thinking not only in designated design schools but in top-level engineering and business schools as well. Design as strategy is as important, if not more important than design as aesthetics①. Bringing students, professors, consultants and practitioners of design together to teach and learn design is a model that may have application in India.

India has immense innovation possibility. Now is the time to build out its innovation capability.

Thank you.

(1,138 words)

---

① aesthetics [iːsˈθetiks] *n.* 美学

设计思维领域的神奇和美妙

共同教授和学习设计是一种理论模式，可以应用于印度。

印度有巨大的创新可能性。 现在是构建其创新能力的时候了。

谢谢大家。

知识链接 🔍

Bruce Nussbaum   布鲁斯·努斯鲍姆是"商业周刊"的一位管理编辑，负责新闻报道的设计和创新。他也是一个经济和社会问题的评论家。努斯鲍姆先生编辑每周的经济观点栏目，也经常写关于设计的文章，分析工业设计师的年度优秀奖和商业周刊/建筑实录协会奖。努斯鲍姆先生还是《石油之后的世界：移轴的权力和财富》和《美好愿望：医学研究内部对艾滋病的认识》这两本书的作者。他获得过由美国工业设计协会颁发的青铜苹果个人奖。

题　记

　　美国最初的门罗主义目标是让欧洲人滚开，如今英国的门罗主义是阻止美国靠得太近，以防止美国的次贷危机感染英国的抵押贷款市场，出现金融市场版的坟前跳舞——幸灾乐祸。英国金融服务管理局主席卡伦·麦克卡西在商务年度晚宴演讲中表达了对抵押贷款市场的信心，重申了如何更好地履行其承诺的实施抵押贷款政策的责任，强调了英国金融服务管理局与 AMI 公司之间的关系发展。卡伦向公众传达了他对市场的信心，以及使市场有效运作、让生产者和消费者双方获益的决心；对增加原则条款的使用并减少细节条款依赖的渴望；对 AMI 公司在未来市场继续扮演其不可或缺、坚强有力和中流砥柱角色、并使其成员和原则运行持续受益的展望。

Our Belief in the Mortgage Markets

— A Speech by Sir. Callum McCarthy,
Chairman of FSA, at AMI Annual Dinner

I am grateful for this opportunity to address the annual AMI dinner. What I would like to do this evening is first to be brief: I have yet to hear the comment on any after dinner speech "what a pity he did not go on longer". Second, and substantially, I want to address two issues: what have we been trying to do in implementing the mortgage regime since we took on those responsibilities; and how do I see the relationship between the AMI and the FSA developing — other than on the basis of after dinner addresses: more generally, how should regulator and regulated co exist, interrelate and-I hope and believe — help each other?

First: what have we been trying to achieve in implementing the mortgage regime? The FSA has been concerned, and will continue to be concerned, to identify those actions we can take to encourage the market for mortgages to flourish as a competitive, efficient and fair market. Central to this is the provision of information to the prospective customer which is clear, fair, and not misleading.

So central to our approach has been our concern that firms should produce information which makes it easier for the customer to understand

我们对抵押贷款市场的信心

——英国金融服务管理局主席卡伦·麦克卡西爵士在 AMI 咨询公司年度晚宴上的演说

受邀在 AMI 咨询公司一年一度的庆祝晚宴上演讲，我感到十分荣幸。首先我要说的是，今晚的演讲将是短小精悍的，我经常在晚宴之后听到这样的抱怨："真遗憾，他怎么没有再讲长一点。"其次，我想主要谈两个问题：一是自承担责任以来，我们在执行抵押贷款政策方面尽心尽力地做了些什么；二是我如何看待 AMI 咨询公司与英国金融服务管理局之间的关系发展，这种关系不是建立在餐后演说之上，更普遍的感觉应该是一种管理者与被管理者共生而又相互联系的关系，我希望并相信，二者应该是相互扶持的。

首先，我们究竟为实施抵押贷款政策做了哪些工作？人们一直以来对英国金融服务管理局能否促进抵押贷款市场的进一步繁荣并使之更具竞争性、高效性和公平性的一举一动十分关注，而且这种关注还将持续。对潜在客户提供明确、公平的信息，而不是对他们进行误导，这一点是关注的中心。

因此，我们一直十分关注如何编制信息，公司应该使客户更容易理解提供给他们的产品，并将之与竞争对手提供的产品作比较。

261

what he or she is being offered, and easier for him or her to compare competing offers. It is this objective — a more competitive and efficient market — which lies behind our work on key fact illustrations and initial disclosure documents.

I am very conscious that one way in which we can help is to make sure that those among you who act in accordance with the principles we wish to see adopted — the great majority — are not put at a disadvantage relative to those — a minority — who choose to ignore or flout those principles.

It is frustrating for those in the majority if they see non compliant competitors apparently acting without sanction taken against them. I can assure you that we are taking action against mortgage firms which issue non compliant promotions. To date, much of this action has been educational and — when it deals with a particular firm — has occurred mainly away from the public arena, by means of raising questionable promotions directly with the firm concerned, for rapid correction.

We intend to continue this educational approach: at the start of June we will be issuing a guide to financial promotions, designed to help you produce compliant financial promotions; and will be organising workshops at which both the principles behind our work and specific case studies will be discussed. I encourage you to book quickly while places are still going.

But we will also go beyond educational work and private conversations. It is important for the law abiding majority that those who persist in non compliant behaviour should be stopped, and I think it appropriate that we now add to our continuing emphasis on education a

这种保障市场更具竞争力和高效的目标正是我们发表的公共文件中核心内容所反映的精髓所在。

我十分清楚，有一种我们可以帮助你们的方式，那就是保证你们这些大部分遵守规章制度的企业处于有利地位，不受其他小部分蔑视规章制度的企业的挤兑。 我们希望看到你们遵守规章制度。

对于大部分遵纪守法的企业来说，如果看到小部分违规企业为非作歹是极为痛苦的事。 我向你们承诺，我们已经开始对那些不遵守制度的抵押贷款企业采取行动。 到目前为止，大部分违规行为都受到了教育，且已远离公众视线。 在处理特定对象时，我们通常使用直接对违规企业进行质疑、并要求立即纠正其错误行为的方式。

我们会继续推进这种教育方式。 从六月开始，我们将制定关于金融创新的指导方针，以帮助你们推出合适的金融产品。 我们还将成立专门的研究小组，讨论特定的规章和对特例进行研究。 我鼓励你们在研究小组席位还未满之前尽快预定。

但教育学习和私人对话远不是我们工作的全部。 重要的是大多数企业遵守规章制度，并禁止违规行为。 我认为，应该适当关注我们对挑选出来的企业继续加强教育，并使用大量的执法，就好像我们已经对企业采取了严厉的措施一样，以保护所有遵守新规章制度的企业，打击少部分试图进行违规业务的贷款抵押公司。 在这两种情况下，我们应对守法企业实施补助，以使他们不至于在违规企业的不正当竞争中受损。

当然，正如你们所期望的那样，我们对抵押企业的很多具体活动也十分感兴趣：公平地对待不同的、但责任相关的产品供应商和产品分销商客户（这一点我们打算在夏季公文中予以说明）；以自我

greater use of enforcement in selected cases — just as we have already taken firm action, to the benefit of all those who have adopted the new regulatory regime, against the small number of mortgage firms which have tried to do unauthorised business. In both contexts, we owe it to the law abiding majority to protect them from improper and unfair competition.

There are, of course, many specifics of the activities of mortgage firms in which we have been interested — as you would expect: the implications of treating customers fairly for the different but related responsibilities of product provider and product distributor on which we plan to publish a discussion document this summer; affordability, with particular reference to self certification and to the sub prime market; outsourcing; how to make it easier for you to report your returns to the FSA.

It is all too easy to see each of these as yet another regulatory enquiry, cost or constraint, without seeing any pattern. So I repeat that our approach has been driven by the objective of making the market for mortgages work as an efficient, competitive and fair market; it has centred on providing fair, clear and not misleading information; and it has been based on education and discussion, with enforcement action playing a small part.

Now, you will have noted that the approach I have described is based on principles, not on detailed rules. We at the FSA see great advantage — for both regulated and regulator, more generally for the efficient attainment[①] of public policy objectives — in making greater use

---

① attainment [ə'teinmənt] *n.* 成就

认证和次级市场为参考的支付能力；外购；如何更简便地向英国金融服务管理局汇报财政情况等。

显而易见，我所提到的上述原则并不像其他的规章制度一样有种种要求和限制，他们是没有固定形式的。在此，我要再次重申，我们使用的方法一直受房贷市场的工作目标驱策，以建立一个高效、竞争、公平的抵押市场。它的重心是提供公正、明确、非误导的信息。它的基础是教育和讨论，强制执行的方法只是其中的一小部分。

现在，你们应该已经注意到，我所描述的这个方法建立在原则之上，而非卷帙浩繁的各种条款之上。我们在更广泛地使用原则和减少对细节条款的依赖方面已经看到了极大的优势，对英国金融服务管理局的管理者和被管理者来说，可以更普遍地有效实现公共政策目标。需要指出的是，这是一个相互平衡的问题：我们永远无法逃避广泛的规则，一部分原因是这些条款起源于欧盟规定的官方指示或条例，一部分原因是他们的确存在适用性。这两个范畴既不互相排斥，却也不尽相同。

我们常常要面对约翰·蒂纳描述的原则和规则这种令人不快的混合体。但只要能正确平衡好二者之间的关系，将会大有裨益，所以我们更多地依赖原则，较少依赖细节条款。更大范围地依赖原则将减少监管抑制创新的风险。它将减少一本超过 8 000 页的规则书引起的纯粹的困惑；它将集中关注真正重要的问题；它将使金融服务公司彻底全面考虑现实问题，而不是伸手去拿规则手册，或者是听取任何个人按照规则手册对他们给出的建议。

因此，我今晚要传达的信息是我对市场的信心，以及使市场有

of principles, and reducing the reliance on specific rules. Please note that this is a question of balance: we will never escape extensive rules-some because they are derived from EU directives or regulations which require detailed rules, some because they are appropriate, the two categories are neither mutually exclusive, nor congruent①.

We will always be faced with what John Tiner has characterised as the unhappy hybrid of both principles and rules. But there is great advantage to be won in correcting this balance, so that we rely more on principles, and less on detailed rules. Greater reliance on principles will reduce the risk that regulation inhibits innovation; it will reduce the sheer bafflement② induced by a rule book of more than 8000 pages; it will concentrate attention on what really matters; and it will make managers in financial services firms think through the real issues rather than reach for the rule book, or for whoever advises them on the rule book.

So my message this evening is one of a belief in markets, and a determination to make them work efficiently to the benefit of both producers and their customers; an aspiration that we will move towards this by greater use of principles and lesser use of rules; and confidence that AMI will play an important, powerful and constructive part in that process to the benefit of you the members as well as to the benefit of better regulation.

(979 words)

---

① congruent ['kɔŋgruənt] *adj.* 一致的
② bafflement ['bæfəlmənt] *n.* 阻碍

我们对抵押贷款市场的信心

效运作、让生产者和消费者双方获益的决心。 我们渴望通过更多地使用原则、更少地使用规则来逐步达到这个目标。 我相信，AMI 咨询公司在这个过程中将扮演一个重要的、强大的和建设性的角色，从而使你们这些公司成员受益，使更好的监管制度受益。

知识链接 🔍

Sir Callum McCarthy 卡伦·麦克卡西爵士是英国金融服务管理局 2003 年 9 月至 2008 年 9 月的前任主席，目前是洲际交易所的独立董事。他在此前是资深的金融服务行业人士，担任过英国天然气和电力市场办公室的首席执行官、北美和日本巴克莱银行的主管等职位。

FSA 英国金融服务管理局（Financial Services Authority，简称 FSA）是英国权威的金融监管机构，宗旨是对金融服务行业进行监管。保持高效、有序、廉洁的金融市场。帮助中小消费者取得公平交易机会。金融服务管理局于1997 年由证券投资委员会（Securities and Investments Board，SIB）改制而成，为独立的非政府组织，成为英国金融市场统一的监管机构，行使法定职责，直接向财政部负责。

题　记

　　作为专门制造和销售电子计算机的跨国公司，IBM 在
强手如林的电子计算机市场独树一帜。IBM 董事会主席兼
执行总裁塞缪尔·帕姆沙努在演讲中历数了 IBM 成功的理
由。首先，IBM 在地理范围覆盖率方面的优势和广泛的全
球影响力使其竞争对手望尘莫及，尤其是在全球新兴市场保
持持续强劲的增长。其次，IBM 具备快速适应顾客变化多
端的需求能力，公司将数据中心设计专长、先进系统技术、
虚拟化和新软件与控制能源使用、利用和配置结合在一起，
为客户提供了高额的投资回报率。随着全球经济一体化进程
的加速推进，新计算机型号更新的周期日益缩短，微电子技
术领域的变革风起云涌，但 IBM 仍然在这一虽有较高风险
但很有发展前途的领域中收获着丰厚的利润。

Reasons for the Success of IBM

— A Speech by Samuel J. Palmisano,

IBM Chairman and CEO

It was a superb year for IBM. It is a pleasure to report to you that IBMers around the world turned in a strong performance, which you saw in our results. We achieved record revenue, profit, earnings per share and cash performance. In terms of our long-term EPS[1] objectives, which we described to you last year — that is, that IBM could generate $ 10 to $ 11 in earnings per share-we made strong progress on each element of our roadmap, growing 18 percent and surpassing our objective of 14-16 percent. And I trust you saw our results for the first quarter, which we announced two weeks ago. We continued to achieve solid performance-growing revenue by 11 percent, and earnings per share by 36 percent while generating substantial cash.

There are many reasons for this performance, and for why we believe it is sustainable. Let me comment on two — our geographic reach

---

① EPS:每股盈利

IBM 成功的理由

——IBM 董事会主席兼执行总裁
塞缪尔·帕姆沙努的演讲

今年对 IBM 来说是辉煌的一年。 我很高兴地告诉大家，正如你们所看到的业绩，全球的 IBM 人奉献了优异的业绩。 我们取得了创纪录的收入、利润、每股收益和现金表现。 我们根据去年描述的每股收益长期目标，即争取每股收益达到 10~11 美元，在这个路线图的每一个组成部分上都取得了长足的进步，增长了 18 个百分点，超过既定目标 14-16 个百分点。 相信大家已经看了两周前宣布的第一季度经营报告。 今年我们仍在稳定增长，在取得巨额现金收益的同时，增长收益达 11%，每股收益达 36%。

取得这种成绩以及为什么我们相信这种状况可以持续下去的原因很多。 我解释一下其中的两点：一是我们地理范围的覆盖率，二是快速适应顾客变化多端的需求能力。 如你所知，我们在当今的许多主要市场目睹了经济环境的不断变化。 但是客户仍然乐意在信息技术上投资，比如，我们的全球技术服务团队在第四季度签署了 3

and our ability to quickly adjust to changing client demand. As you know, in many of the major markets today we see a changing economic environment. Yet clients are still willing to invest in information technology, for example, in the fourth quarter, our Global Technology Services team signed $300 million in "Green" services contracts and had more than 700 engagements. Demand is very strong because we have solutions that offer ROI① now. These solutions combine things like data center design expertise, advanced systems technology, virtualization and new software to control energy use, utilization and provisioning.

IBM also performed well because of our broad global presence. The first quarter saw continued robust growth in the world's emerging markets, as we focus on building out the infrastructures in these countries. For example, we're helping Telecom Egypt construct a state-of-the-art data center with sophisticated energy-efficient green technologies, based on our mainframe platform. In Korea, we're working with a leading bank to build an infrastructure to develop and sell capital markets products, as they expand into investment banking. In Indonesia, we're part of a collaborative effort to deliver a microfinance solution for rural communities. These are all examples of the build-out of public and private infrastructures to support three billion people moving into the middle class. In each of more than 50 countries-including Poland, Malaysia, Singapore, South Africa and Mexico-we grew revenues by more than 10

---

① ROI:投资收益率/感兴趣的区域

亿美元的"绿色"服务合同，签约项目达到 700 多个。 需求如此之大正是因为我们采取措施，为客户提供了目前的投资回报率。 这些解决方案将数据中心设计专长，先进系统技术，虚拟化和新软件与控制能源使用、利用和配置结合在一起。

IBM 的良好经营状况也要归因于我们广泛的全球影响力。 由于我们专注于构建在各国的基础设施，我们在第一季度取得了全球新兴市场持续强劲增长的佳绩。 例如，我们基于公司的大型平台，帮助埃及电信公司利用复杂的节能环保技术构建了一个最先进的数据中心。 我们在韩国与一家主要银行合作，构建了开发和销售资本市场产品的基础设施，这些产品又拓展了投资银行业务。 在印度尼西亚，我们参与了部分合作项目，为农村社区提供小额信贷解决方案。 这些都是建设公共和私人基础设施以支持 30 亿人进入中产阶级的例子。 在波兰、马来西亚、新加坡、南非和墨西哥等 50 多个国家中，我们去年的收益都超过了 10%。

我们最近建立了一个新的"增长型市场"组织，总部设在上海，旨在更好地利用这次机会。 在第一季度，从增长型市场国获得的收入按固定汇率计量达到 11%，占 IBM 收入的 17% 左右。 我们期望这种趋势持续下去，希望这些快速增长的市场继续驱动IBM 的收入和利润引擎。 所以我们对今年的起步感觉良好。 事实上，我们对今年的每股收益预期提高了 25 美分。 我们现在期望全年的每股收益额至少达到 8.50 美元，这比去年报告的结果增长

percent last year.

We recently formed a new "growth markets" organization, headquartered in Shanghai, to make the most of this opportunity. In the first quarter, revenue from the countries in the growth markets unit was up 11 percent at constant currency, and represented about 17 percent of IBM's revenue. We expect these trends to continue, and we expect these rapidly growing markets to continue to fuel IBM's revenue and profit engine. So we feel good about our start this year. In fact, we raised our EPS projection for the year by 25 cents. We now expect the full year earnings per share of at least $ 8.50, which is 18 percent growth over last year's reported results.

In an economic environment where many firms are struggling, we are demonstrating again your company's historic ability to balance an aggressive growth strategy with disciplined attention to productivity and cost. We are operating ambidextrously①, as the times demand, and the results speak for themselves.

IBM is in a strong position today because of focused execution and strategic choices that we made several years ago. Entering the decade, we saw major shifts that would change the economic and competitive landscape of our industry.

First, we saw an accelerating integration of global economies, and with it, the emergence of two important-in fact, historic-opportunities

---

① ambidextrously [ˌæmbiˈdekstrəsli] *adv.* 两手同利地

了 18 个百分点。

当许多公司还挣扎在经济困境之时，我们再次证明了公司具有历史意义的能力，它可以使积极进取的市场策略和对生产力与成本的密切关注保持平衡。 我们坚持两手一起抓，结果应运而生，不言自明。

由于我们几年前制定了集中管理模式和战略选择，IBM 才能处于今天的强势地位。 进入这个 10 年以来，我们目睹了改变行业经济和竞争格局的巨大变化。

首先，我们看到全球经济一体化进程正在加速推进，它为 IBM 带来了两大重要的机遇，事实上，也是划时代的机遇。 我们有机会利用世界各地庞大的技术和专业人才。 当几十个国家大量投资信息技术以实现社会现代化之时，我们也可以捕捉这种快速增长的机遇。

其次，我们见证了新计算机模型的萌芽过程。 20 世纪 80 年代个人计算机型号的重要性在客户心目中不断降低。 这种新型号将以开放的标准和新技术为基础，奠定全球网络的基础设施。所以，如你们所知，我们大刀阔斧地改变了业务组合，摆脱个人计算机和磁盘驱动器商品业务，着手加强新计算机模型需要的技术和技能。

再次，我们期望客户愿意激发创新和一体化进程。 企业和机构希望把这一切先进的技术进一步引进他们的组织，使用技术来推动

Reasons for the Success of IBM

for IBM. We had a chance to capitalize on enormous populations of skills and expertise all over the world. And we could also capture rapid growth in dozens of countries as they heavily invested in information technology to modernize their societies.

Second, we saw the emergence of a new computing model. The PC model of the 1980s was receding in importance to clients. This new model would be built on a new global networked infrastructure-grounded in open standards and new technologies. So, as you know, we changed our business mix dramatically-getting out of commodity businesses like PCs and disk drives — and strengthening our hand in the technologies and skills that the new computing model would require.

Third, we anticipated that clients would place a premium on innovation and integration. Businesses and institutions wanted to take all this advanced technology far deeper into their organizations, to use technology to drive real transformation.

These were the three strategic choices we've made. They were far from obvious to many in our industry only a few years ago, but we made our decisions, and IBMers across the globe went to work. Some people are asking if we can continue to perform, if we can continue to produce profitable growth. I believe we can. Let me offer some reasons:

We have unmatched global reach & scale. IBM is diversified globally operating in 170 countries, with 63 percent of our revenue coming from outside the U.S. last year.

We are the world's preeminent IT infrastructure provider at the

276

IBM 成功的理由

真正的变革。

这就是我们已经实施的三种战略选择。 他们直到几年前才在我们行业的许多人心中一目了然，但是，我们做出了自己的决定，全球的 IBM 员工已经开始行动。 有些人问我们是否可以继续执行这项战略，我们是否可以继续获得利润增长。 我相信我们能够做到。下面我提供几个理由。

我们具有无与伦比的全球影响力和规模。 IBM 在全球 170 个国家多样化运营，去年我们 63% 的收入来自美国境外。

几十年来，在最重要的数据中心转型之初，我们都是世界卓越的 IT 基础设施提供商。 一家分析公司的项目显示，全球 1000 家公司中有超过 70% 的公司在未来 5 年将大幅修改数据中心。 上个月，我们启动了新企业数据中心战略，把面向服务架构中的领先优势能力、"绿色"节能解决方案、虚拟化和"云"计算等新方法结合起来。 我们在这方面正在与谷歌合作。 我们提供独特的客户价值观。 即使在不确定的经济时期，有一件事始终保持不变：企业对信息技术行业的投资。 信息技术为企业省钱，它控制着企业决定性的需求。 我们是商业世界的领导者。 IBM 是先进的信息技术领域不可战胜的冠军。 我们在过去 5 年收购了 60 多家企业，充实和扩大了我们现存的投资组合的规模。 最后，我们有充足和灵活的资金。 我们对高附加值产品的专注有助于推动盈利增长和强劲的现金生成能力。 它促使 IBM 能够给股东带来收益，为增长不

277

beginning of the most significant data center transformation in decades. One analyst firm projects that more than 70 percent of the Global 1000 will modify their data centers significantly in the next 5 years. Last month we launched our strategy for the New Enterprise Data Center, combining leading-edge capabilities in SOA, energy-saving "green" solutions, virtualization and new approaches such as "cloud" computing, on which we are partnering with Google. We deliver unique client value. Even in uncertain economic times, one thing remains constant: Businesses invest in IT. IT saves them money, and it manages business-critical needs. We are the business world's technology leader. IBM is the undefeated champ of advanced information technology. And we have acquired more than 60 companies over the past 5 years to complement and scale our existing portfolio. Finally, we are financially strong and flexible. Our focus on higher-value offerings helps drive profitable growth and strong cash generation. It has enabled IBM to return value to shareholders and to invest opportunistically for growth.

In the end, the success of a company like IBM depends on the persistence and vision of its owners. I and my colleagues are deeply grateful for your support, your continual input and ideas, and your shared commitment to the core values of this unique enterprise.

Thank you.

(1,073 words)

失时机地进行投资。

最后，IBM 公司的成功取决于其所有者的坚持和视野。 我和我的同事们深深地感谢你们的支持，你们持续不断的奉献和思维能力，以及你们对这个独一无二的企业核心价值观的共同承诺。

谢谢大家！

知识链接 🔍

Samuel J. Palmisano 　塞缪尔·帕姆沙努 1973 年加入 IBM。1997 年起，他先后担任高级副总裁兼个人系统集团高管、高级副总裁兼 IBM 全球服务部集团高管、高级副总裁兼企业系统部门集团高管等职位。2002 年就任 IBM 董事会主席兼执行总裁。

IBM 　国际商务机器公司 (International Business Machines Corporation，简称 IBM) 是美国、也是世界最大的电子计算机制造商，创建于 1911 年。IBM 目前在世界 132 个国家和地区设有子公司和营业点，拥有 39 个生产厂、3 个基础研究部、22 个产品研究所的 13 个科学中心、拥有 40 万中层管理人员、520 亿美元资产、年销售额达到 500 多亿美元，利润为 70 多亿美元，是世界上经营最好、管理最成功的公司之一。

题　记

　　亚太经合组织的独一无二不仅在于它的职权范围，更在于它的方法：决策和计划的自愿性和非约束性。亚太经济合作组织经济及技术合作委员会主席胡安深谙此道，积极推动着亚太经合组织的增长和活力。当全球股市岌岌可危、金融巨擘纷纷倒塌、信贷市场风雨飘摇、气候变化黑云压城之时，亚太经合组织中的新兴经济体已经成为世界经济格局中的一支平衡性力量。它借助文化和经济背景的多元化，通过建造、发展和扩大现存的金融体系协调变革；它启动气候变化对经济影响的研究，提供新的区域性合作和能力构建框架；它鼓励地区金融服务行业的发展，确保各国政策机构和监管机构的良好配置和审查监管规则；它鼓励规模较小的厂商进入全球市场。亚太经合组织在全球的金融版图上充当着国际经济秩序的积极主导力量。

Realizing an Authentic
Asia-Pacific Community
— A Speech by Ambassador Juan C. Capunay
at 5th China International Finance Forum

I would like to extend my thanks to the organizing committee of the China International Finance Forum. Indeed, a forum for all relevant institutions is fundamental to a comprehensive and coordinated approach. For this reason I am very happy to share with you the importance of the finance sector to APEC. When it was founded in 1989, APEC was a 12 member organization seeking to promote sustainable economic growth through trade and investment liberalization and facilitation throughout the Asia-Pacific region.

Faithful to its original mandate, APEC has experienced tremendous gains since its formation. It now includes 21 members and is home to both developed and developing economies in the Americas and Asia. Members account for half of world trade, 41 percent of world population and 55 percent of world GDP. Its achievements have been remarkable and have been driven mostly by market forces. From 1994-2004, 195 million new

实现真正的亚太共同体

——胡安·C. 卡普尼亚伊大使

在第 5 届中国国际金融论坛上的演讲

　　我要感谢中国国际金融论坛组委会。 的确，论坛对所有相关机构进行综合和协调的方法非常重要。 基于这个原因，我非常乐意与你们分享亚太经济合作组织金融部门的重要性。 亚太经济合作组织在 1989 年建立之初，有 12 个成员国，致力于发展亚太地区贸易和投资的自由化和便利化，促进可持续的经济增长。

　　亚太经济合作组织忠实履行其原有的使命，它自成立以来已经获得了巨大的收益。 它目前包括 21 个成员国，是美洲和亚洲发达国家和发展中国家的经济体。 成员占世界贸易的一半，拥有 41% 的世界人口和 55% 的世界国内生产总值。 它的成就非凡卓越，而且主要受市场力量的驱动。 1994 年至 2004 年间，这些地区创造了 1.95 亿个新职位，包括低收入经济体中的 1.74 亿个岗位，1.65 亿人摆脱了贫困，即贫困人口减少了三分之一。 出口增长了 113%，外国直接投资增加了 210%。

jobs were created in the region including 174 million in lower-income economies, and 165 million people have been lifted out of poverty — a reduction of one third. Exports increased by 113 percent and foreign direct investment by 210 percent.

This is not to say that the road has been smooth. The financial crisis left an indelible① mark on businesses and individuals alike. For APEC, it served as a springboard to address the inherent weaknesses of the existing financial systems. To this end, the "crisis" was not destructive but served to fortify and invigorate② the state of financial affairs in Asia. In retrospect, it might be observed as a time of restructuring.

Over the long-term, APEC grew stronger and more dynamic. It's purchasing power parity tripled. It's GDP has exceeded the global average. Trade with the rest of the world has risen from US $ 3 trillion to over US $ 13 trillion in this year; exports from US $ 1.5 trillion to US $ 6.5 trillion and tariffs decreased by an average of 11 percent. Intra-APEC merchandise trade has more than doubled and 15 of APEC's 21 members rank among the top 40 exporting nations.

Again, the world is at a critical juncture. For the entire international community, this particular point in time might be considered a catalyst. The world's financial system continues to be influenced by recent dramatic fluctuations in world stock markets as a result of the failure of what was

---

① indelible [in'delibl] *adj.* 不能消除的
② invigorate [in'vigəreit] *vt.* 增添活力

这并不意味着此路畅通无阻。 金融危机给企业和个人留下了不可磨灭的印记。 亚太经合组织作为一个跳板，解决了现有的金融体系固有的弱点。 为此，"危机"不是破坏性的，而是为了巩固和振兴亚洲金融事务的状态。 回想起来，它可能被视作一段重建的时期。

从长期来看，亚太经合组织的经济增长更强大，更有活力。 它的购买力平价增加到 3 倍。 它的国内生产总值已超过全球平均水平。 今年，与世界其他地方的贸易从 3 万亿美元增加到超过 13 万亿美元，出口从 1.5 万亿美元增加到 6.5 万亿美元，而关税平均降低了 11%。 亚太经合组织内部的商品贸易增加了 1 倍以上，亚太经合组织 21 个成员中有 15 个国家已跻身前 40 的出口国。

世界再次处于一个关键的转折点。 对于整个国际社会，这个特别的时间点可能被视为一种催化剂。 全球股市近期的猛烈波动继续影响着全球的金融体系，曾经一度被认为坚不可摧的金融机构以失败而告终。 此外，传统上稳定的货币风雨飘摇；全球随处可见气候变化的影响；石油价格急剧上涨给能源市场带来冲击；即将来临的地区选举可能严重影响未来的政治动态；多哈谈判宣告失败。 我们面临危险的经济形势，它使我们的国际经济体系和社会稳定处于非常危险的局势。

我们可以利用这些不确定的条件寻求积极变革的契机。 最

once thought to be indestructible financial institutions. Combine this with the instability of what was traditionally a stable currency; the consequences of climate change which can be seen throughout the world; the impact on the energy market by the dramatic increase in the price of oil; upcoming elections in the region that could have a significant impact on future political dynamics; and the break down of the Doha negotiations and we have a perilous① economic situation that puts our international economic system and social stability in a very risky situation.

Uncertain conditions might be leveraged as an opportunity for positive change. One of the most notable developments is the increasing interdependence among world economies and, in this respect APEC is uniquely positioned to respond to challenges. Half of world trade is carried out under free trade agreements and of the approximate 300 FTAs in existence, 119 are in the APEC region. Drawing from a multiplicity of cultural and economic contexts, APEC can accommodate change by building upon, developing and expanding financial systems that are already in place.

APEC approaches the financial system from several directions. One way is through the Finance Ministers' Meeting. Coming together annually to share information on regional macroeconomic and financial developments and to exchange views on national and regional policy

---

① perilous ['perilǝs] *adj.* 危险的

值得关注的发展动态之一是全球经济之间日益增长的相互依存，在这方面，亚太经合组织具有应对挑战的独特地位。世界贸易的一半是在自由贸易协定的框架下进行的，在现有的大约 300 个自由贸易区中，119 个在亚太经合组织区内。借助文化和经济背景的多元化，亚太经合组织可以通过建造、发展和扩大现存的金融体系协调变革。

亚太经合组织正在从几个方面着手处理金融系统。一种方法是召开财政部长会议。财政部长们每年聚会，分享区域宏观经济和金融发展的信息，交换对国家和区域政策优先事项的意见，并为全地区可持续和基础广泛的发展推出合理和可信的政策。他们将影响经济增长的问题视作根本利益，给领导人提供与区域政策相应的有用观点。

亚太经合组织的财长们断定，气候变化和能源安全已经严重影响了区域的经济增长。亚太经合组织已经通过世界银行启动了一项研究——气候变化对经济的影响，旨在提供新的区域性合作和能力构建框架。财长们还致力于深化私人资本市场和确保政府财政的透明度和可持续性。财政部长们预计将通过发展安全和可持续的粮食生产、监管、分销和营销系统，同意在地区实施经济稳定政策的新举措，强化亚太经合组织区域的资本市场。为了这个目的，作为原则性工具的公共私营伙伴关系将会受到特别关注。

priorities, Ministers promote sound and credible policies for sustainable and broad-based developments throughout the region. They have a fundamental interest in issues with implications for economic growth and provide Leaders with useful perspectives on regional policy responses.

APEC Finance Ministers determined that climate change and energy security have a critical impact on economic growth in the region. A World Bank study has now been launched through APEC on the Economic Impacts of Climate Change, to provide a new framework for collaboration and capacity building in the region. Ministers also committed to deepening private capital markets and to securing the transparency and sustainability of government finances. Finance Ministers are expected to agree to new initiatives in the area of economic stabilization policies through the development of secure and sustainable food production, regulation, distribution and marketing systems; and to strengthening capital markets in the APEC region. To this end, particular attention will be given to Public Private Partnerships as a principle vehicle.

The development of the financial services industry is a recurrent topic of discussion by Ministers. APEC's Finance Ministers encourage the development of the financial services industry in the region by ensuring that domestic policy agencies and regulators are well-equipped to develop, enforce and review regulation. An excellent example of capacity-building initiatives is the Asia-Pacific Finance and Development Program (AFDP), which is run by the Asia-Pacific Finance and Development Centre (AFDC) in China. The AFDP focuses on issues of regional concern and capacity building in finance and development, such as SME financing and

　　金融服务行业的发展是一个财长们经常讨论的议题。 亚太经合组织的财长们通过确保国内政策机构和监管机构的良好配置来发展、强化和审查监管规则，鼓励该地区金融服务行业的发展。 亚太金融与发展项目（AFDP）就是能力建设举措的优秀案例。 它是由在中国的亚太财经与发展中心运营的。 金融与发展项目重点关注金融和发展方面的地域关系和能力构建，如中小企业融资和银行风险管理。

　　中小企业的融资能力在金融危机之后受到部分地区投资水平下降的不利影响。 因此，资本商品的创新和更新能力受到负面挤压。中小企业对亚太经合组织具有至关重要的价值：就业机会导致社会稳定。 稳定的、有信心的社会有助于资本流动和健康的宏观经济环境。 亚太经合组织认为，当前的这个时期是一次契机，可以改善中小企业的状况，并将他们提供的尚未开发的资源大量输送至金融机构。 鼓励规模较小的厂商进入全球市场是一个可长期持续发展的前兆。 发展微型银行并改善微型融资的准入，是帮助这些小型厂商进入出口市场的一种方式。

　　为此，亚太经合组织多年来殚精竭虑，创造有利于中小企业的发展环境，并努力排除他们面临的一些障碍。 除了尽量减少总成本和开展业务的难度，还为他们提供融资的便利性，这是一个对小型企业来说最沮丧的因素。 正是通过资金的实际分配，才能决定经济

bank risk-management.

The ability of SMEs to access capital was adversely affected by the decline in investment levels in parts of the region after the financial crisis. As a result the capacity for innovation and renewal of capital goods was negatively impacted. SMEs are of critical importance to APEC : employment opportunities lead to community stability. Stable, confident communities facilitate the flow of capital and contribute to a healthy macro-economic environment. APEC sees this current time period as an opportunity to improve the circumstances of SMEs, and to draw from the untapped resources they offer to the financial community at large. Encouraging the entry of smaller players into the global market is a precursor to long-term sustainable development. Developing micro-banking and thereby improving access to micro-financing is one way in which to assist these smaller players to enter into the export market.

To this end, APEC has exerted considerable efforts over the years to create an environment conducive to the development of SMEs and to address some of the barriers they face. Aside from minimizing the overall cost and difficulty of conducting business, this has included the facilitation of accessing finance — one of the single most discouraging factors to smaller businesses. It is through the actual distribution of financing that the economic future is determined. It is through financial institutions that power is distributed and through which businesses are entrusted for an authentic Asia-Pacific Community.

(1,086 words)

实现真正的亚太共同体

的未来。 正是通过金融机构权利的被分配，并通过这些企业的委托，才能实现真正的亚太共同体。

知识链接 🔍

Juan C. Capunay　亚太经济合作组织经济及技术合作委员会主席。秘鲁人。

Asia-Pacific Economic Cooperation　亚太经济合作组织（简称 APEC）是亚太地区最具影响的经济合作官方论坛。1989 年 11 月 5 日至 7 日，澳大利亚、美国、加拿大、日本、韩国、新西兰和东南亚国家联盟 6 国在澳大利亚首都堪培拉举行亚太经济合作会议首届部长级会议，这标志着亚太经济合作会议的成立，1993 年 6 月改名为亚太经济合作组织。它的宗旨是：保持经济的增长和发展；促进成员间经济的相互依存；加强开放的多边贸易体制；减少区域贸易和投资壁垒，维护本地区人民的共同利益。

题 记

　　追求卓越，成功就会在不经意间降临。艾萨克·牛顿发现万有引力定律是他在自然科学中最辉煌的成就，他坦言：如果说我比别人看得更远，那是因为我站在了巨人的肩上。迈克尔·戴尔一直将此引为座右铭，创造了 21 世纪电脑行业的奇迹。站在巨人肩上的戴尔，在史密森尼慈善捐赠仪式上的演讲中透露了自己成功的秘密：对消费者顶礼膜拜。戴尔的整个业务模式一直基于听取客户意见并直接与他们互动的理念。过去，戴尔团队在原始的涡轮电脑里装上一张客户可以填写、提供反馈的卡片，并虔诚地根据客户需求改进技术；现在，戴尔团队建了一个名为"谋略风暴"的网站，发布产品和服务的帖子，供客户投票和评判，然后运用这些理念生产更好的产品。将来，戴尔团队会一如既往，虚心地倾听消费者的意见，冷静地揣摩消费者心的归属。

Putting Customers
at the Center of Business
— A Speech by Michael Dell at
Smithsonian Charity Contribution Ceremony

Thank you, Brent, David, Mr. Ambassador. Thank you for coming today. Thank you all for joining us. And I especially in particular want to thank the Johnsons, Barbara and Clint, who traveled here today from Ashe County, North Carolina. The Johnsons are among our longest standing customers, and past owners of this 1985 PCs Limited Turbo PC that we're contributing to the museum. The Johnsons have had many computers since then, and while they've all been quite durable, they can also attest① that they've changed quite a bit during that time.

And that's why it's a great honor for me to be here today. It's also a strange feeling. To be honest, looking back at what our company was 21 or 23 years ago, and remembering what I might have looked like when I was 19, I'm not sure I want to think about that too much. Never really

---

① attest [əˈtest] vt. 作为或提供某事物的证明

对消费者顶礼膜拜

——迈克尔·戴尔在史密森尼
慈善捐赠仪式上的演讲

感谢布伦特、戴维和大使先生。 欢迎大家今天的到来。 谢谢参与我们活动的所有人。 我特别要感谢从北卡罗来纳州阿士县远道而来的芭芭拉和科林特·约翰逊夫妇。 约翰逊一家是我们最早的忠实客户的代表,那个年代的业主使用的是 1985 年版的有限涡轮电脑,这种产品已经被我们送进了博物馆。 约翰逊夫妇从那时至今换过许多代产品,虽然它们已经相当耐用,但它们也可以证实,它们在那段时间发生了很大的变化。

这也是我今天在此感到十分荣幸的原因。 这是一种奇特的感觉。 说实话,回想公司 21 年前或 23 年前的模样,再想想我 19 岁时的模样,我敢肯定我并没有太多的奢望。 我从未真正想过电脑会成为历史的一部分,当然也从未打算把他们送进历史的博物馆。

但是,对于像我一样在上世纪后四分之一的时间里花了大部分时间做科技产业的人来说,有一点可能是真实的,即我们在戴尔的

295

intended to be part of history, and certainly never planned to be a museum piece.

But it's probably true for anyone like me who spent most of their time in the last quarter of the century in the technology industry, our teams at Dell spend a lot more time thinking about our customers' needs, and how they'll be using technology in the future rather than the past.

What our teams like to do is what Isaac Newton said he did, seeing further by standing on the shoulders of giants. Our real passion is stirred by what's new and what's next and what the potential and what the possibilities are for technology.

As a result of that, history is not often a very good guide for us, but what makes today very special for us is the opportunity to really pause and look back and acknowledge how far we have come, and the impact that technology has made on our society in a very short period of time.

So, I'm very grateful to the Smithsonian for helping us to step back from the furious① pace of our industry and our business to capture this important milestone. And if we do our jobs right, I suspect that much of the technology that we develop right now will be ready for the museum in another 23 years or so. And who knows, I might still be CEO of Dell, and I'll be ready to come back and contribute some more.

The innovation in our industry, the pace of innovation is pretty amazing, and it's pretty simple why it's driven by all the underlying

---

① furious ['fjuəriəs] *adj.*飞快的(指工作非常努力而速度快的)

团队花了很多时间思考客户的需要，他们在未来（而不是在过去）将如何使用技术。

我们团队喜欢做的事就是艾萨克·牛顿曾说过的他所做的事，即站在巨人的肩膀上看得更远。技术的创新、未来、潜力和可能性激发了我们真正的激情。

因此，历史通常并没有对我们起到很好的指导作用，使我们今天非同一般的是真正停下来、回首过去、并承认我们已经走了多远的机会，还有技术在很短的一段时期内已经造成的影响力。

所以，我非常感激史密森尼博物馆，帮助我们从行业和业务高速发展的步伐中后退一步，捕获这个重要的里程碑。只要我们做好本职工作，我猜想，我们现在开发的大部分技术在大约 23 年后也会进博物馆。谁知道呢，也许我仍然是戴尔的首席执行官，我会重来此地，捐赠更多的物品。

我们行业的创新、创新的速度真是令人瞠目结舌，它完全受底层技术驱动的原因非常简单，它也是客户的需求所致。20 年前，我们的大多数用户运用电脑做文字处理便心满意足。当然，他们现在有各种各样的需求：收发邮件、在线工作、听歌上网、下载电影、看电视、写博客、资源共享、唱卡拉 OK，等等。

戴尔非常幸运，我们的成功，事实上我们的整个业务模式一直基于听取客户意见并直接与他们互动的理念，这就是我们成功的真

technologies, and it's also what our customers want. The needs and demands, and desires for technology are changing at a very fast pace. Twenty years ago, most of our customers were pretty happy just doing word processing on their PCs. Now, of course, then they're wanting e-mail and creating networks and listening to music and getting on the Internet, downloading movies, watching television, blogging, file sharing, singing karaoke, whatever turns you on.

Fortunately for Dell, our success, in fact our entire business model has been based on the idea of listening to customers, interacting directly with customers and that's been a real foundation of how we have succeeded. Customers continue to provide us enormous feedback, and we've found that when we listen and we respond, we succeed. In fact, this original Turbo PC came with it a card which was affectionately called a "Dear Michael" card, and this was a card that a customer could fill in and provide feedback to us, and I used to read those quite religiously, and our teams would read them, and I'd hand them out to people and say, "Look at this. This says 'here's what we need to do, here's what we need to fix.'"

Well, a few months ago, we set up a Web site at Dell called IdeaStorm, and it's, if you will, the modern version of the Dear Michael card. And the way IdeaStorm works is that a customer or a non-customer can go online to this site and post an idea about our products and our services, and then other customers can vote whether they think that's a good idea or a bad idea. And then there are comments. In many cases

实基础。 客户持续不断地给我们大量的反馈，我们发现，只要我们认真倾听和回复，我们就会成功。 实际上，这个原始的涡轮电脑装有一张卡，被亲切地称为"亲爱的迈克尔"。 这是一张客户可以填写、并给我们提供反馈的卡片。 我过去常常非常虔诚地阅读这些卡片，我们团队也会阅读这些卡片，我会把他们分发给大家，告诉他们："看一下这张卡片。 上面写着'这是我们需要做的，这是我们需要改进的'。"

几个月前，我们在戴尔建了一个名为"谋略风暴"的网站，如果你愿意这样说的话，它就是"亲爱的迈克尔"卡片的现代版本。"谋略风暴"的工作方式如下：客户或非客户可以登录这个网站，发布关于我们产品和服务的帖子，接下来其他客户可以投票，评判这是个好主意还是坏主意。 然后还可以添加评论。 在很多情况下，有些想法差不多可以吸引成千上万条评论。 这是一种实时跟进的方式，使我们及时了解客户的思想动态，然后运用这些理念生产更好的产品，非常虚心地倾听顾客的意见，了解什么是客户的需要。

大家都知道当年亨利·福特发布 T 型车时的名言：只要车是黑色，客户就能够拥有它的任何颜色。 为了给亨利·福特尊重，科技行业长期以来礼貌地忽略这个建议，我很高兴我们做到了。 我认为我们的客户从中受益匪浅，我很乐意向大家展示我们在这么短的时

certain ideas have attracted literally thousands of comments. And so it's a real time way for us to tap into the power of customers' ideas, and then use those ideas to make our products even better, and keep our ear very close to the ground and what customers' needs are.

So, everyone knows that when Henry Ford released the Model The was famous for saying that customers could have it in any color so long as it was black. With all due respect to Henry Ford, the technology industry has come a long way by politely ignoring that advice, and I'm glad we did. I think our customers have benefited from that, and I'm very happy that by showing us how much we can change in such a short period of time, the Smithsonian is able to highlight Dell's contribution to the idea of paying homage to the consumers.

Thank you all very much for joining us today.

(866 words)

对消费者顶礼膜拜

期内发生了多么大的变化，史密森尼博物馆能够烘托戴尔对这个理念的贡献：对消费者顶礼膜拜。

非常感谢今天所有的与会人士！

知识链接

Dell 戴尔公司。总部设在德克萨斯州奥斯汀的戴尔公司于 1984 年由迈克尔·戴尔创立。戴尔是目前计算机行业内任期最长的首席执行官。戴尔公司在全球的产品销量高于任一家计算机厂商，它受益于独特的直接经营模式，致力于倾听客户需求，提供客户所信赖和注重的创新技术与服务。戴尔公司目前在全球约有 75 100 名雇员。

题 记

　　当埃克森美孚远离拥抱替代能源的时尚潮流之际，英国石油公司仍然沉浸在崇尚环保的浓浓绿意之中，为"超越石油"、加速转向可替代能源奔走相告。英国石油公司替代能源部执行副总裁和首席执行官维维恩妮·考克斯在首届世界未来能源峰会上呼吁，一方面要充分理解开发新能源所面临的困难，另一方面要认识到开发可再生能源和可替代能源的机会，重要的是保持两者之间的正常平衡。它意味着公司组成合资企业和形成其他的合作伙伴关系，它意味着公司与政府之间的紧密合作，它意味着国有企业与跨国公司之间的合作，它意味着学者、专家、非政府组织在给予企业和政府建议和鼓励方面必须发挥作用。创建可靠的、能够消费得起的清洁能源的未来需要国际社会的共同努力与合作。

Working Together with
the Future of Energy

— A Speech by Vivienne Cox, Executive
Vice President and CEO of Alternative Energy,
BP, at World Future Energy Summit

Your highnesses, your excellencies, ladies and gentlemen, good afternoon. Thank you very much for inviting me to join you today. This is a fantastic event — at a fantastic location. And it's great to be among so many people who are enthusiastic and optimistic about the future of energy.

We're hearing views today from a range of people who all have a lot of experience in trying to build that future — and I think it's important to get the right balance between understanding the difficulties we face on one hand — and the real opportunities we have for change and progress on the other. We need to be realistic — not too gloomy — but certainly not complacent. I think the truth is that we do face some unprecedented challenges, but we can overcome them because we also have unprecedented skills, technologies and assets. The fundamental challenge

共同创建能源的未来

——英国石油公司替代能源部执行副总裁
和首席执行官维维恩妮·考克斯
在首届世界未来能源峰会上的演讲

尊敬的殿下，尊敬的阁下，女士们，先生们，大家下午好！　非常感谢你们邀请我参加今天的会议。　这是一次非常美妙的活动——在一个非常美妙的地方举行。　如此多的人对能源的未来充满热情，态度乐观，与大家在一起，感觉真是太棒了。

我们今天听取了一部分人的观点，他们都在努力创建能源未来方面积累了丰富的经验。　我认为，重要的是保持两者之间的正常平衡，一方面要充分理解我们面临的困难，另一方面要认识我们已有的变革和进步的机会。　我们需要认清现实，不要太沮丧，当然也不能太自满。　我认为，事实是我们确实面临前所未有的挑战，但是我们可以战胜这些挑战，因为我们同样拥有前所未有的技能、技术和有利条件。　我们行业未来面临的根本挑战在于人们不仅需要更多的能源，由于经济和人口持续增长，他们也需要可靠的、能够消费得起的、清洁的能源，即我们可以依靠的能源和未来几代人可持续使

for the future of our industry is that people are not only demanding more energy — because economies and populations are growing; they're also demanding energy that's reliable, affordable and clean: energy we can depend on and energy that is sustainable for future generations.

New technologies can be developed. Renewable and alternative energies can be deployed at scale. Policy-makers can take the bold decisions needed to support low-carbon energy. There are many different ways to create sustainable energy. And different countries are approaching the issue in different ways. And that is good, because there is no one single, obvious answer. To meet the challenges of the future we will need a whole range of approaches and technologies. But what is absolutely clear is that the new possibilities require new partnerships. We need to bring together people with different skills and different experiences to work together in new ways and come up with new solutions.

That means companies forming joint ventures and other partnerships. It means companies working closely with governments. It means national companies working with international companies. It means academics, experts and NGOs playing their part in advising and encouraging companies and governments. It means bringing together existing technologies to create new opportunities. And here in Abu Dhabi-as you may know if you've been keeping an eye on the many press releases being issued — we have just announced some plans that provide a very clear example of these themes. These plans have been announced by Masdar — with whom we are delighted to partner — and Hydrogen Energy, our

用的能源。

我们可以开发新技术，可以大规模开发可再生能源和可替代能源。决策者们可以制定支持低碳能源的大胆决策。有多种创造可持续能源的不同方法。不同的国家正采用不同的方式达到这一目标。这种做法很好，因为没有一个单一的、明确的答案。为了应对未来的挑战，我们需要多种多样的方法和技术。但是可以完全确定的是，新的可能性需要新的合作者。我们需要把具有不同的技术和不同经验的人联合在一起，以新的方式共同工作，提出新的解决方案。

它意味着公司组成合资企业和形成其他的合作伙伴关系。它意味着公司与政府之间的紧密合作。它意味着国有企业与跨国公司之间的合作。它意味着学者、专家、非政府组织在给予企业和政府建议和鼓励方面发挥了他们的作用。它意味着综合现有技术，创造新的机会。如果你一直在密切关注大量新闻稿件的发布，正如你可能知道的，我们在阿布扎比这里刚刚公布了一些计划，为这些主题提供了明确的示例。马斯达已经宣布了这些计划，我们很高兴能与他们成为合作伙伴，同时我们还与力拓矿业集团成立了氢能合资公司。

简要介绍一下该计划，设计如下：天然气将被分成二氧化碳和氢气流体。氢气用来产生约 420 兆瓦的低碳发电。这大约相当于阿布扎比目前发电能力的 5%。然后将二氧化碳输送和注入生产油

joint venture with Rio Tinto.

To briefly explain the project, the design is as follows: Natural gas would be separated into streams of carbon dioxide and hydrogen. The hydrogen would then be used to generate around 420MW of low carbon power. That's equivalent to around five percent of Abu Dhabi's current power generation capacity. The carbon dioxide would then be transported and injected into a producing oil field where it would enable previously unrecoverable oil to be produced. Using carbon dioxide for this purpose would enable the gas that is currently used to be produced and marketed. The carbon dioxide would then remain stored securely in the oil field.

This is our plan — and if we can make it a reality — it will meet several needs. It would generate a substantial volume of power. It would enable more natural gas to be used domestically or exported. And because the carbon dioxide does not go into the atmosphere, it would avoid around 1.7 million tones of emissions per year. That is equivalent to eliminating the carbon dioxide emissions from all of Abu Dhabi's cars. What's more it would provide a source of expertise and capability and make Abu Dhabi a leader in this vital emerging technology.

So the next year will be all about detailed engineering and design work and negotiating the commercial arrangements. If these progress well, we hope we might be able to make the final investment decision in about a year's time. The plant could then conceivably be in commercial operation in 2012. One reason I am so positive about this project is that I believe it is right in line with several of the most positive trends in the

田，对以前不可回收的石油进行再加工。 用于这种目的的二氧化碳可以使目前使用的石油现产现卖。 而二氧化碳也可以安全地储存在油田里。

这就是我们的计划，如果我们可以将它变成现实的话，它将可以满足几种需要。 它将产生大量的电力。 它将使更多的天然气用于本国消费或者出口。 由于二氧化碳不会进入大气层，它每年可以减少 170 万吨的排放量。 这相当于消除了阿布扎比所有汽车的二氧化碳排放。 此外，它还是提供专业技术和能力的一个来源，使阿布扎比成为这项重要的新兴技术的领导者。

因此，明年的工作将全部围绕详细的工程、设计工作和安排商业谈判展开。 如果这些进展顺利，我们希望，我们可以在大约一年内做出最后的投资决定。 该工厂预计可以在 2012 年进入商业运作。 我很看好这个项目的原因之一就是我相信，它符合目前能源领域中的几个最积极的趋势，这些趋势可以带领我们走向更可持续的未来。

请允许我花一两分钟的时间对项目逐条做个介绍。 碳氢化合物仍然在起作用。 首先，该项目表明，可持续的世界并不是一个没有碳氢化合物的世界。 事实上，几乎任何关于未来能源的方案倾向于显示可再生能源与碳氢化合物的混合。 当然，至关重要的问题是这种混合是什么样的。"一切照常"的状况展示出极少份额的可再生能源和超大份额的碳氢化合物，到 2030 年，每年的二氧化碳排放量将

energy world at the moment — the trends that can lead us to a more sustainable future.

Let me spend a moment or two on each of them.Hydrocarbons① still have a role. First of all the project shows that a sustainable world does not have to be a world without hydrocarbons. In fact almost any scenario for the future of energy tends to show a blend of renewable energy and hydrocarbons. The crucial question, of course, is what that mix will be.

"Business-as-usual" scenarios tend to show a very small share of renewables and a very large share of hydrocarbons, with annual carbon dioxide emissions rising by over 50% by 2030.

To start with, if renewables are propelled forward by supportive policies and technology breakthroughs, then they may grow much faster than today's projections suggest. Already, wind power is growing at up to 30% a year, solar PV at up to 50% and biofuels② at up to 20%. It's been calculated that around $70 billion was invested in sustainable energy last year and over 50 countries have adopted targets for future shares of renewable energy.

Technology is fundamental to the progress of both renewable energy and new uses of hydrocarbons. For example, carbon capture itself is in action today. In BP, we are already injecting around one million tones of carbon dioxide each year into a reservoir at our upstream gas production

---

① hydrocarbon [ˌhaidrə'kɑːbən] *n.* 碳氢化合物
② biofuel [baiəu'fjuːəl] *n.* 生物燃料(指曾经为活质的燃料,如煤)

增加 50％以上。

首先，如果扶持性政策和技术突破能够推动可再生能源的话，那么他们增长的速度可能会远远超过今天的预测。 风力发电每年已经增长 30％左右，太阳能光伏发电已经增长 50％，生物燃料发电已经增长 20％。 根据计算，去年大约有 700 亿美元投资于可持续能源，50 多个国家已经将开发可再生能源作为未来共享的目标。

技术是可再生能源和碳氢化合物新用途发展的根本。 例如，目前正在进行碳内提取工作。 在英国石油公司，我们每年会对阿尔及利亚萨拉赫上游天然气生产工程注入约 100 万吨的二氧化碳库存。 所有这些技术都有提高能源效率和未来可持续性的潜力。 碳捕集与封存具有特别重要的意义。 由于它可用于铁、钢和水泥生产等工业过程，所以它除了发电外，还有一个主要的作用。 它在电力部门的影响可能是最大的。 大约 40％与排放相关的能源来自电力，这几乎是运输的两倍。 而在 2030 年需要的发电能力大约有 65％尚未建立。 不过一旦建成，电厂将持续数十年。 所以，如果更多的能源也可以成为清洁能源，那么目前对清洁能源发电容量的投资就迫在眉睫。

谢谢你们的关注。 我很高兴能来这里参加这个新的项目，这说明我们的行业存在很多积极的发展趋势。 然而，最重要的趋势还是使用技术来创造可持续能源，并结成伙伴关系，以加速开发和部署这些新技术，正如我们在阿布扎比这里所做的事情。

project at In Salah in Algeria. All of these technologies have potential for providing energy more efficiently and sustainably in the future. CCS is particularly significant. It can have a major role beyond power generation because it can be applied to industrial processes such as iron, steel and cement manufacture. But it is in power where the impact is likely to be greatest. Around 40% of energy related emissions come from power — that's almost twice as much as transport. And around 65% of the power capacity needed in 2030 is not yet built. Once they are built, though, power plants last for decades. So if more energy is also to be cleaner energy, there is an urgent need to invest in clean generation capacity today.

So thank you for your attention. I'm delighted to be here and to be taking part in a new project that illustrates so many of the positive trends in the development of our industry. And the most important trends are using technology to create sustainable energy and forming partnerships to accelerate the development and deployment of those new technologies — as we are doing here in Abu Dhabi.

None of us can do it alone. But all of us can certainly do it together. I am confident about the future and we look forward to working with you to create it.

(1,140 words)

共同创建能源的未来

我们任何人都无法独自做到这一点。 但是，只要我们大家团结起来，就一定能够做到。 我对未来充满信心，我们期待着与您共同创建能源的未来。

知识链接 🔍

World Future Energy Summit 首届世界未来能源峰会(简称 WFES)。首届世界未来能源峰会由进行探测、开发和商业化运用未来能源的马斯达公司(Masdar Initiative) 主办，于 2008 年 1 月 21 日至 23 日在阿布扎比举行，为期三天。此次峰会聚集了来自可替代能源领域的全球领先的创新者、教育家、科学家、风险投资商，以及另类和再生能源专家，4 000 多名企业家、分析家和官员，其中包括绿色设计师威廉·麦克唐纳和冰岛总统奥拉维尔·拉格纳·格里姆松。英国查尔斯王子也通过全息影像发表了讲话。阿布扎比皇太子在峰会上宣布，首期投资 150 亿美元用于太阳能、风能和水能项目，碳还原和管理，可持续发展，教育，制造，研究和发展。此次峰会是世界领导人首次聚集在一起交流最新解决方案和技术、并寻找合作伙伴的场所。

题 记

公共演讲的艺术与科学直接影响到公司的对外形象。遗憾的是，高管们的演讲经常步入表达的误区："我想讲个笑话来开头"；"练习太多对我没有好处"以及"最好直接进入问答环节"。这三种最常见的谬误设下陷阱，让演讲的高管坠入熊熊烈焰之中，浑身上下焦躁不安。大部分高管既缺乏技巧又缺乏实践，当他们无法把一个好笑话表达清楚时，就会神经紧张，备受折磨，不出所料地彻底败下阵来。高管们常常找借口推脱演讲排练，结果演讲时精神疲乏，彷徨不安，甚至语无伦次，让自己的形象黯然失色。观众和他们的即席提问存在太多碰运气的风险，而放弃演讲、直接进入问答环节的高管往往不可能完全控制所提的问题。职场生涯的成功与充满自信和有说服力的表述能力息息相关，熟练的公共演说者在广阔的世界中游刃有余地将公司管理玩弄于股掌之间。

Three Big Myths of Executive Public Speaking

— A Speech by Nick Morgan, the President of Public Words, a Communications Consulting Company

Do yourself a favor and don't believe them.

In my two decades of work with executives on their communications, I've seen some myths come up over and over again about how best to succeed at speaking in public. The three most common are: "I want to begin with a joke"; "Too much rehearsal is bad for me"; and "It's better to go right to Q and A." Let me debunk each one in turn, in the hope I may save executives and their audiences from future mishap.

I want to begin with a joke. There's nothing wrong with humor; of course it's a great thing when done right. The problem is that most executives lack both the skill and the practice to put a good joke across, although they're infected with plenty of inclination to try. Add to that the initial nerves that afflict most speakers at the beginning of a talk, and you

行政公共演说的三种谬误

——公关咨询公司"公共演讲"
总裁尼克·摩根的演讲

帮自己一个忙，不要相信他们。

20 年来，在我与公司高管打交道的过程中，我一而再、再而三地见证了如何在公共场合达到最佳成功演说效果的一些秘诀。最常见的三种是："我想讲个笑话来开头"；"练习太多对我没有好处"以及"最好直接进入问答环节"。让我依次揭穿真相，希望我可以将高管和他们的听众从未来的不幸中拯救出来。

我想讲个笑话来开头，幽默本身无错，如果处理得当肯定是一件了不起的事情。问题是大部分高管既缺乏技巧又缺乏实践，尽管他们欲望强烈，反复尝试，也不可能把一个好笑话表达清楚。大部分演讲者一开始讲话就神经紧张，备受折磨，不出所料会彻底败下阵来。结果是高管紧张地讲着笑话，听众也随之紧张，对笑话却毫无反应，高管心想，我即将坠入这儿的熊熊烈焰之中，浑身上下越来越焦躁不安，听众开始嗅到了灾难的味道。这是一个恶性的交际循环，难以终止。

have a surefire① flop. What happens is the executive delivers the joke tensely, the audience responds to the tension and not the joke, the executive thinks, I'm going down in flames here and radiates more nervousness, and the audience begins to smell disaster. It's a vicious communications circle, and it's hard to stop.

My advice: Don't put that kind of pressure on yourself, at least initially. One-liners are very hard to deliver well. Just ask any stand-up comic; comics get many of their laughs from their follow-ups to failed jokes. Instead, allow yourself to have fun with the material — if the topic makes it appropriate — once you've gotten through those crucial opening moments.

Also you probably should avoid a certain kind of humor that executives are particularly prone to: self-deprecation. Self-deprecation② is fine if you're already firmly established on a pedestal above the crowd; the act brings you down to crowd level, which can be very humanizing. But most executives aren't as elevated in their audiences' minds as they think. If you're not speaking from a height, self-deprecation merely puts you lower than the audience, and you have to spend the rest of your talk climbing back up.

Too much rehearsal is bad for me. Executives often try to avoid rehearsing. They're busy, and they like to appear in control. Rehearsal

---

① surefire [ˈʃɔˈfaiə] *adj.* 准不会有错的，一定成功的
② self-deprecation [ˈselfˌdepriˈkeiʃən] *n.* 自嘲

我的建议是不要给自己施加那种压力，至少在初始阶段没有必要。俏皮话很难讲好，只要问问任何一位单人脱口秀的喜剧演员就知道了。由于不成功的笑话，他们多次招到观众的嘲笑。相反，如果话题合适，一旦你挺过了开头的关键时刻，就要让自己在笑话中获得愉悦。

你还应该避免高管们特别容易受影响的某种幽默：自嘲。如果听众对你已经佩服得五体投地，自嘲何尝不是一种好的方式。这种行为使你与听众处于同样的地位，显得极富人情味。但是大多数高管在听众心目中的形象并不像他们想象中的那样高大。如果你演讲的角度定位不高，自嘲只会降低你在听众心目中的地位，你不得不占用演讲的其余时间，重新回到以往的水平。

练习太多对我没有好处。高管们常常试图避免排练。他们很忙，他们喜欢看起来牢牢控制着局面。排练消耗时间，还牵涉不完全受控的状态，所以他们找借口推脱，不想丧失元气。到了该发表演讲的时候，他们看上去像是一边练习一边演讲，一副与权威人士不相称的表现。他们的身体无意识地出卖了自己的不安，听众很快便明白了这种无意识举动的含义。最糟糕的是，听众将这种不安解读为伪装。

事实是，只要你现身演讲时精力充沛，精神集中，即使大量的排练也不会伤害你的元气。这就是关键。如果你不知道自己在做什么，你不可能精力充沛、精神集中。

所以，排练吧。我看过很多排练不足的演讲，但是我也可以用

eats up time and involves not being completely in control, so they put it off, using the excuse of not wanting to go stale. Then when it comes time to deliver the speech, they look like they're learning as they go, an appearance incommensurate with authority. Their bodies unconsciously give away their unease, and the audience is very quick to pick up that unconscious behavior. Worst of all, the audience reads the unease as inauthenticity[1].

The truth is you can't go stale even with copious rehearsal, as long as you show up for the speech itself up with energy and focus. That's the key. And you can't be fully energized and focused if you don't know what you're doing.

So rehearse. I've seen many under-rehearsed performances, but I can count the number of over-rehearsed speeches I've experienced on the fingers of one hand, and still have digits left over.

It's better to go right to Q and A. This myth is at least consistent with the preceding one. If you don't rehearse, you'll be uncomfortable with a script. So it makes sense to ditch the script and go right to questions and answers. Many executives have told me that they feel better responding to questions than speaking outright.

That's only natural, but here's the problem with dumping the speech and taking questions. You can't entirely control what's asked. You can't control the order in which it's asked. And most important, you can't

---

① inauthenticity [ˌinɔ'θɛn'tisiti] *n.* 不真实;伪造

一只手的手指头历数我经历过的排练过多的演讲，而且还有剩余的数字。

最好直接进入问答环节。 这种谬误至少与前面的荒诞说法相一致。 如果你不排练，拿着讲稿就不自在。 那么，抛开讲稿、直接进入问答环节就言之有理了。 很多高管告诉我，回答问题比当场演说感觉更好。

这是很自然的，但放弃演讲、转而回答问题又引起了麻烦。你不可能完全控制所提的问题。 你不可能控制所提问题的顺序。 最重要的是，你不可能控制最后提出的问题。 通常发生的情况是，率先提出的问题更明显和重要，所以，结束时的提问显得模糊不清，无关紧要或愚蠢至极。 而人们倾向于记住他们听到的最后一件事。

你还记得奥巴马总统在 2009 年 7 月 22 日召开的关于卫生保健的记者招待会吗？ 当然不记得了。 但是你肯定记得他最后的评论。他说，马萨诸塞州剑桥的警察逮捕小亨利·路易斯·盖茨一事是"愚蠢"的行为，当时这位学者刚从中国归来，试图进入自己的家。 这一评论连续数日在舆论界激起轩然大波，使奥巴马那天晚上发表的关于卫生保健的所有言论都黯然失色。

最重要的是，对试图向特殊听众传达特殊信息的高管来说，毫无条理和次序混乱的问答环节，使这种交流工具变得不那么有效。

为什么要冒次序混乱的风险呢？ 当然，不论问题是什么，你都可以接受训练，链接到某些答案，但是这样做可能比简单地做一场

control the question that's asked last. What usually happens is that the more obvious and important questions are asked first, so there's a tendency to end on the obscure, the unimportant or the merely idiotic. And people tend to remember the last thing they hear.

Do you recall President Obama's news conference on health care on July 22, 2009? Of course not. But you do remember the last comment he made. He said that the Cambridge, Mass., police had acted "stupidly" in arresting Henry Louis Gates, Jr., when the scholar was trying to get into his house after returning from China. That remark started a media brouhaha that lasted for days and completely eclipsed anything Obama had said about health care that evening.

Above all it's the shapelessness and anarchy of Q and A that makes it a not very effective communication vehicle for an executive trying to get specific messages across to specific audiences.

Why take a chance on anarchy? Of course, you can be trained to bridge to certain answers no matter the question, but doing that will probably be even less satisfactory than simply giving a speech.

If you're going to take questions, the best way is to take them toward the end of your speech but save a few minutes for final comments, so you can end on a high note, saying something clear and clearly appropriate. Don't wing it. There's too much at stake for you to be gambling on audiences and their off-the-cuff questions.

(867 words)

演讲更加令人不满。

如果你打算回答问题，最好的方法是让他们处于你演讲的结尾部分，但要留出几分钟来做最后的解释，这样你可以高调地结束，说一些清楚和明显合适的话。不要即兴表演。观众和他们的即席提问存在太多碰运气的风险。

知识链接

Nick Morgan 是一家交流咨询公司"公共演讲"（Public Words）的总裁，也是《相信我：迈向真实和魅力的四步》（Trust Me：Four Steps to Authenticity and Charisma）一书的作者。

题　记

　　实现全球的千年发展目标是每一位世界公民的主要使命之一。"千年发展目标"确定到 2015 年实现消除极端贫困和饥饿，普及初等教育，促进男女平等并赋予妇女权利，降低儿童死亡率，改善产妇保健，与艾滋病毒/艾滋病、疟疾及其他疾病作斗争，确保环境的可持续能力，全球合作促进发展等八项发展目标。达到这些目标我们仍然要走如此遥远的路程，但只有我们每个人都发挥自己的作用才会实现这些目标，而企业所起的作用比以往任何时候都要更大。作为企业不仅拥有技术、技能和专业知识，如果为了全球化的目的充分调动企业的积极性，就会在整个发展中的世界创造财富和就业。使最贫穷的国家融入全球经济，并创造一个无所不包的全球化，这也正是作为企业的最佳利益所在。

Meeting the World's
Millennium Development Goals
— A Speech by Gordon Brown at the
Business Call to Action Meeting

President Kufuor, President Kagame, distinguished guests.

Today the most dynamic and far-sighted of the world's business leaders have come together to lead the world in change.

We are agreed that the worst of injustices demand the most strenuous of our efforts.

And that the greatest of wrongs require nothing less than the united endeavours of the whole global community — business, governments, faith groups and non-governmental organisations all working as one.

And that is the reason for this historic meeting today — for business and government to join the Call to Action and for us to dedicate ourselves to work together to eliminate, in our time and in the poorest of countries, the worst of deprivation and poverty.

Our aim: to meet the world's Millennium Development Goals.

So great is the distance we still have to travel to achieve them that they can only be met by each of us playing our part.

326

实现全球的千年发展目标

——英国首相戈登·布朗在"呼吁大企业行动会议"上的演讲

库福尔总统，卡加梅总统，尊敬的各位来宾：

今天，最具活力和远见的全球商界领袖聚集在一起，引领着世界的变化。

我们一致认为，最严重的不公正行为要求我们做出最艰苦的努力。

而最大的错误行为只不过是要求企业、政府、宗教团体和非政府组织等整个国际社会联合起来，竭尽全力，共同努力。

这就是今天举行这个历史性会议的原因，即呼吁企业和政府加入大企业行动，让我们全力以赴，共同努力消除当代和最贫穷国家中最糟糕的匮乏和贫穷。

我们的目的是实现全球的千年发展目标。

达到这些目标我们仍然要走如此遥远的路程，而只有我们每个人都发挥自己的作用才会实现这些目标。

因为我们知道，如果没有非凡的努力，我们就会失败。

For we know that, without an extraordinary effort, we will fail.

Our Millennium Development Goal is to reduce infant mortality by two-thirds, but so far do we still have to go that, unless we act now, it will not be met by 2015, not even by 2030 — not, in fact, until 2050.

Our Millennium Development Goal is primary education for every child, but unless we act now it will not be met by 2015, not even by 2050, but by 2100 at best.

And unless we act now, the planet will by 2015 be suffering not less but more environmental degradation, millions of people will still be struggling on less than a dollar a day, and millions of children will still be hungry.

It is because of the scale and the scope of our ambitions — to eradicate poverty, illiteracy, disease and environmental degradation across the world — that we need all those with skills, expertise, innovation and creativity to contribute.

And let me thank for their attendance this morning two Presidents who are changing Africa for the better.

Presidents Kagame and Kufuor — men I congratulate as leaders of a new wave of successful, reforming African countries.

And I am pleased at this conference organised with the United Nations — and in the presence of Dr Kerim and Kemal Dervis — to be joined by so many distinguished business leaders from corporations across the world, some of whom I thank for traveling thousands of miles to be here today.

Next month, European leaders will meet in Brussels to agree an E.U. plan on education, health and infrastructure; in July, the G8 will

我们的千年发展目标是使婴儿的死亡率降低三分之二，但迄今为止我们仍然在做努力，除非我们现在就采取行动，否则，这个目标到 2015 年都不可能实现，甚至到 2030 年也不可能实现，事实上，到 2050 年才可能实现这一目标。

我们的千年发展目标是使每个孩子接受初等教育，但是，除非我们现在就采取行动，否则这个目标到 2015 年都不可能实现，甚至到 2050 年也不可能实现，至多是到 2100 年才有可能实现。

除非我们现在就采取行动，否则地球在 2015 年之前将会遭遇不是更少、而是更多的环境恶化问题，数以百万计的人将仍然挣扎在一天不到 1 美元的日子里，数以百万计的儿童仍然在挨饿。

我们的抱负是消除世界各地的贫困、文盲、疾病和环境恶化，它的规模和范围是我们需要具有技能、专门知识、创新和创造力人才的原因。

我要感谢今天上午出席会议的两位总统，他们正在使非洲变得越来越好。

卡加梅总统和库福尔总统，祝贺你们作为领导人成功进行了非洲国家新一轮的改革。

我很高兴出席联合国组织的本次会议，加入到众多杰出的世界各地公司的商界领袖中来，在场的还有克里姆和凯末尔·德尔维什博士，感谢大家今天不远千里来到这里。

下个月，欧盟领导人将在布鲁塞尔举行会议，制定欧盟教育、医疗卫生和基础设施协议。今年 7 月，八国集团将对卫生工作者、

decide new measures on health workers, malaria① and food prices; and in September governments, businesses, NGOs and faith groups will come together at a special UN summit to agree what more we need to do to accelerate action.

But, as I said at the United Nations in July, business has a bigger role than ever to play in helping to achieve our goals.

And as I said then, "for too long we have talked the language of development without defining its starting point in wealth creation — the dignity of individuals empowered to trade and to be economically self-sufficient".

There is no need, to this audience, to emphasise the role of global business in driving economic growth.

And it is growth and prosperity, not aid, that is our objective.

While aid is an essential means, the purpose of aid is to no longer require it.

And my argument today is that not only do you as businesses have the technology, the skills and the expertise that, if fully mobilized for global purpose, will generate wealth and jobs throughout the developing world.

It is also in your best interests as businesses to bring the poorest countries into the global economy and to create a globalisation that is inclusive for all.

So I'm not talking just about a moral imperative② but about a strategic and an economic one as well. Ours is already a world where the

---

① malaria [mə'leəriə] *n.* 疟疾
② imperative [im'perətiv] *n.* 必须完成的事

疟疾和食品价格出台新的措施。 政府、企业、非政府组织和宗教团体9月份将共同举行一次联合国特别首脑会议,在我们需要进一步做些什么以加速行动这个问题上达成一致。

但是,诚如我7月份在联合国发言所说,在帮我们实现目标方面,企业起着比以往任何时候都更大的作用。

正如我当时所说,"我们长期以来一直在谈论语言的发展,忽视了其创造财富的初衷,即个人享有贸易和在经济上自给自足的权利和尊严"。

对于在座的听众,没有必要强调全球企业在推动经济增长方面的作用。

它是增长和繁荣,而不是援助,这是我们的目标。

虽然援助是必不可少的手段,但援助的目的是不再需要援助。

我如今的观点是,作为企业不仅拥有技术、技能和专业知识,如果为了全球化的目的充分调动企业的积极性,就会在整个发展中的世界创造财富和就业。

使最贫穷的国家融入全球经济,并创造一个无所不包的全球化,这也正是你们作为企业的最佳利益所在。

所以,我不只是在谈论一种道德责任,而是在强调战略和经济上的当务之急。 在我们所处的世界里,最贫穷国家中的最贫穷公民的行为能够影响最富有国家中的最富有公民,所有的不发达国家、甚至是整个落后的大陆是直接造成全球不稳定的根源。

这就是为什么今天的活动会非常重要。

actions of the poorest citizen in the poorest country can have an impact on the richest citizen in the richest country — and where whole countries and even a whole continent left behind are a source of instability right around the globe.

That is why today's event is so important.

Some argue that it is the presence of big international corporations that is the cause of the problems in developing countries, but I disagree. Indeed, I believe it is the absence of business — and not the presence of business — that blights① the lives of poor people, leaving them dependent on aid and denying them the opportunity to work, denying them the chance to support their families and denying them the means to ensure their children get the chance to succeed.

Economic growth alone has lifted more than 500 million people out of poverty over the last 25 years, accounting for over 80 per cent of poverty reduction.

And the countries whose economies are growing fastest, like Rwanda and Ghana represented here today, are those that are making progress on the Millennium Development Goals — with countries whose economies are growing more slowly falling behind.

So we need to fully acknowledge the critical importance of the private sector in driving development — focusing our attention not on an old one-dimensional welfarist approach but on enterprise, on free and fair trade and open markets, and on harnessing the power of innovation — the building blocks of growth.

---

① blight [blait] vt. 使摧残

有些人认为，大型国际企业的出现是引起发展中国家问题的原因，但我不同意这种观点。事实上，我认为是企业匮乏、而不是企业存在摧残了穷人的生活，使他们依赖救济，剥夺了他们的工作机会，剥夺了他们赡养家人的机会，剥夺了他们确保子女有机会获得成功的手段。

在过去的 25 年里，仅靠经济增长已使 500 多万人摆脱了贫困，占贫困缩减量的 80％多。

那些经济增长速度最快的国家正在取得千年发展目标的进展，如今天在座的卢旺达和加纳，而有些国家的经济增长越来越慢，逐渐落后。

因此，我们需要完全承认私营企业在推动发展中的重要性，我们不仅要关注过去那种一味追求福利主义的做法，而且要关注企业、自由、公平贸易和公开市场，利用创新的力量，构建增长模块。

包括加纳和卢旺达在内的发展中国家已经在努力稳定宏观经济，积极调控环境和出台整治腐败的措施，这些都是商业贸易繁荣的必要手段。

富国也必须发挥自己的作用，郑重履行他们在格伦伊格尔斯达成的援助和债务承诺，并在未来数周达成新的世界贸易组织的贸易协议。

但是，今天这个会议室里在座的各位，以及许多世界各地的其他企业也都发挥着至关重要的作用。你们的创新、专业技能和技术

Developing countries — including Ghana and Rwanda — are already working hard to put in place the macroeconomic stability, supportive regulatory environment and measures to tackle corruption that are necessary for business and trade to thrive.

And rich countries must also play their part — delivering on the solemn promises they made at Gleneagles on aid and debt and agreeing a new W.T.O. trade deal over the coming weeks.

But all of you here in this room today — and many more businesses around the world — have a vital role to play as well — using your innovation, your specialist skills and your technology to deliver solutions that governments alone cannot.

Too often in the past, business involvement in reducing poverty in developing countries has focused on philanthropy in its old Fordist guise.

Today we need a new approach — moving beyond minimum standards, beyond philanthropy and beyond traditional corporate social responsibility — important though they are — to develop long-term business initiatives that mobilize the resources and talents that are the central strengths of global business.

And I am pleased that this morning more than a dozen global companies are announcing trailblazing projects that showcase this approach.

From delivering financial services via mobile phones so that millions of people have access to basic bank accounts for the first time; to providing rural farmers with electronic price and weather information so they can decide when best to harvest and sell their crops; to sourcing ingredients from local supply chains to develop the base of the local

实现全球的千年发展目标

提供了单靠政府无法解决的方案。

过去，企业参与减少发展中国家贫困的活动往往集中于老福特式的慈善事业。

今天，我们需要一种新的方法来发展长期商业行为，即超越最低标准、超越慈善事业和超越传统企业的社会责任（尽管他们很重要），从而调动全球商业主要优势中的资源和人才。

我很高兴，今天上午有十多个全球公司宣布了采取这一做法的开创性项目。

从通过手机提供金融服务、使数以百万计的人们第一次进入基本的银行账户，到向农民提供电子价格和天气信息，以便他们可以决定最佳收获和销售农作物的时间，以及从当地供应链采购原料以发展地方的经济基础，这些举措中的每一条都提出了我们所面临问题的创新解决方案，在发展中国家扩张企业和寻找机会。

如果仅是首批的少数公司就能取得这么大的成就，想一想如果更多的企业加入这场运动，我们可以取得多么大的成就。

因此，我们今天要敦促更多的企业响应我们的行动倡议，并制定符合这一新做法的具体措施：运用你的专业技能当场解决问题，不管这些问题是缺乏技能还是缺乏信息；尝试新的创新，并使之随时间的推移按比例增加，复制到整个发展中国家；根据新的和创造性的方式运用核心商业模式，改变经济和人民的生活。

我们需要在这重要的一年中积蓄力量，为联合国 9 月份召开的历史性首脑会议做好准备，并呼吁每一位关注贫困危机的人采取紧

335

economy — each one of these initiatives is providing innovative solutions to the problems we face and spreading enterprise and opportunity across the developing world.

And if we can achieve so much with only the first handful of companies, just think how much we can achieve as more businesses join the campaign.

So today we are urging even more of you to join us in our call to action and to develop specific initiatives in line with this new approach: bringing your specialist skills to bear on solving problems on the ground — whether that be a shortage of skills or a lack of information; trying out new innovations that can be scaled up over time and replicated throughout the developing world; and using your core business models in new and creative ways that transform both economies and people's lives.

And we need to build momentum throughout this important year in the run-up to the historic United Nations summit in September, summoning everyone who is concerned about this poverty emergency to take urgent action to meet our goals — and I urge all of the companies here today to develop an initiative in time for that meeting in the autumn.

So to every private sector company in the world, in Britain and here in the City of London my message today is: join us. You can make a difference.

Already, because of both public and private sector action since 2000, 41 million more children are in school, 3 million more children are surviving to their fifth birthday each year, and 2 million more people are receiving treatment for aids.

Already, we have seen what a difference private sector engagement

急行动，以达到我们的目标。 我敦促所有今天在这里的公司，为秋季会议及时制订行动计划。

因此，对全球、英国以及伦敦市这里的每一家私营部门公司，我今天要传递的信息是：加入我们的行列。 你可以有所作为。

由于自 2000 年以来公共和私营部门采取的行动，4 100 多万儿童早已能够上学，每年有 300 多万儿童可以度过 5 岁的生日，200 多万人正在接受艾滋病治疗。

我们早已见证了私营部门参与和创新产生的差异。 例如，我们了解到，发展中国家的增长率每上升 0.6 个百分点，每 100 人中就有 10 个人买手机。

我们早已通过国际金融免疫机制等举措，展示了一个真正的公私合作伙伴关系的影响力，到 2010 年，我们按照捐助国对金融市场杠杆的长期承诺，计划拯救 500 万人的生命。

我们早已知道，如果我们能够共同工作，打造一个新的和有远见的变革联盟，我们就可以确保全球经济一体化带来的好处，这种好处不只是惠及极少数人和幸运的国家，而是眷顾全球社会的每个部分。

当良心与良心叠加，道德力量与道德力量汇聚……想想我们会有多么大的力量去行善，我们会有多么大的力量去改变可以实现的生活。

让每一个儿童受教育；

消除可避免的疾病；

and innovation can make-we know, for example, that the growth rate in developing countries increases by 0.6 per cent for every 10 extra mobile phones per 100 people.

Already, through initiatives like the international financial facility for immunisation, we have shown the impact of a genuine public-private partnership — long term commitments from donor countries leveraged on the financial markets to save, by 2010, 5 million lives.

And already, we know that if we can work together to forge a new and far-sighted coalition for change we can ensure that the benefits of globalisation flow not just to the few and fortunate but to every part of our global society.

And when conscience is joined to conscience, moral force to moral force... think how much our power to do good and our power to change lives can achieve.

Education for every child;

The eradication of avoidable diseases;

Millions moving from poverty to prosperity;

Governments and business coming together to make globalisation a force for justice on a truly global scale.

Together, that is our aim.

Together, that is our challenge.

And together, in this generation, that is what we can achieve.

(1,617 words)

338

实现全球的千年发展目标

帮助数以百万计的人从贫穷走向富裕;

政府和企业共同合作，使全球化真正在全球范围内成为实现公平的力量。

这是我们共同的目标。

这是我们共同的挑战。

这是我们这一代人能够共同实现的目标。

知识链接 🔍

President Kufuor 加纳总统库福尔。他在担任非洲联盟负责人期间赢得了世界各国领导人的尊敬。

President Kagame 卢旺达总统卡加梅。